HESI A²
SECRETS

Study Guide
Your Key to Exam Success

HESI A² Test Review for the
**Health Education Systems, Inc.
Admission Assessment Exam**

Published by
Mometrix Test Preparation
Mometrix HESI A² Exam Secrets Test Prep Team

Copyright © 2015 by Mometrix Media LLC

All rights reserved. This book, or parts thereof, may not be reproduced, stored in a retrieval system, or transmitted in any form or by any means—electronic, mechanical, photocopy, recording, scanning, or other—except for brief quotations in critical reviews or articles, without the prior written permission of the publisher.

Written and edited by the Mometrix HESI A2 Exam Secrets Test Prep Team

Printed in the United States of America

This paper meets the requirements of ANSI/NISO Z39.48-1992 (Permanence of Paper).

Mometrix offers volume discount pricing to institutions. For more information or a price quote, please contact our sales department at sales@mometrix.com or 888-248-1219.

HESI is a registered trademark of the Health Education Systems Inc., which was not involved in the production of, and does not endorse, this product.

ISBN 978-1-5167-0536-8

Dear Future Exam Success Story:

Congratulations on your purchase of our study guide. Our goal in writing our study guide was to cover the content on the test, as well as provide insight into typical test taking mistakes and how to overcome them.

Standardized tests are a key component of being successful, which only increases the importance of doing well in the high-pressure high-stakes environment of test day. How well you do on this test will have a significant impact on your future- and we have the research and practical advice to help you execute on test day.

The product you're reading now is designed to exploit weaknesses in the test itself, and help you avoid the most common errors test takers frequently make.

How to use this study guide

We don't want to waste your time. Our study guide is fast-paced and fluff-free. We suggest going through it a number of times, as repetition is an important part of learning new information and concepts.

First, read through the study guide completely to get a feel for the content and organization. Read the general success strategies first, and then proceed to the content sections. Each tip has been carefully selected for its effectiveness.

Second, read through the study guide again, and take notes in the margins and highlight those sections where you may have a particular weakness.

Finally, bring the manual with you on test day and study it before the exam begins.

Your success is our success

We would be delighted to hear about your success. Send us an email and tell us your story. Thanks for your business and we wish you continued success-

Sincerely,

Mometrix Test Preparation Team

Need more help? Check out our flashcards at: http://MometrixFlashcards.com/HESI

TABLE OF CONTENTS

- TOP 20 TEST TAKING TIPS 1
- EXAM OVERVIEW 2
- ENGLISH LANGUAGE 3
    - Reading Comprehension 3
    - Vocabulary 11
    - Grammar 16
    - Punctuation 23
    - Improving Sentences and Paragraphs 28
- MATHEMATICS 42
    - Basic Math 42
    - Algebra 51
    - Final Notes 53
    - Mathematics Application 55
    - Algebraic Applications 68
- BIOLOGY 70
    - General Knowledge 70
    - Water 71
    - Metabolism 72
    - The Cell 72
    - Cellular Respiration 76
    - Photosynthesis 76
    - Cellular Reproduction 76
    - Genetics 77
    - DNA 80
- CHEMISTRY 82
    - Scientific Notation, Metric System, and Temperature 82
    - The Atom 83
    - Periodic Table 84
    - Chemical Equations 85
    - Solutions 86
    - Chemical Reactions 88
    - Oxidation-Reduction Reactions 90
    - Acids and Bases 91
    - Nuclear Chemistry 92
    - Biochemistry 94
- ANATOMY AND PHYSIOLOGY 97
    - Anatomical Planes and Direction 97
    - Histology 97
    - Mitosis and Meiosis 98
    - Body Systems 99
- PROFESSIONAL PRACTICE 109
- TESTING 113
- PRACTICE TEST 117
    - Reading Comprehension Questions 117
    - Vocabulary and General Knowledge Questions 130

    Grammar Questions 137
    Mathematics Questions 145
    Biology Questions 153
    Chemistry Questions 157
    Anatomy and Physiology Questions 161

ANSWER KEY AND EXPLANATIONS **165**
    Reading Comprehension Answer Key and Explanations 165
    Vocabulary and General Knowledge Answer Key and Explanations 173
    Grammar Answer Key and Explanations 181
    Mathematics Answer Key and Explanations 189
    Biology Answer Key and Explanations 199
    Chemistry Answer Key and Explanations 203
    Anatomy and Physiology Answer Key and Explanations 206

SECRET KEY #1 - GUESSING IS NOT GUESSWORK **211**
    Monkeys Take the Test 211
    $5 Challenge 212
    Specific Guessing Techniques 213

SECRET KEY #2 - PREPARE, DON'T PROCRASTINATE **214**

SECRET KEY #3 - TEST YOURSELF **215**

GENERAL STRATEGIES **216**

ADDITIONAL BONUS MATERIAL **221**

Top 20 Test Taking Tips

1. Carefully follow all the test registration procedures
2. Know the test directions, duration, topics, question types, how many questions
3. Setup a flexible study schedule at least 3-4 weeks before test day
4. Study during the time of day you are most alert, relaxed, and stress free
5. Maximize your learning style; visual learner use visual study aids, auditory learner use auditory study aids
6. Focus on your weakest knowledge base
7. Find a study partner to review with and help clarify questions
8. Practice, practice, practice
9. Get a good night's sleep; don't try to cram the night before the test
10. Eat a well balanced meal
11. Know the exact physical location of the testing site; drive the route to the site prior to test day
12. Bring a set of ear plugs; the testing center could be noisy
13. Wear comfortable, loose fitting, layered clothing to the testing center; prepare for it to be either cold or hot during the test
14. Bring at least 2 current forms of ID to the testing center
15. Arrive to the test early; be prepared to wait and be patient
16. Eliminate the obviously wrong answer choices, then guess the first remaining choice
17. Pace yourself; don't rush, but keep working and move on if you get stuck
18. Maintain a positive attitude even if the test is going poorly
19. Keep your first answer unless you are positive it is wrong
20. Check your work, don't make a careless mistake

Exam Overview

Every nursing program is different, and you will need to know heading into the test which sections your program requires. Below is a list of all the sections offered on the HESI A².

Scored sections:
- Basic Math Skills: 50-item exam. Focuses on math needed for calculation of dosages and solutions.
- Reading Comprehension: 47-item exam. Reading scenarios that are health related.
- Vocabulary and General Knowledge: 50-item exam. Contains basic vocabulary that is often used in health care fields.
- Grammar: 50-item exam. Contains basic grammar.
- Chemistry: 25-item exam.
- Anatomy and Physiology (A&P): 25-item exam.
- Biology: 25-item exam.

Unscored Sections:
- Learning Styles: 14 items. Identifies individual learning style and prints test-taking and study tips best suited for the individual's learning style and relates these recommendations to nursing curricula.
- Personality Style: 15 items. Uses concepts related to introversion and extroversion to classify the student's personality style. Explanations are printed at the conclusion of the exam to let the student know how to use his/her personality style to be successful in a nursing education program.

None of the sections is individually timed, but your full test session has a limit of 4 hours. If there are some sections you are required to take and others that are optional, you should work on the required sections first so you don't feel rushed. Once those are out of the way, you can use the leftover time to work on the optional sections.

English Language

Reading Comprehension

The reading comprehension portion of the exam requires the student to answer questions based on a passage that they have read. These questions are related to comprehension of reading measure the students' ability to comprehend meaning, identify the main idea, finding meaning of words in context, passage comprehension, making logical inferences, etc. There are 47 reading comprehension items.

Preparation

One of the best techniques for increasing reading comprehension is to read as much and as often as possible. Expand your literary horizons by reading a variety of publications. Read things like fiction stories, medical journals, comic books, and newspapers. This forces your mind to encounter new words and concepts. Keep reading materials in places where you will have idle time, such as the bathroom and your car. When you are waiting in line at the bank or pumping gas, you can thumb through a news magazine or read a chapter of a book. Tuck a book or pamphlet into your purse or pocket and read while standing in line at the grocery store. If you are using the Internet to decide which movie to see, read some reviews for each movie.

Understanding a Passage

One of the most important skills in reading comprehension is the identification of **topics** and **main ideas.** There is a subtle difference between these two features. The topic is the subject of a text (i.e., what the text is all about). The main idea, on the other hand, is the most important point being made by the author. The topic is usually expressed in a few words at the most while the main idea often needs a full sentence to be completely defined. As an example, a short passage might have the topic of penguins and the main idea could be written as *Penguins are different from other birds in many ways.*

In most nonfiction writing, the topic and the main idea will be stated directly and often appear in a sentence at the very beginning or end of the text. When being tested on an understanding of the author's topic, you may be able to skim the passage for the general idea, by reading only the first sentence of each paragraph. A body paragraph's first sentence is often--but not always--the main topic sentence which gives you a summary of the content in the paragraph. However, there are cases in which the reader must figure out an unstated topic or main idea. In these instances, you must read every sentence of the text and try to come up with an overarching idea that is supported by each of those sentences.

Note: A thesis statement should not be confused with the main idea of the passage. While the main idea gives a brief, general summary of a text, the thesis statement provides a specific perspective on an issue that the author supports with evidence.

> **Review Video: Topics and Main Ideas**
> Visit *mometrix.com/academy* and enter **Code: 691033**

Supporting details provide evidence and backing for the main point. In order to show that a main idea is correct, or valid, authors add details that prove their point. All texts contain details, but they are only classified as supporting details when they serve to reinforce some larger point. Supporting details are most commonly found in informative and persuasive texts. In some cases, they will be clearly indicated with terms like *for example* or *for instance*, or they will be enumerated with terms like *first*, *second*, and *last*. However, you need to be prepared for texts that do not contain those indicators. As a reader, you should consider whether the author's supporting details really back up his or her main point. Supporting details can be factual and correct, yet they may not be relevant to the author's point. Conversely, supporting details can seem pertinent, but they can be ineffective because they are based on opinion or assertions that cannot be proven.

> ➢ **Review Video: Supporting Details**
> Visit **mometrix.com/academy** and enter *Code:* **396297**

An example of a main idea is: *Giraffes live in the Serengeti of Africa.* A supporting detail about giraffes could be: *A giraffe in this region benefits from a long neck by reaching twigs and leaves on tall trees.* The main idea gives the general idea that the text is about giraffes. The supporting detail gives a specific fact about how the giraffes eat.

The Meaning of Words

The **denotative** meaning of a word is the literal meaning. The **connotative** meaning goes beyond the denotative meaning to include the emotional reaction that a word may invoke. The connotative meaning often takes the denotative meaning a step further due to associations which the reader makes with the denotative meaning. Readers can differentiate between the denotative and connotative meanings by first recognizing how authors use each meaning. Most non-fiction, for example, is fact-based and authors do not use flowery, figurative language. The reader can assume that the writer is using the denotative meaning of words. In fiction, the author may use the connotative meaning. Readers can determine whether the author is using the denotative or connotative meaning of a word by implementing context clues.

> ➢ **Review Video: Denotative and Connotative Meanings**
> Visit **mometrix.com/academy** and enter *Code:* **736707**

Readers of all levels will encounter words that they have either never seen or encountered on a limited basis. The best way to define a word in **context** is to look for nearby words that can assist in learning the meaning of the word. For instance, unfamiliar nouns are often accompanied by examples that provide a definition. Consider the following sentence: *Dave arrived at the party in hilarious garb: a leopard-print shirt, buckskin trousers, and high heels.* If a reader was unfamiliar with the meaning of garb, he or she could read the examples (i.e., a leopard-print shirt, buckskin trousers, and high heels) and quickly determine that the word means *clothing*. Examples will not always be this obvious. Consider this sentence: *Parsley, lemon, and flowers were just a few of items he used as garnishes.* Here, the word *garnishes* is exemplified by parsley, lemon, and flowers. Readers who have eaten in a few restaurants will probably be able to identify a garnish as something used to decorate a plate.

> ➢ **Review Video: Context**
> Visit **mometrix.com/academy** and enter *Code:* **613660**

In addition to looking at the context of a passage, readers can use contrasts to define an unfamiliar word in context. In many sentences, the author will not describe the unfamiliar word directly; instead, he or she will describe the opposite of the unfamiliar word. Thus, you are provided with some information that will bring you closer to defining the word. Consider the following example: *Despite his intelligence, Hector's low brow and bad posture made him look obtuse.* The author writes that Hector's appearance does not convey intelligence. Therefore, *obtuse* must mean unintelligent. Here is another example: *Despite the horrible weather, we were beatific about our trip to Alaska.* The word *despite* indicates that the speaker's feelings were at odds with the weather. Since the weather is described as *horrible*, then *beatific* must mean something positive.

In some cases, there will be very few contextual clues to help a reader define the meaning of an unfamiliar word. When this happens, one strategy that readers may employ is **substitution**. A good reader will brainstorm some possible synonyms for the given word, and he or she will substitute these words into the sentence. If the sentence and the surrounding passage continue to make sense, then the substitution has revealed at least some information about the unfamiliar word. Consider the sentence: *Frank's admonition rang in her ears as she climbed the mountain.* A reader unfamiliar with *admonition* might come up with some substitutions like *vow, promise, advice, complaint,* or *compliment*. All of these words make general sense of the sentence though their meanings are diverse. The process has suggested; however, that an admonition is some sort of message. The substitution strategy is rarely able to pinpoint a precise definition, but this process can be effective as a last resort.

Occasionally, you will be able to define an unfamiliar word by looking at the descriptive words in the context. Consider the following sentence: *Fred dragged the recalcitrant boy kicking and screaming up the stairs.* The words *dragged, kicking,* and *screaming* all suggest that the boy does not want to go up the stairs. The reader may assume that *recalcitrant* means something like unwilling or protesting. In this example, an unfamiliar adjective was identified.

Additionally, using description to define an unfamiliar noun is a common practice compared to unfamiliar adjectives, as in this sentence: *Don's wrinkled frown and constantly shaking fist identified him as a curmudgeon of the first order.* Don is described as having a *wrinkled frown and constantly shaking fist* suggesting that a *curmudgeon* must be a grumpy man. Contrasts do not always provide detailed information about the unfamiliar word, but they at least give the reader some clues.

When a word has more than one meaning, readers can have difficulty with determining how the word is being used in a given sentence. For instance, the verb *cleave*, can mean either *join* or *separate*. When readers come upon this word, they will have to select the definition that makes the most sense. Consider the following sentence: *Hermione's knife cleaved the bread cleanly.* Since, a knife cannot join bread together, the word must indicate separation. A slightly more difficult example would be the sentence: *The birds cleaved together as they flew from the oak tree.* Immediately, the presence of the word *together* should suggest that in this sentence *cleave* is being used to mean *join*. Discovering the intent of a word with multiple meanings requires the same tricks as defining an unknown word: look for contextual clues and evaluate the substituted words.

When you understand how words relate to each other, you will discover more in a passage. This is explained by understanding **synonyms** (e.g., words that mean the same thing) and **antonyms** (e.g., words that mean the opposite of one another). As an example, *dry* and *arid* are synonyms, and *dry* and *wet* are antonyms. There are many pairs of words in English that can be considered synonyms, despite having slightly different definitions. For instance, the words *friendly* and *collegial* can both be used to describe a warm interpersonal relationship, and one would be correct to call them synonyms. However, *collegial* (kin to *colleague*) is often used in reference to professional or academic relationships, and *friendly* has no such connotation. If the difference between the two words is too great, then they should not be called synonyms. *Hot* and *warm* are not synonyms because their meanings are too distinct. A good way to determine whether two words are synonyms is to substitute one word for the other word and verify that the meaning of the sentence has not changed. Substituting *warm* for *hot* in a sentence would convey a different meaning. Although warm and hot may seem close in meaning, warm generally means that the temperature is moderate, and hot generally means that the temperature is excessively high.

Antonyms are words with opposite meanings. *Light* and *dark*, *up* and *down*, *right* and *left*, *good* and *bad*: these are all sets of antonyms. Be careful to distinguish between antonyms and pairs of words that are simply different. *Black* and *gray*, for instance, are not antonyms because gray is not the opposite of black. *Black* and *white*, on the other hand, are antonyms. Not every word has an antonym. For instance, many nouns do not: What would be the antonym of chair? During your exam, the questions related to antonyms are more likely to concern adjectives. You will recall that adjectives are words that describe a noun. Some common adjectives include *purple*, *fast*, *skinny*, and *sweet*. From those four adjectives, *purple* is the item that lacks a group of obvious antonyms.

> **Review Video: Synonyms and Antonyms**
> Visit **mometrix.com/academy** and enter **Code: 105612**

Authors often use analogies to add meaning to their passages. An **analogy** is a comparison of two things. The words in the analogy are connected by a certain, often undetermined relationship. Look at this analogy: *moo is to cow as quack is to duck*. This analogy compares the sound that a cow makes with the sound that a duck makes. Even if the word *quack* was not given, one could figure out the correct word to complete the analogy based on the relationship between the words *moo* and *cow*.

Purposes for Writing

In order to be an effective reader, one must pay attention to the author's **position** and purpose. Even those texts that seem objective and impartial, like textbooks, have a position and bias. Readers need to take these positions into account when considering the author's message. When an author uses emotional language or clearly favors one side of an argument, his or her position is clear. However, the author's position may be evident not only in what he or she writes, but also in what he or she doesn't write. In a normal setting, a reader would want to review some other texts on the same topic in order to develop a view of the author's position. If this was not possible, then you would want to acquire some background about the author. However, since you are in the middle of an exam and the only source of information is the text, you should look for language and argumentation that seems to indicate a particular stance on the subject.

> **Review Video: Author's Position**
> Visit **mometrix.com/academy** and enter **Code: 478923**

Usually, identifying the **purpose** of an author is easier than identifying his or her position. In most cases, the author has no interest in hiding his or her purpose. A text that is meant to entertain, for instance, should be written to please the reader. Most narratives, or stories, are written to entertain, though they may also inform or persuade. Informative texts are easy to identify, while the most difficult purpose of a text to identify is persuasion because the author has an interest in making this purpose hard to detect. When a reader discovers that the author is trying to persuade, he or she should be skeptical of the argument. For this reason persuasive texts often try to establish an entertaining tone and hope to amuse the reader into agreement. On the other hand, an informative tone may be implemented to create an appearance of authority and objectivity.

An author's purpose is evident often in the organization of the text (e.g., section headings in bold font points to an informative text). However, you may not have such organization available to you in your exam. Instead, if the author makes his or her main idea clear from the beginning, then the likely purpose of the text is to inform. If the author begins by making a claim and provides various arguments to support that claim, then the purpose is probably to persuade. If the author tells a story or seems to want the attention of the reader more than to push a particular point or deliver information, then his or her purpose is most likely to entertain. As a reader, you must judge authors on how well they accomplish their purpose. In other words, you need to consider the type of passage (e.g., technical, persuasive, etc.) that the author has written and if the author has followed the requirements of the passage type.

> **Review Video:** Purpose of an Author
> *Visit **mometrix.com/academy** and enter **Code: 497555***

Facts and Opinions

Critical thinking skills are mastered through understanding various types of writing and the different purposes of authors in writing their passages. Every author writes for a purpose. When you understand their purpose and how they accomplish their goal, you will be able to analyze their writing and determine whether or not you agree with their conclusions.

Readers must always be conscious of the distinction between fact and opinion. A **fact** can be subjected to analysis and can be either proved or disproved. An **opinion**, on the other hand, is the author's personal thoughts or feelings which may not be alterable by research or evidence. If the author writes that the distance from New York to Boston is about two hundred miles, then he or she is stating a fact. If an author writes that New York is too crowded, then he or she is giving an opinion because there is no objective standard for overpopulation.

An opinion may be indicated by words like *believe*, *think*, or *feel*. Readers must be aware that an opinion may be supported by facts. For instance, the author might give the population density of New York as a reason for an overcrowded population. An opinion supported by fact tends to be more convincing. On the other hand, when authors support their opinions with other opinions, readers should not be persuaded by the argument to any degree.

When you have an argumentative passage, you need to be sure that facts are presented to the reader from reliable sources. An opinion is what the author thinks about a given topic. An opinion is not common knowledge or proven by expert sources, instead the information is the personal beliefs and thoughts of the author.

To distinguish between fact and opinion, a reader needs to consider the type of source that is presenting information, the information that backs-up a claim, and the author's motivation to have a certain point-of-view on a given topic. For example, if a panel of scientists has conducted multiple studies on the effectiveness of taking a certain vitamin, then the results are more likely to be factual than a company that is selling a vitamin and claims that taking the vitamin can produce positive effects. The company is motivated to sell their product, and the scientists are using the scientific method to prove a theory. Remember: if you find sentences that contain phrases such as "I think...", then the statement is an opinion.

> **Review Video:** Fact or Opinion
> Visit *mometrix.com/academy* and enter **Code: 870899**

Evaluating a Passage

When reading informational texts, there is importance in understanding the logical conclusion of the author's ideas. **Identifying a logical conclusion** can help you determine whether you agree with the writer or not. Coming to this conclusion is much like making an inference: the approach requires you to combine the information given by the text with what you already know in order to make a logical conclusion. If the author intended the reader to draw a certain conclusion, then you can expect the author's argumentation and detail to be leading in that direction. One way to approach the task of drawing conclusions is to make brief notes of all the points made by the author. When the notes are arranged on paper, they may clarify the logical conclusion. Another way to approach conclusions is to consider whether the reasoning of the author raises any pertinent questions. Sometimes you will be able to draw several conclusions from a passage. On occasion these will be conclusions that were never imagined by the author. Therefore, be aware that these conclusions must be supported directly by the text.

> **Review Video:** Identifying a Logical Conclusion
> Visit *mometrix.com/academy* and enter **Code: 281653**

The term **text evidence** refers to information that supports a main point or minor points and can help lead the reader to a conclusion. Information used as text evidence is precise, descriptive, and factual. A main point is often followed by supporting details that provide evidence to back-up a claim. For example, a passage may include the claim that winter occurs during opposite months in the Northern and Southern hemispheres. Text evidence based on this claim may include countries where winter occurs in opposite months along with reasons that winter occurs at different times of the year in separate hemispheres (due to the tilt of the Earth as it rotates around the sun).

> **Review Video:** Text Evidence
> Visit *mometrix.com/academy* and enter **Code: 486236**

Drawing conclusions from information implied within a passage requires confidence on the part of the reader. **Implications** are things that the author does not state directly, but readers can assume based on what the author does say. Consider the following passage: *I stepped outside and opened my umbrella. By the time I got to work, the cuffs of my pants were soaked*. The author never states that it is raining, but this fact is clearly implied. Conclusions based on implication must be well supported by the text. In order to draw a solid conclusion, readers should have multiple pieces of evidence. If readers have only one piece, they must be assured that there is no other possible explanation than their conclusion. A good reader will be able to draw many conclusions from information implied by the text which will be a great help in the exam.

When reading a good passage, readers are moved to engage actively in the text. One part of being an active reader involves making predictions. A **prediction** is a guess about what will happen next. Readers constantly make predictions based on what they have read and what they already know. Consider the following sentence: *Staring at the computer screen in shock, Kim blindly reached over* *for the brimming glass of water on the shelf to her side.* The sentence suggests that Kim is agitated, and that she is not looking at the glass that she is going to pick up. So, a reader might predict that Kim is going to knock over the glass. Of course, not every prediction will be accurate: perhaps Kim will pick the glass up cleanly. Nevertheless, the author has certainly created the expectation that the water might be spilled. Predictions are always subject to revision as the reader acquires more information.

> ➢ **Review Video:** Predictions
> *Visit* **mometrix.com/academy** *and enter* **Code: 437248**

Test-taking tip: To respond to questions requiring future predictions, your answers should be based on evidence of past or present behavior.

Readers are often required to understand a text that claims and suggests ideas without stating them directly. An **inference** is a piece of information that is implied but not written outright by the author. For instance, consider the following sentence: *After the final out of the inning, the fans were filled with joy and rushed the field.* From this sentence, a reader can infer that the fans were watching a baseball game and their team won the game. Readers should take great care to avoid using information beyond the provided passage before making inferences. As you practice with drawing inferences, you will find that they require concentration and attention.

> ➢ **Review Video:** Inference
> *Visit* **mometrix.com/academy** *and enter* **Code: 379203**

Test-taking tip: While being tested on your ability to make correct inferences, you must look for contextual clues. An answer can be *true* but not *correct*. The contextual clues will help you find the answer that is the best answer out of the given choices. Be careful in your reading to understand the context in which a phrase is stated. When asked for the implied meaning of a statement made in the passage, you should immediately locate the statement and read the context in which the statement was made. Also, look for an answer choice that has a similar phrase to the statement in question.

In addition to inference and prediction, readers must often **draw conclusions** about the information they have read. When asked for a *conclusion* that may be drawn, look for critical "hedge" phrases, such as *likely, may, can, will often*, among many others. When you are being tested on this knowledge, remember the question that writers insert into these hedge phrases to cover every possibility. Often an answer will be wrong simply because there is no room for exception. Extreme positive or negative answers (such as always or never) are usually not correct. The reader should not use any outside knowledge that is not gathered from the passage to answer the related questions. Correct answers can be derived straight from the passage.

Summarizing a Passage

As an aid to drawing conclusions, **outlining** the information contained in the passage should be a familiar skill to readers. An effective outline will reveal the structure of the passage and will lead to solid conclusions. An effective outline will have a title that refers to the basic subject of the text though the title needs not recapitulate the main idea. In most outlines, the main idea will be the first major section. Each major idea of the passage will be established as the head of a category. For instance, the most common outline format calls for the main ideas of the passage to be indicated with Roman numerals. In an effective outline of this kind, each of the main ideas will be represented by a Roman numeral and none of the Roman numerals will designate minor details or secondary ideas. Moreover, all supporting ideas and details should be placed in the appropriate place on the outline. An outline does not need to include every detail listed in the text, but the outline should feature all of those that are central to the argument or message. Each of these details should be listed under the appropriate main idea.

Ideas from a text can also be organized using **graphic organizers**. A graphic organizer is a way to simplify information and take key points from the text. A graphic organizer such as a timeline may have an event listed for a corresponding date on the timeline while an outline may have an event listed under a key point that occurs in the text. Each reader needs to create the type of graphic organizer that works the best for him or her in terms of being able to recall information from a story. Examples include a *spider-map,* which takes a main idea from the story and places it in a bubble with supporting points branching off the main idea. An *outline* is useful for diagramming the main and supporting points of the entire story, and a *Venn diagram* classifies information as separate or overlapping.

> **Review Video: Graphic Organizers**
> Visit *mometrix.com/academy* and enter **Code: 665513**

A helpful tool is the ability to **summarize** the information that you have read in a paragraph or passage format. This process is similar to creating an effective outline. First, a summary should accurately define the main idea of the passage though the summary does not need to explain this main idea in exhaustive detail. The summary should continue by laying out the most important supporting details or arguments from the passage. All of the significant supporting details should be included, and none of the details included should be irrelevant or insignificant. Also, the summary should accurately report all of these details. Too often, the desire for brevity in a summary leads to the sacrifice of clarity or accuracy. Summaries are often difficult to read because they omit all of the graceful language, digressions, and asides that distinguish great writing. However, an effective summary should contain much the same message as the original text.

Paraphrasing is another method that the reader can use to aid in comprehension. When paraphrasing, one puts what they have read into their words by rephrasing what the author has written, or one "translates" all of what the author shared into their words by including as many details as they can.

Vocabulary

The Vocabulary and General Knowledge exam has 50 items, and contains basic vocabulary that is often used in health care fields.

Increasing Verbal Ability

Nursing, like many professions, requires the ability to communicate effectively. Students should prepare for standardized testing and their nursing careers by utilizing some basic techniques for increasing vocabulary. Writing down new words is a good way to increase vocabulary. While reading, watching TV, or talking to others, make a note of any unfamiliar words you encounter. Look up the definition of those words and then attempt to use them in conversation. This will help the word become part of your general store of knowledge. Reading new and different material will also increase vocabulary. For example, if you normally read fashion magazines, try thumbing through a professional journal of archaeology or mathematics. This will introduce new words that you would not encounter in everyday life. Playing games like Scrabble and solving crossword puzzles can also help build verbal ability.

Etymology

Etymology is the study of words. It specifically focuses on the origins of words: how they have developed over time and between languages. Language is made up of words from different cultures and areas of the world. Some words we use today mean something completely different from what they meant hundreds of years ago. Words are constantly being redefined, changed, and created. New words appear as technology increases. Some words are formed by combining root words with prefixes and suffixes. Students who must improve verbal ability for standardized testing can do so by studying common prefixes and suffixes. By understanding the prefix pre, a student increases their chances of understanding words like predate. The prefix pre means "before", so it can be reasoned that predate means to date something in advance, such as predating a check.

Glossary of Important Terms

A
Abrupt - describes a sudden change that occurs without warning
Abstain - the deliberate effort to refrain from an action, such as drinking alcohol or eating junk food
Access - the freedom to use something as one chooses; the permission or ability to enter or approach a specific entity or area
Accountable - responsible for actions or explanations
Adhere - the process of binding one thing to another using glue, tape, or another agent; refers to the action of maintaining loyalty or support
Adverse - in a contrary fashion; can cause harm; may also refer to something that is in opposition to one's interests
Affect - a clear influence on one's emotions
Annual - the duration of a single year; an occurrence that takes place once each year
Apply - to put something to use; having a relevant or valid connection to something else
Audible - capable of being heard

B

Bilateral - having two sides; may refer to something that affects both side of the human body

C

Cardiac - concerning the heart
Cast - the process by which something is given shape through the pouring of a liquid substance into a mold; may also refer to the throwing of an object
Cease - to bring about a gradual end; refers to something that dies out or becomes extinct
Compensatory - an equivalent; the action of making a payment that serves as a counterbalance for another action
Complications - a factor that presents a degree of difficulty; may also refer to a secondary disease or condition
Comply - to carry out the wishes of another person; to perform in the manner prescribed by law
Concave - a surface that is rounded inward like a bowl; surface that is arched or curved
Concise - straightforward and to the point; absent of all excessive detail
Consistency - the agreement of each of the parts that constitute a whole
Constrict - to make something narrow by squeezing or compressing
Contingent - something that may happen; may also refer to something that is dependent upon or conditioned by something else
Contour - the line that represents the shape of a curvy figure
Contract - an agreement between two parties that binds each to perform certain actions
Contraindication - the presence of a symptom or condition that will make a specific treatment unadvisable

D

Defecate - to have feces removed from the bowels
Deficit - a lack in an amount or quality of something, such as money or rainfall
Depress - to press down; the lessening of activity or strength; an action in which something moves to a lower position
Depth - a quality of being complete and thorough
Deteriorating - to make inferior in quality; to diminish in function or condition
Device - something that is devised or thought up; may be a piece of equipment designed for a specific task
Diagnosis - determining the dysfunction/disease
Diameter - the length of a line that passes through the body of an object
Dilate - to enlarge, extend, or widen; to become wide like the pupil of the eye
Dilute - to make a substance thinner or less potent; diminish in flavor or intensity
Discrete - a separate entity; unique and separate from other things
Distended - something that has been enlarged by the force of internal pressure
Dysfunction - a hindered function a body system or organ

E

Elevate - to lift or make something higher; to lift in rank or title
Endogenous - the growth from a deep tissue; refers to conditions that arise from factors that are internal to an organism
Exacerbate - to cause something to become more intense in nature; especially an increase in violence or severity
Excess - surpassing usual limitations; unnecessary indulgence
Exogenous - the growth from superficial or shallow tissue; refers to conditions caused by factors that are external to an organism

Expand - to open or unfold; refers to an increase in number, size, or scope; may refer to the expression of an idea in greater depth
Exposure - being subject to a condition or influence; making a secret fact known publicly
External - being outside the human body; existing outside the confines of a specific space or institution

F

Fatal - something that may cause death; relating to fate or proceeding in a manner that follows a fixed sequence of events
Fatigue - the state of tiredness brought on by labor, exertion, or stress; the tendency of a specified material to break under stress
Flaccid - the state of not being firm; lacking vigor, force, or youthful firmness
Flushed - blushing or an area of the body that becomes reddened

G

Gaping - something that is wide open and exposed
Gastrointestinal - concerning the stomach and intestines
Gender - the behavioral, cultural, or psychological traits that are associated with a specific sex

H

Hematologic - concerning blood
Hygiene - the science of health - inducing practices; the condition or practice of activities that can maintain physical health

I

Impaired - a condition in which one cannot perform or function properly; often refers to a person who is under the influence of drugs or alcohol
Impending - hanging overhead threateningly; bound to occur in the near future
Incidence - the arrival of something at a surface; something that occurs or affects something else
Infection - an area of body tissue that been invaded with pathogenic organisms
Inflamed - to incite an intensely emotional state; also refers to something that has been set on fire
Ingest - to take into one's mouth for digestion
Initiate - to cause something to begin or to set events in motion; as initiation, can also refer to the process through which a person is allowed entry into a club or organization
Insidious - something or someone who is enticing but dangerous; slow - developing dangerousness
Intact - something that remains whole or untouched by destructive forces; having no relevant part removed or altered
Internal - things inside of the body or the mind; something that exists within the limits and confines of something else
Invasive - tending to spread or infringe upon something; may also refer to something that will enter the human body

L

Labile - unstable; constantly undergoing a chemical or physical change or breakdown
Laceration - wound with irregular borders, knife like in appearance
Latent - not presently active but with the potential to become active
Lethargic - sluggish, indifferent, or apathetic

M

Manifestation - the act of becoming outwardly visible; can refer to the occult phenomenon of a supernatural materialization
Musculoskeletal - concerning the connections of the muscle and the skeleton

N

Neurologic - concerning the nervous system
Neurovascular - concerning the blood vessels and the nerves
Nutrient - something that provides nourishment

O

Occluded - closed or blocked off
Ominous - exhibiting an omen; refers to something evil or disastrous that appears likely to occur
Ongoing - in the process of occurring; continuously advancing or moving ahead
Oral - spoken by the mouth; of or relating to the mouth
Overt - something that is openly displayed or obvious

P

Parameter - a limit or boundary; in math, it is an arbitrary value that is used to describe a statistical population
Paroxysmal - characterized by a sudden fit or attack of symptoms; may be a sudden emotion or uncontrollable action
Patent - a clear and easily accessible passage
Pathogenic - disease causing
Pathology - the study of diseases
Posterior - related to the rear/back position
Potent - able to copulate as a male; refers to something that is chemically or medically effective
Potential - having the possibility of becoming a reality
Precaution - the act of taking care in advance; refers to measures taken in advance in order to prevent harm
Precipitous - very steep or difficult to climb or overcome
Predispose - to dispose in advance of or to make susceptible to
Pre-existing - the state of existing before or previous to something else
Primary - first in order; a rank of importance
Priority - the state of being before; coming first in order of date or position; a preferential rating
Prognosis - the possibility of recovery after the diagnosis of an illness or disease

R

Rationale - an explanation regarding the principles, opinions, beliefs, or practices held by a specific party
Recur - something that is revisited for consideration; a thought or idea that enters one's mind for a second time
Renal - concerning the kidneys
Respiration - the act of breathing in and out of air
Restrict - to confine something or someone within specific limitations or boundaries
Retain - to keep in one's possession; to maintain an item or person in security

S

Site - the physical location of a structure; the physical space reserved for a building; the place or scene of an occurrence
Status - the position or rank held in relation to others; a person or object's condition with respect to circumstances
Strict - inflexible; maintained in such a manner that cannot be changed or altered
Sublingual - beneath the tongue
Supplement - an item that completes something else
Suppress - to restrain by authority or force; to omit something from memory; to keep from public knowledge
Symmetric - exhibiting symmetry; capable of being divided by a longitudinal plane into equal sections
Symptom - the evidence of a disease or illness; the presence of a symptom is indicative of something else
Syndrome - a group of symptoms that happen close together and suggest an illness or irregular condition

T

Therapeutic - concerning the treatment of an illness or irregular condition
Transdermal - passing through skin
Transmission - passing something from one place to another
Trauma - an injury done by an outside object
Triage - a system that helps to determine which patients need the most care by evaluating their condition and chances of responding positively to treatment

U

Untoward - difficult to manage; marked by trouble or unpleasantness
Urinate - to expel urine

V

Vascular - concerning the blood vessels
Verbal - relating to or consisting of words; involving words rather than meaning or substance
Virus - a microscopic pathogen that replicates in living cells and can cause disease
Vital - necessary or essential to the existence of life
Void - not occupied or empty; of no legal force or effect
Volume - printed pages bound in a book form; space occupied by a three - dimensional form; degree of loudness

Grammar

The Eight Parts of Speech

<u>Nouns</u>
When you talk about a person, place, thing, or idea, you are talking about nouns. The two main types of nouns are common and proper nouns. Also, nouns can be abstract (i.e., general) or concrete (i.e., specific).

Common nouns are the class or group of people, places, and things (Note: Do not capitalize common nouns). Examples of common nouns:
People: boy, girl, worker, manager
Places: school, bank, library, home
Things: dog, cat, truck, car

Proper nouns are the names of a specific person, place, or thing (Note: Capitalize all proper nouns). Examples of proper nouns:
People: Abraham Lincoln, George Washington, Martin Luther King, Jr.
Places: Los Angeles, California / New York / Asia
Things: Statue of Liberty, Earth*, Lincoln Memorial

*Note: When you talk about the planet that we live on, you capitalize *Earth*. When you mean the dirt, rocks, or land, you lowercase *earth*.

General nouns are the names of conditions or ideas. **Specific nouns** name people, places, and things that are understood by using your senses.

General nouns:
Condition: beauty, strength
Idea: truth, peace

Specific nouns:
People: baby, friend, father
Places: town, park, city hall
Things: rainbow, cough, apple, silk, gasoline

Collective nouns are the names for a person, place, or thing that may act as a whole. The following are examples of collective nouns: *class, company, dozen, group, herd, team,* and *public*.

Pronouns

Pronouns are words that are used to stand in for a noun. A pronoun may be grouped as personal, intensive, relative, interrogative, demonstrative, indefinite, and reciprocal.

Personal: Nominative is the case for nouns and pronouns that are the subject of a sentence. Objective is the case for nouns and pronouns that are an object in a sentence. Possessive is the case for nouns and pronouns that show possession or ownership.

Singular

	Nominative	Objective	Possessive
First Person	I	me	my, mine
Second Person	you	you	your, yours
Third Person	he, she, it	him, her, it	his, her, hers, its

Plural

	Nominative	Objective	Possessive
First Person	we	us	our, ours
Second Person	you	you	your, yours
Third Person	they	them	their, theirs

Intensive: I myself, you yourself, he himself, she herself, the (thing) itself, we ourselves, you yourselves, they themselves

Relative: which, who, whom, whose

Interrogative: what, which, who, whom, whose

Demonstrative: this, that, these, those

Indefinite: all, any, each, everyone, either/neither, one, some, several

Reciprocal: each other, one another

> ➢ **Review Video: Nouns and Pronouns**
> Visit *mometrix.com/academy* and enter *Code:* **312073**

Verbs

If you want to write a sentence, then you need a verb in your sentence. Without a verb, you have no sentence. The verb of a sentence explains action or being. In other words, the verb shows the subject's movement or the movement that has been done to the subject.

Transitive and Intransitive Verbs

A transitive verb is a verb whose action (e.g., drive, run, jump) points to a receiver (e.g., car, dog, kangaroo). Intransitive verbs do not point to a receiver of an action. In other words, the action of the verb does not point to a subject or object.

Transitive: He plays the piano. | The piano was played by him.

Intransitive: He plays. | John writes well.

A dictionary will let you know whether a verb is transitive or intransitive. Some verbs can be transitive and intransitive.

Action Verbs and Linking Verbs

An action verb is a verb that shows what the subject is doing in a sentence. In other words, an action verb shows action. A sentence can be complete with one word: an action verb. Linking verbs are intransitive verbs that show a condition (i.e., the subject is described but does no action).

Linking verbs link the subject of a sentence to a noun or pronoun, or they link a subject with an adjective. You always need a verb if you want a complete sentence. However, linking verbs are not able to complete a sentence.

Common linking verbs include *appear, be, become, feel, grow, look, seem, smell, sound,* and *taste*. However, any verb that shows a condition and has a noun, pronoun, or adjective that describes the subject of a sentence is a linking verb.

Action: He sings. | Run! | Go! | I talk with him every day. | She reads.

Linking:
Incorrect: I am.
Correct: I am John. | I smell roses. | I feel tired.

Note: Some verbs are followed by words that look like prepositions, but they are a part of the verb and a part of the verb's meaning. These are known as phrasal verbs and examples include *call off, look up,* and *drop off*.

Voice

Transitive verbs come in active or passive voice. If the subject does an action or receives the action of the verb, then you will know whether a verb is active or passive. When the subject of the sentence is doing the action, the verb is active voice. When the subject receives the action, the verb is passive voice.

Active: Jon drew the picture. (The subject *Jon* is doing the action of *drawing a picture*.)

Passive: The picture is drawn by Jon. (The subject *picture* is receiving the action from Jon.)

Verb Tenses

A verb tense shows the different form of a verb to point to the time of an action. The present and past tense are shown by changing the verb's form. An action in the present *I talk* can change form for the past: *I talked*. However, for the other tenses, an auxiliary (i.e., helping) verb is needed to show the change in form. These helping verbs include *am, are, is | have, has, had | was, were, will* (or *shall*).

Present: I talk   Present perfect: I have talked
Past: I talked   Past perfect: I had talked
Future: I will talk   Future perfect: I will have talked

Present: The action happens at the current time.
Example: He *walks* to the store every morning.
To show that something is happening right now, use the progressive present tense: I *am walking*.

Past: The action happened in the past.
Example: He *walked* to the store an hour ago.

Future: The action is going to happen later.
Example: I *will walk* to the store tomorrow.

Present perfect: The action started in the past and continues into the present.
Example: I *have walked* to the store three times today.

Past perfect: The second action happened in the past. The first action came before the second.
Example: Before I walked to the store (Action 2), I *had walked* to the library (Action 1).

Future perfect: An action that uses the past and the future. In other words, the action is complete before a future moment.
Example: When she comes for the supplies (future moment), I *will have walked* to the store (action completed in the past).

Conjugating Verbs
When you need to change the form of a verb, you are conjugating a verb. The key parts of a verb are first person singular, present tense (dream); first person singular, past tense (dreamed); and the past participle (dreamed). Note: the past participle needs a helping verb to make a verb tense. For example, I *have dreamed* of this day. | I *am dreaming* of this day.

Present Tense: Active Voice

	Singular	Plural
First Person	I dream	We dream
Second Person	You dream	You dream
Third Person	He, she, it dreams	They dream

Mood
There are three moods in English: the indicative, the imperative, and the subjunctive.

The **indicative mood** is used for facts, opinions, and questions.
Fact: You can do this.
Opinion: I think that you can do this.
Question: Do you know that you can do this?

The **imperative** is used for orders or requests.
Order: You are going to do this!
Request: Will you do this for me?

The **subjunctive mood** is for wishes and statements that go against fact.
Wish: I wish that I were going to do this.
Statement against fact: If I were you, I would do this. (This goes against fact because I am not you. You have the chance to do this, and I do not the chance.)

The mood that causes trouble for most people is the subjunctive mood. If you have trouble with any of the moods, then be sure to practice.

<u>Adjectives</u>
An adjective is a word that is used to modify a noun or pronoun. An adjective answers a question: *Which one?*, *What kind of?*, or *How many?*. Usually, adjectives come before the words that they modify.

Which one?: The *third* suit is my favorite.
What kind?: The *navy blue* suit is my favorite.
How many?: Can I look over the *four* neckties for the suit?

Articles
Articles are adjectives that are used to mark nouns. There are only three: the definite (i.e., limited or fixed amount) article *the*, and the indefinite (i.e., no limit or fixed amount) articles *a* and *an*. Note: *An* comes before words that start with a vowel sound (i.e., vowels include *a, e, i, o, u,* and *y*). For example, Are you going to get an **u**mbrella?

Definite: I lost *the* bottle that belongs to me.
Indefinite: Does anyone have *a* bottle to share?

Comparison with Adjectives
Some adjectives are relative and other adjectives are absolute. Adjectives that are relative can show the comparison between things. Adjectives that are absolute can show comparison. However, they show comparison in a different way. Let's say that you are reading two books. You think that one book is perfect, and the other book is not exactly perfect. It is not possible for the book to be more perfect than the other. Either you think that the book is perfect, or you think that the book is not perfect.

The adjectives that are relative will show the different degrees of something or someone to something else or someone else. The three degrees of adjectives include positive, comparative, and superlative.

The positive degree is the normal form of an adjective.
Example: This work is *difficult*. | She is *smart*.

The comparative degree compares one person or thing to another person or thing.
Example: This work is *more difficult* than your work. | She is *smarter* than me.

The superlative degree compares more than two people or things.
Example: This is the *most difficult* work of my life. | She is the *smartest* lady in school.

> **Review Video: What is an Adjective?**
> *Visit* **mometrix.com/academy** *and enter* **Code: 809578**

Adverbs
An adverb is a word that is used to modify a verb, adjective, or another adverb. Usually, adverbs answer one of these questions: *When?, Where?, How?,* and *Why?* . The negatives *not* and *never* are known as adverbs. Adverbs that modify adjectives or other adverbs strengthen or weaken the words that they modify.

Examples:
He walks quickly through the crowd.
The water flows smoothly on the rocks.

Note: While many adverbs end in *-ly*, you need to remember that not all adverbs end in *-ly*. Also, some words that end in *-ly* are adjectives, not adverbs. Some examples include: *early, friendly, holy,* *lonely*, *silly*, and *ugly*. To know if a word that ends in *-ly* is an adjective or adverb, you need to check your dictionary.

Examples:
He is *never* angry.
You talk *too* loud.

Comparison with Adverbs
The rules for comparing adverbs are the same as the rules for adjectives.

The positive degree is the standard form of an adverb.
Example: He arrives soon. | She speaks softly to her friends.

The comparative degree compares one person or thing to another person or thing.
Example: He arrives sooner than Sarah. | She speaks more softly than him.

The superlative degree compares more than two people or things.
Example: He arrives soonest of the group. | She speaks most softly of any of her friends.

> ➢ **Review Video: Adverbs**
> *Visit* **mometrix.com/academy** *and enter* **Code: 713951**

Prepositions
A preposition is a word placed before a noun or pronoun that shows the relationship between an object and another word in the sentence.

Common prepositions:

about	before	during	on	under
after	beneath	for	over	until
against	between	from	past	up
among	beyond	in	through	with
around	by	of	to	within
at	down	off	toward	without

Examples:
The napkin is *in* the drawer.
The Earth rotates *around* the Sun.
The needle is *beneath* the haystack.
Can you find me *among* the words?

> ➢ **Review Video: What is a Preposition?**
> *Visit* **mometrix.com/academy** *and enter* **Code: 946763**

Conjunctions
Conjunctions join words, phrases, or clauses, and they show the connection between the joined pieces. There are coordinating conjunctions that connect equal parts of sentences. Correlative conjunctions show the connection between pairs. Subordinating conjunctions join subordinate (i.e., dependent) clauses with independent clauses.

Coordinating Conjunctions
The coordinating conjunctions include: *and, but, yet, or, nor, for,* and *so*
Examples:
The rock was small, but it was heavy.
She drove in the night, and he drove in the day.

Correlative Conjunctions
The correlative conjunctions are: *either...or | neither...nor | not only... but also*
Examples:
Either you are coming, *or* you are staying. | He ran *not only* three miles, *but also* swam 200 yards.

> ➤ **Review Video: Coordinating and Correlative Conjunctions**
> Visit *mometrix.com/academy* and enter **Code: 390329**

Subordinating Conjunctions
Common subordinating conjunctions include:

after	since	whenever
although	so that	where
because	unless	wherever
before	until	whether
in order that	when	while

Examples:
I am hungry *because* I did not eat breakfast.
He went home *when* everyone left.

> ➤ **Review Video: Subordinating Conjunctions**
> Visit *mometrix.com/academy* and enter **Code: 958913**

<u>Interjections</u>
An interjection is a word for exclamation (i.e., great amount of feeling) that is used alone or as a piece to a sentence. Often, they are used at the beginning of a sentence for an introduction. Sometimes, they can be used in the middle of a sentence to show a change in thought or attitude.

Common Interjections: Hey! | Oh,... | Ouch! | Please! | Wow!

Punctuation

Capitalization

The rules for capitalization are:
1. Capitalize the first word of a sentence and the first word in a direct quotation
   Examples:
   First Word: *Football* is my favorite sport.
   Direct Quote: She asked, "*What* is your name?"

2. Capitalize proper nouns and adjectives that come from proper nouns
   Examples:
   Proper Noun: My parents are from *Europe*.
   Adjective from Proper Noun: My father is *British,* and my mother is *Italian*.

3. Capitalize the names of days, months, and holidays
   Examples:
   Day: Everyone needs to be here on *Wednesday*.
   Month: I am so excited for *December*.
   Holiday: *Independence Day* comes every July.

4. Capitalize the names on a compass for specific areas, not when they give direction
   Examples:
   Specific Area: James is from the *West*.
   Direction: After three miles, turn *south* toward the highway.

5. Capitalize the first word for each word in a title (Note: Articles, Prepositions, and Conjunctions are not capitalized.)
   Examples:
   Titles: <u>Romeo and Juliet</u> is a beautiful drama on love.
   Incorrect: <u>The Taming Of The Shrew</u> is my favorite. (Remember that prepositions and articles are not capitalized.)

   Note: Books, movies, plays (more than one act), newspapers, magazines, and long musical pieces are put in italics. The two examples of Shakespeare's plays are underlined to show their use as an example.

End Punctuation

<u>Periods</u>
Use a period to end all sentences except direct questions, exclamations, and questions.

Declarative Sentence
A declarative sentence gives information or makes a statement.
Examples: I can fly a kite. | The plane left two hours ago.

Imperative Sentence
An imperative sentence gives an order or command.
Examples: You are coming with me. | Bring me that note.

Periods for Abbreviations
Examples: 3 P.M. | 2 A.M. | Mr. Jones | Mrs. Stevens | Dr. Smith | Bill Jr. | Pennsylvania Ave.
Note: an abbreviation is a shortened form of a word or phrase.

Question Marks
Question marks should be used following a direct question. A polite request can be followed by a period instead of a question mark.

Direct Question: What is for lunch today? | How are you? | Why is that the answer?

Polite Requests:
Can you please send me the item tomorrow. | Will you please walk with me on the track.

Exclamation Marks
Exclamation marks are used after a word group or sentence that shows much feeling or has special importance. Exclamation marks should not be overused. They are saved for proper exclamatory interjections.
Examples: We're going to the finals! | You have a beautiful car! | That's crazy!

Commas

The comma is a punctuation mark that can help you understand connections in a sentence. Not every sentence needs a comma. However, if a sentence needs a comma, you need to put it in the right place. A comma in the wrong place (or an absent comma) will make a sentence's meaning unclear. These are some of the rules for commas:

1. Use a comma between a coordinating conjunction joining independent clauses
   Example: *Bob caught three fish, and I caught two fish.*

2. Use a comma after an introductory phrase or an adverbial clause
   Examples:
   After the final out, we went to a restaurant to celebrate.
   Studying the stars, I was surprised at the beauty of the sky.

3. Use a comma between items in a series.
   Example: I will bring *the turkey, the pie, and the coffee.*

4. Use a comma between coordinate adjectives not joined with *and*
   Incorrect: The kind, brown dog followed me home.
   Correct: The *kind, loyal* dog followed me home.

   Note: Not all adjectives are coordinate (i.e., equal or parallel). There are two simple ways to know if your adjectives are coordinate. One, you can join the adjectives with *and*: *The kind and loyal dog.* Two, you can change the order of the adjectives: *The loyal, kind dog.*

5. Use commas for interjections and after *yes* and *no* responses
   Examples:
   Interjection: Oh, I had no idea. | Wow, you know how to play this game.
   Yes and No: *Yes,* I heard you. | *No,* I cannot come tomorrow.

6. Use commas to separate nonessential modifiers and nonessential appositives
   Examples:
   Nonessential Modifier: John Frank, who is coaching the team, was promoted today.
   Nonessential Appositive: Thomas Edison, an American inventor, was born in Ohio.

7. Use commas to set off nouns of direct address, interrogative tags, and contrast
   Examples:
   Direct Address: You, *John,* are my only hope in this moment.
   Interrogative Tag: This is the last time, *correct?*
   Contrast: You are my friend, *not my enemy.*

8. Use commas with dates, addresses, geographical names, and titles
   Examples:
   Date: *July 4, 1776,* is an important date to remember.
   Address: He is meeting me at *456 Delaware Avenue,* tomorrow morning.
   Geographical Name: *Paris, France,* is my favorite city.
   Title: John Smith, *Ph. D.,* will be visiting your class today.

9. Use commas to separate expressions like *he said* and *she said* if they come between a sentence of a quote
   Examples:
   "I want you to know," he began, "that I always wanted the best for you."
   "You can start," Jane said, "with an apology."

> ➤ **Review Video: Commas**
> Visit **mometrix.com/academy** and enter **Code: 644254**

Semicolons

The semicolon is used to connect major sentence pieces of equal value. Some rules for semicolons include:

1. Use a semicolon between closely connected independent clauses that are not connected with a coordinating conjunction.
   Examples:
   She is outside; we are inside.
   You are right; we should go with your plan.

2. Use a semicolon between independent clauses linked with a transitional word.
   Examples:
   I think that we can agree on this; *however,* I am not sure about my friends.
   You are looking in the wrong places; *therefore,* you will not find what you need.

3. Use a semicolon between items in a series that has internal punctuation.
   Example: I have visited *New York, New York; Augusta, Maine; and Baltimore, Maryland*.

> **Review Video: Semicolon Usage**
> Visit *mometrix.com/academy* and enter **Code: 370605**

Colons

The colon is used to call attention to the words that follow it. A colon must come after an independent clause. The rules for colons are as follows:
1. Use a colon after an independent clause to make a list
   Example: I want to learn many languages: Spanish, French, German, and Italian.

2. Use a colon for explanations or to give a quote
   Examples:
   Quote: The man started with an idea: "We are able to do more than we imagine."

   Explanation: There is one thing that stands out on your resume: responsibility.

3. Use a colon after the greeting in a formal letter, to show hours and minutes, and to separate a title and subtitle
   Examples:
   Greeting in a formal letter: Dear Sir: | To Whom It May Concern:

   Time: It is 3:14 P.M.

   Title: The essay is titled "America: A Short Introduction to a Modern Country"

Parentheses

Parentheses are used for additional information. Also, they can be used to put labels for letters or numbers in a series. Parentheses should be not be used very often. If they are overused, parentheses can be a distraction instead of a help.

Examples:
Extra Information: The rattlesnake (see Image 2) is a dangerous snake of North and South America.

Series: Include in the email (1) your name, (2) your address, and (3) your question for the author.

Quotation Marks

Use quotation marks to close off direct quotations of a person's spoken or written words. Do not use quotation marks around indirect quotations. An indirect quotation gives someone's message without using the person's exact words. Use single quotation marks to close off a quotation inside a quotation.

Direct Quote: Nancy said, "I am waiting for Henry to arrive."

Indirect Quote: Henry said that he is going to be late to the meeting.

Quote inside a Quote: The teacher asked, "Has everyone read 'The Gift of the Magi'?"

Quotation marks should be used around the titles of short works: newspaper and magazine articles, poems, short stories, songs, television episodes, radio programs, and subdivisions of books or web sites.

Examples:

"Rip van Winkle" (short story by Washington Irving)

"O Captain! My Captain!" (poem by Walt Whitman)

Quotation marks may be used to set off words that are being used in a different way from a dictionary definition. Also, they can be used to highlight irony.

Examples:

The boss warned Frank that he was walking on "thin ice."

(Frank is not walking on real ice. Instead, Frank is being warned to avoid mistakes.)

The teacher thanked the young man for his "honesty."

(Honesty and truth are not always the same thing. In this example, the quotation marks around *honesty* show that the teacher does not believe the young man's explanation.)

> ➢ **Review Video: Quotation Marks**
> *Visit mometrix.com/academy and enter Code:* **118471**

Note: Periods and commas are put inside quotation marks. Colons and semicolons are put outside the quotation marks. Question marks and exclamation points are placed inside quotation marks when they are part of a quote. When the question or exclamation mark goes with the whole sentence, the mark is left outside of the quotation marks.

Examples:

Period and comma: We read "Peter Pan," "Alice in Wonderland," and "Cinderella."

Semicolon: They watched "The Nutcracker"; then, they went home.

Exclamation mark that is a part of a quote: The crowd cheered, "Victory!"

Question mark that goes with the whole sentence: Is your favorite book "The Hobbit"?

Apostrophes

An apostrophe is used to show possession or the deletion of letters in contractions. An apostrophe is not needed with the possessive pronouns *his, hers, its, ours, theirs, whose,* and *yours*.

Singular Nouns: David's car | a book's theme | my brother's board game

Plural Nouns with *-s*: the scissors' handle | boys' basketball

Plural Nouns without *-s*: Men's department | the people's adventure

> ➢ **Review Video: Apostrophes**
> *Visit mometrix.com/academy and enter Code:* **213068**

Improving Sentences and Paragraphs

Subjects and Predicates

<u>Subjects</u>
Every sentence has two things: a subject and a verb. The subject of a sentence names who or what the sentence is all about. The subject may be directly stated in a sentence, or the subject may be the implied *you*.

In imperative sentences, the verb's subject is understood (e.g., |You| Run to the store). So, the subject may not be in the sentence. Normally, the subject comes before the verb. However, the subject comes after the verb in sentences that begin with *There are* or *There was*.

Direct:
John knows the way to the park.
(Who knows the way to the park? Answer: John)

The cookies need ten more minutes.
(What needs ten minutes? Answer: The cookies)

By five o' clock, Bill will need to leave.
(Who needs to leave? Answer: Bill)

Remember: The subject can come after the verb.
There are five letters on the table for him.
(What is on the table? Answer: Five letters)

There were coffee and doughnuts in the house.
(What was in the house? Answer: Coffee and doughnuts)

Implied:
Go to the post office for me.
(Who is going to the post office? Answer: You are.)

Come and sit with me, please?
(Who needs to come and sit? Answer: You do.)

The complete subject has the simple subject and all of the modifiers. To find the complete subject, ask *Who* or *What* and insert the verb to complete the question. The answer is the complete subject. To find the simple subject, remove all of the modifiers in the complete subject. When you can find the subject of a sentence, you can correct many problems. These problems include sentence fragments and subject-verb agreement.

Examples:
The small red car is the one that he wants for Christmas.
(The complete subject is *the small red car*.)

The young artist is coming over for dinner.
(The complete subject is *the young artist*.)

> ➤ **Review Video:** <u>Subjects</u>
> Visit **mometrix.com/academy** *and enter* **Code: 444771**

Predicates
In a sentence, you always have a predicate and a subject. A predicate is what remains when you have found the subject. The subject tells what the sentence is about, and the predicate explains or describes the subject.

Think about the sentence: *He sings*. In this sentence, we have a subject (He) and a predicate (sings). This is all that is needed for a sentence to be complete. Would we like more information? Of course, we would like to know more. However, if this all the information that you are given, you have a complete sentence.

Now, let's look at another sentence:
John and Jane sing on Tuesday nights at the dance hall.

What is the subject of this sentence?
Answer: John and Jane.

What is the predicate of this sentence?
Answer: Everything else in the sentence besides John and Jane.

Subject-Verb Agreement

Verbs agree with their subjects in number. In other words, singular subjects need singular verbs. Plural subjects need plural verbs. Singular is for one person, place, or thing. Plural is for more than one person, place, or thing. Subjects and verbs must also agree in person: first, second, or third. The present tense ending *-s* is used on a verb if its subject is third person singular; otherwise, the verb takes no ending.

> ➤ **Review Video: Subjects and Verbs**
> Visit *mometrix.com/academy* and enter **Code: 987207**

Number Agreement Examples:
Single Subject and Verb: *Dan calls home.*
(Dan is one person. So, the singular verb *calls* is needed.)

Plural Subject and Verb: *Dan and Bob call home.*
(More than one person needs the plural verb *call*.)

Person Agreement Examples:
First Person: I *am* walking.
Second Person: You *are* walking.
Third Person: He *is* walking.

Problems with Subject-Verb Agreement

- Words between Subject and Verb
  The joy of my life returns home tonight.
  (**Singular Subject**: joy. **Singular Verb**: returns)
  The phrase *of my life* does not influence the verb *returns*.

The question that still remains unanswered is "Who are you?"
(**Singular Subject**: question. **Singular Verb**: is)
Don't let the phrase "*that still remains…*" trouble you. The subject *questions* goes with *is*.

- Compound Subjects
  You and Jon are invited to come to my house.
  (**Plural Subject**: You and Jon. **Plural Verb**: are)

  The pencil and paper belong to me.
  (**Plural Subject**: pencil and paper. **Plural Verb**: belong)

- Subjects Joined by *Or* and *Nor*
  Today or tomorrow is the day.
  (**Subject**: Today / tomorrow. **Verb**: is)

  Stan or Phil wants to read the book.
  (**Subject**: Stan / Phil. **Verb**: wants)

  Neither the books nor the *pen is* on the desk.
  (**Subject**: Books / Pen. **Verb**: was)

  Either the blanket or *pillows arrive* this afternoon.
  (**Subject**: Blanket / Pillows. **Verb**: arrive)

  Note: Singular subjects that are joined with the conjunction *or* need a singular verb. However, when one subject is singular and another is plural, you make the verb agree with the closer subject. The example about books and the pen has a singular verb because the pen (singular subject) is closer to the verb.

- Indefinite Pronouns: Either, Neither, and Each
  Is either of you ready for the game?
  (**Singular Subject**: Either. **Singular Verb**: is)

  Each man, woman, and child is unique.
  (**Singular Subject**: Each. **Singular Verb**: is)

- The adjective Every and compounds: Everybody, Everyone, Anybody, Anyone
  Every day passes faster than the last.
  (**Singular Subject**: Every day. **Singular Verb**: passes)

  Anybody is welcome to bring a tent.
  (**Singular Subject**: Anybody. **Singular Verb**: is)

- Collective Nouns
  The family eats at the restaurant every Friday night.
  (The members of the family are one at the restaurant.)

  The team are leaving for their homes after the game.
  (The members of the team are leaving as individuals to go to their own homes.)

- <u>Who, Which, and That as Subject</u>
  This is the man who is helping me today.
  He is a good man who serves others before himself.
  This painting that is hung over the couch is very beautiful.

- <u>Plural Form and Singular Meaning</u>
  Some nouns that are singular in meaning but plural in form: news, mathematics, physics, and economics
      The news is coming on now.
      Mathematics is my favorite class.

  Some nouns that are plural in meaning: athletics, gymnastics, scissors, and pants
      Do these pants come with a shirt?
      The scissors are for my project.

  Note: There are more nouns in plural form and are singular in meaning than plural in meaning. Look to your dictionary for help when you don't know about the meaning of a verb.

  Addition, Multiplication, Subtraction, and Division are normally singular.
      One plus one is two.
      Three times three is nine.

Complements

A complement is a noun, pronoun, or adjective that is used to give more information about the verb in the sentence.

<u>Direct Objects</u>
A direct object is a noun that takes or receives the action of a verb. Remember: a complete sentence does not need a direct object. A sentence needs only a subject and a verb. When you are looking for a direct object, find the verb and ask *who* or *what*.
    Example: I took the blanket. (Who or what did I take? *The blanket*)
                   Jane read books. (Who or what does Jane read? *Books*)

<u>Indirect Objects</u>
An indirect object is a word or group of words that show how an action had an influence on someone or something. If there is an indirect object in a sentence, then you always have a direct object in the sentence. When you are looking for the indirect object, find the verb and ask *to/for whom or what*.
    Examples: We taught the old dog a new trick.
                   (To/For Whom or What was taught? *The old dog*)

                  I gave them a math lesson.
                  (To/For Whom or What was given? *Them*)

<u>Predicate Nouns</u> are nouns that modify the subject and finish linking verbs.
    Example: My father is a lawyer.
                    Father is the subject. Lawyer is the predicate noun.

Predicate Adjectives are adjectives that modify the subject and finish linking verbs.
Example: Your mother is patient.
            Mother is the subject. Patient is the predicate adjective.

Pronoun Usage

Pronoun - antecedent agreement - The antecedent is the noun that has been replaced by a pronoun. A pronoun and the antecedent agree when they are singular or plural.

Singular agreement: *John* came into town, and *he* played for us.
(The word *He* replaces *John*.)

Plural agreement: *John and Rick* came into town, and *they* played for us.
(The word *They* replaces *John* and *Rick*.)

To know the correct pronoun for a compound subject, try each pronoun separately with the verb. Your knowledge of pronouns will tell you which one is correct.
Example: Bob and (I, me) will be going.
(Answer: Bob and I will be going.)

Test: (1) *I will be going* or (2) *Me will be going*. The second choice cannot be correct because *me* is not used as a subject of a sentence. Instead, *me* is used as an object.

When a pronoun is used with a noun immediately following (as in "we boys"), try the sentence without the added noun.
Example: (We/Us) boys played football last year.
(Answer: We boys played football last year.)

Test: (1) *We* played football last year or (2) *Us* played football last year. Again, the second choice cannot be correct because *us* is not used as a subject of a sentence. Instead, *us* is used as an object.

> **Review Video: Pronoun Usage**
> Visit **mometrix.com/academy** and enter **Code: 666500**

Pronoun reference - A pronoun should point clearly to the antecedent. Here is how a pronoun reference can be unhelpful if it is not directly stated or puzzling.

Unhelpful: Ron and Jim went to the store, and he bought soda.
(Who bought soda? Ron or Jim?)

Helpful: Jim went to the store, and he bought soda.
(The sentence is clear. Jim bought the soda.)

Personal pronouns - Some pronouns change their form by their placement in a sentence. A pronoun that is a subject in a sentence comes in the subjective case. Pronouns that serve as objects appear in the objective case. Finally, the pronouns that are used as possessives appear in the possessive case.

Subjective case: *He* is coming to the show.
(The pronoun *He* is the subject of the sentence.)

Objective case: Josh drove *him* to the airport.
(The pronoun *him* is the object of the sentence.)

Possessive case: The flowers are *mine*.
(The pronoun *mine* shows ownership of the flowers.)

Who or whom - *Who*, a subjective-case pronoun, can be used as a subject. *Whom*, an objective case pronoun, can be used as an object. The words *who* and *whom* are common in subordinate clauses or in questions.

Subject: He knows who wants to come.
(*Who* is the subject of the verb *wants*.)

Object: He knows whom we want at the party.
(*Whom* is the object of *we want*.)

Word Confusion

Which is used for things only.
    Example: John's dog, *which was called Max,* is large and fierce.

That is used for people or things.
    Example: Is this the only book *that Louis L'Amour wrote?*
    Example: Is Louis L'Amour the author *that wrote Western novels?*

Who is used for people only.
    Example: Mozart was the composer *who wrote those operas.*

Homonyms
Homonyms are words that sound alike, but they have different spellings and definitions.

To, Too, and Two

To can be an adverb or a preposition for showing direction, purpose, and relationship. See your dictionary for the many other ways use *to* in a sentence.
Examples: I went to the store. | I want to go with you.

Too is an adverb that means *also, as well, very, or more than enough.*
Examples: I can walk a mile too. | You have eaten too much.

Two is the second number in the series of numbers (e.g., one (1), two, (2), three (3)...)
Example: You have two minutes left.

There, Their, and They're

There can be an adjective, adverb, or pronoun. Often, *there* is used to show a place or to start a sentence.
Examples: I went there yesterday. | There is something in his pocket.

Their is a pronoun that is used to show ownership.
Examples: He is their father. | This is their fourth apology this week.

They're is a contraction of *they are*.
Example: Did you know that they're in town?

Knew and New

Knew is the past tense of *know*.
Example: I knew the answer.

New is an adjective that means something is current, has not been used, or modern.
Example: This is my new phone.

Its and It's

Its is an adjective that shows ownership.
Example: The guitar is in its case.

It's is a contraction of *it is*.
Example: It's an honor and a privilege to meet you.
Note: The *h* in honor is silent. So, the sound of the vowel *o* must have the article *an*.

Your and You're

Your is an adjective that shows ownership.
Example: This is your moment to shine.

You're is a contraction of you are.
Example: Yes, you're correct.

Affect and Effect

Affect can be used as a noun for feeling, emotion, or mood. Effect can be used as a noun that means result. Affect as a verb means to influence. Effect as a verb means to bring about.
Affect: The sunshine affects plants.
Effect: The new rules will effect order in the office.

Clauses

There are two groups of clauses: independent and dependent. Unlike phrases, a clause has a subject and a verb. So, what is the difference between a clause that is independent and one that is dependent? An independent clause gives a complete thought. A dependent clause does not share a complete thought. Instead, a dependent clause has a subject and a verb, but it needs an independent clause. Subordinate (i.e., dependent) clauses look like sentences. They may have a subject, a verb, and objects or complements. They are used within sentences as adverbs, adjectives, or nouns.

Examples:
Independent Clause: I am running outside.
(The sentence has a subject *I* and a verb *am running*.)

Dependent Clause: I am running because I want to stay in shape.

The clause *I am running* is an independent clause. The underlined clause is dependent. Remember: a dependent clause does not give a complete thought. Think about the dependent clause: *because I want to stay in shape.*

Without any other information, you think: So, you want to stay in shape. What are you are doing to stay in shape? Answer: *I am running.*

<u>Types of Dependent Clauses</u>
An **adjective clause** is a dependent clause that modifies nouns and pronouns. Adjective clauses begin with a relative pronoun (*who, whose, whom, which,* and *that*) or a relative adverb (*where, when,* and *why*). Also, adjective clauses come after the noun that the clause needs to explain or rename. This is done to have a clear connection to the independent clause.
Examples:
I learned the reason *why I won the award.*
This is the place *where I started my first job.*

An adjective clause can be an essential or nonessential clause. An essential clause is very important to the sentence. Essential clauses explain or define a person or thing. Nonessential clauses give more information about a person or thing. However, they are not necessary to the sentence.
Examples:
Essential: A person *who works hard at first* can rest later in life.
Nonessential: Neil Armstrong, *who walked on the moon*, is my hero.

An **adverb clause** is a dependent clause that modifies verbs, adjectives, and other adverbs. To show a clear connection to the independent clause, put the adverb clause immediately before or after the independent clause. An adverb clause can start with *after, although, as, as if, before, because, if, since, so, so that, unless, when, where,* or *while*.
Examples:
When you walked outside, I called the manager.
I want to go with you *unless you want to stay.*

A **noun clause** is a dependent clause that can be used as a subject, object, or complement. Noun clauses can begin with *how, that, what, whether, which, who,* or *why*. These words can also come with an adjective clause. Remember that the entire clause makes a noun or an adjective clause, not the word that starts a clause. So, be sure to look for more than the word that begins the clause. To show a clear connection to the independent clause, be sure that a noun clause comes after the verb. The exception is when the noun clause is the subject of the sentence.
Examples:
The fact *that you were alone* alarms me.
What you learn from each other depends on your honesty with others.

Phrases

A phrase is not a complete sentence. So, a phrase cannot be a statement and cannot give a complete thought. Instead, a phrase is a group of words that can be used as a noun, adjective, or adverb in a sentence. Phrases strengthen sentences by adding explanation or renaming something.

Prepositional Phrases - A phrase that can be found in many sentences is the prepositional phrase. A prepositional phrase begins with a preposition and ends with a noun or pronoun that is used as an object. Normally, the prepositional phrase works as an adjective or an adverb.

Examples:
The picnic is *on the blanket*.
I am sick *with a fever* today.
Among the many flowers, a four-leaf clover was found by John.

Verbals and Verbal Phrases
A verbal looks like a verb, but it is not used as a verb. Instead, a verbal is used as a noun, adjective, or adverb. Be careful with verbals. They do not replace a verb in a sentence.

Correct: Walk a mile daily.
(*Walk* is the verb of this sentence. As in, "*You* walk a mile daily.")

Incorrect: To walk a mile.
(*To walk* is a type of verbal. But, verbals cannot be a verb for a sentence.)

A verbal phrase is a verb form that does not function as the verb of a clause. There are three major types of verbal phrases: participial, gerund, and infinitive phrases.

Participles - A participle is a verbal that is used as an adjective. The present participle always ends with *-ing*. Past participles end with *-d, -ed, -n,* or *-t.*

Examples: Verb: *dance* | Present Participle: *dancing* | Past Participle: *danced*

Participial phrases are made of a participle and any complements or modifiers. Often, they come right after the noun or pronoun that they modify.

Examples:
Shipwrecked on an island, the boys started to fish for food.
Having been seated for five hours, we got out of the car to stretch our legs.
Praised for their work, the group accepted the first place trophy.

Gerunds - A gerund is a verbal that is used as a noun. Gerunds can be found by looking for their *-ing* endings. However, you need to be careful that you have found a gerund, not a present participle. Since gerunds are nouns, they can be used as a subject of a sentence and the object of a verb or preposition.

Gerund Phrases are built around present participles (i.e., *-ing* endings to verbs) and they are always used as nouns. The gerund phrase has a gerund and any complements or modifiers.

Examples:
We want to be known for *teaching the poor*. (Object of Preposition)
Coaching this team is the best job of my life. (Subject)
We like *practicing our songs* in the basement. (Object of the verb: *like*)

Infinitives - An infinitive is a verbal that can be used as a noun, an adjective, or an adverb. An infinitive is made of the basic form of a verb with the word *to* coming before the verb.

Infinitive Phrases are made of an infinitive and all complements and modifiers. They are used as nouns, adjectives, or adverbs.

Examples:
To join the team is my goal in life. (Noun)
The animals have enough food *to eat for the night*. (Adjective)
People lift weights *to exercise their muscles*. (Adverb)

Appositive Phrases
An appositive is a word or phrase that is used to explain or rename nouns or pronouns. In a sentence they can be noun phrases, prepositional phrases, gerund phrases, or infinitive phrases.

Examples:
Terriers, *hunters at heart*, have been dressed up to look like lap dogs.
(The phrase *hunters at heart* renames the noun *terriers*.)

His plan, *to save and invest his money*, was proven as a safe approach.
(The italicized infinitive phrase renames the plan.)

Appositive phrases can be essential or nonessential. An appositive phrase is essential if the person, place, or thing being described or renamed is too general.
Essential: Two Founding Fathers George Washington and Thomas Jefferson served as presidents.

Nonessential: George Washington and Thomas Jefferson, two Founding Fathers, served as presidents.

Absolute Phrases
An absolute phrase is a phrase with a participle that comes after a noun. The absolute phrase is never the subject of a sentence. Also, the phrase does not explain or add to the meaning of a word in a sentence. Absolute phrases are used independently from the rest of the sentence. However, they are still a phrase, and phrases cannot give a complete thought.

Examples:
The alarm ringing, he pushed the snooze button.
The music paused, she continued to dance through the crowd.

Note: Appositive and absolute phrases can be confusing in sentences. So, don't be discouraged if you have a difficult time with them.

Sentence Structures

The four major types of sentence structure are:
1. Simple Sentences - Simple sentences have one independent clause with no subordinate clauses. A simple sentence can have compound elements (e.g., a compound subject or verb).
   Examples:
   Judy watered the lawn. (Singular Subject & Singular Predicate)
   Judy and Alan watered the lawn. (Compound Subject: Judy and Alan)

2. Compound Sentences - Compound sentences have two or more independent clauses with no dependent clauses. Usually, the independent clauses are joined with a comma and a coordinating conjunction, or they can be joined with a semicolon.
   Example:
   The time has come, and we are ready.
   I woke up at dawn; then I went outside to watch the sun rise.

3. Complex Sentences - A complex sentence has one independent clause and one or more dependent clauses.
   Examples:
   Although he had the flu, Harry went to work.
   Marcia got married after she finished college.

4. Compound-Complex Sentences - A compound-complex sentence has at least two independent clauses and at least one dependent clause.
   Examples:
   John is my friend who went to India, and he brought souvenirs for us.
   You may not know, but we heard the music that you played last night.

> **Review Video: Sentence Structure**
> Visit mometrix.com/academy and enter **Code: 700478**

Sentence Fragments

A part of a sentence should not be treated like a complete sentence. A sentence must be made of at least one independent clause. An independent clause has a subject and a verb. Remember that the independent clause can stand alone as a sentence. Some fragments are independent clauses that begin with a subordinating word (e.g., as, because, so, etc.). Other fragments may not have a subject, a verb, or both.

A sentence fragment can be repaired in several ways. One way is to put the fragment with a neighbor sentence. Another way is to be sure that punctuation is not needed. You can also turn the fragment into a sentence by adding any missing pieces. Sentence fragments are allowed for writers who want to show off their art. However, for your exam, sentence fragments are not allowed.

Fragment: Because he wanted to sail for Rome.
Correct: He dreamed of Europe because he wanted to sail for Rome.

Run-on Sentences

Run-on sentences are independent clauses that have not been joined by a conjunction. When two or more independent clauses appear in one sentence, they must be joined in one of these ways:
1. Correction with a comma and a coordinating conjunction.
   Incorrect: I went on the trip and I had a good time.
   Correct: I went on the trip, and I had a good time.

2. Correction with a semicolon, a colon, or a dash. Used when independent clauses are closely related and their connection is clear without a coordinating conjunction.
   Incorrect: I went to the store and I bought some eggs.
   Correct: I went to the store; I bought some eggs.

3. Correction by separating sentences. This correction may be used when both independent clauses are long. Also, this can be used when one sentence is a question and one is not.
   Incorrect: The drive to New York takes ten hours it makes me very tired.
   Correct: The drive to New York takes ten hours. So, I become very tired.

4. Correction by changing parts of the sentence. One way is to turn one of the independent clauses into a phrase or subordinate clause.
   Incorrect: The drive to New York takes ten hours it makes me very tired.
   Correct: During the ten hour drive to New York, I become very tired.

Note: Normally, one of these choices will be a clear correction to a run-on sentence. The fourth way can be the best correction but needs the most work.

> **Review Video: Fragments and Run-on Sentences**
> Visit *mometrix.com/academy* and enter **Code: 541989**

Dangling and Misplaced Modifiers

Dangling Modifiers
A dangling modifier is a verbal phrase that does not have a clear connection to a word. A dangling modifier can also be a dependent clause (the subject and/or verb are not included) that does not have a clear connection to a word.

Examples:
Dangling: *Reading each magazine article*, the stories caught my attention.
Corrected: Reading each magazine article, *I* was entertained by the stories.

In this example, the word *stories* cannot be modified by *Reading each magazine article*. People can read, but stories cannot read. So, the pronoun *I* is needed for the modifying phrase *Reading each magazine article*.

Dangling: Since childhood, my grandparents have visited me for Christmas.
Corrected: Since childhood, I have been visited by my grandparents for Christmas.

In this example, the dependent adverb clause *Since childhood* cannot modify grandparents. So, the pronoun *I* is needed for the modifying adverb clause.

Misplaced Modifiers
In some sentences, a modifier can be put in more than one place. However, you need to be sure that there is no confusion about which word is being explained or given more detail.

Incorrect: He read the book to a crowd that was filled with beautiful pictures.
Correct: He read the book that was filled with beautiful pictures to a crowd.

The crowd is not filled with pictures. The book is filled with pictures.

Incorrect: John only ate fruits and vegetables for two weeks.
Correct: John ate *only* fruits and vegetables for two weeks.

John may have done nothing else for two weeks but eat fruits and vegetables and sleep. However, it is reasonable to think that John had fruits and vegetables for his meals. Then, he continued to work on other things.

Split Infinitives
A split infinitive is when something comes between the word *to* and the verb that pairs with *to*.
Incorrect: To *clearly* explain | To *softly* sing
Correct: *To explain* clearly | *To sing* softly

Double Negatives

Standard English allows two negatives when a positive meaning is intended. For example, "The team was not displeased with their performance." Double negatives that are used to emphasize negation are not part of Standard English.

Negative modifiers (e.g., never, no, and not) should not be paired with other negative modifiers or negative words (e.g., none, nobody, nothing, or neither). The modifiers *hardly, barely*, and *scarcely* are also considered negatives in Standard English. So, they should not be used with other negatives.

Parallelism and Subordination

Parallelism
Parallel structures are used in sentences to highlight similar ideas and to connect sentences that give similar information. Parallelism pairs parts of speech, phrases, or clauses together with a matching piece. To write, *I enjoy reading and to study* would be incorrect. An infinitive does not match with a gerund. Instead, you should write *I enjoy reading and studying*.

Be sure that you continue to use certain words (e.g., articles, linking verbs, prepositions, infinitive sign (to), and the introductory word for a dependent clause) in sentences.

Incorrect: Will you bring the paper and pen with you?
Correct: Will you bring *the* paper and *a* pen with you?

Incorrect: The animals can come to eat and play.
Correct: The animals can come *to* eat and *to* play.

Incorrect: You are the person who remembered my name and cared for me.
Correct: You are the person *who* remembered my name and *who* cared for me.

Subordination

When two items are not equal to each other, you can join them by making the more important piece an independent clause. The less important piece can become subordinate. To make the less important piece subordinate, you make it a phrase or a dependent clause. The piece of more importance should be the one that readers want or will need to remember.

Example:

(1) The team had a perfect regular season. (2) The team lost the championship.

Despite having a perfect regular season, *the team lost the championship.*

Mathematics

The Mathematics Test section of the HESI A² exam consists of 50 questions. All numbers used are real numbers.

Basic Math

Numbers and their Classifications

Numbers are the basic building blocks of mathematics. Specific features of numbers are identified by the following terms:

Integers – The set of whole positive and negative numbers, including zero. Integers do not include fractions ($\frac{1}{3}$), decimals (0.56), or mixed numbers ($7\frac{3}{4}$).

Prime number – A whole number greater than 1 that has only two factors, itself and 1; that is, a number that can be divided evenly only by 1 and itself.

Composite number – A whole number greater than 1 that has more than two different factors; in other words, any whole number that is not a prime number. For example: The composite number 8 has the factors of 1, 2, 4, and 8.

Even number – Any integer that can be divided by 2 without leaving a remainder. For example: 2, 4, 6, 8, and so on.

Odd number – Any integer that cannot be divided evenly by 2. For example: 3, 5, 7, 9, and so on.
Decimal number – a number that uses a decimal point to show the part of the number that is less than one. Example: 1.234.

Decimal point – a symbol used to separate the ones place from the tenths place in decimals or dollars from cents in currency.

Decimal place – the position of a number to the right of the decimal point. In the decimal 0.123, the 1 is in the first place to the right of the decimal point, indicating tenths; the 2 is in the second place, indicating hundredths; and the 3 is in the third place, indicating thousandths.

The decimal, or base 10, system is a number system that uses ten different digits (0, 1, 2, 3, 4, 5, 6, 7, 8, 9). An example of a number system that uses something other than ten digits is the binary, or base 2, number system, used by computers, which uses only the numbers 0 and 1. It is thought that the decimal system originated because people had only their 10 fingers for counting.

Rational, irrational, and real numbers can be described as follows:
Rational numbers include all integers, decimals, and fractions. Any terminating or repeating decimal number is a rational number.

Irrational numbers cannot be written as fractions or decimals because the number of decimal places is infinite and there is no recurring pattern of digits within the number. For example, pi (π) begins with 3.141592 and continues without terminating or repeating, so pi is an irrational number.

Real numbers are the set of all rational and irrational numbers.

Operations

There are four basic mathematical operations:

Addition
Addition increases the value of one quantity by the value of another quantity. Example: $2 + 4 = 6$; $8 + 9 = 17$. The result is called the sum. With addition, the order does not matter. $4 + 2 = 2 + 4$.

Subtraction
Subtraction is the opposite operation to addition; it decreases the value of one quantity by the value of another quantity. Example: $6 - 4 = 2$; $17 - 8 = 9$. The result is called the difference. Note that with subtraction, the order does matter. $6 - 4 \neq 4 - 6$.

Subtracting with Regrouping
Example 1
Demonstrate how to subtract 189 from 525 using regrouping.

First, set up the subtraction problem:
```
  525
- 189
```

Notice that the numbers in the ones and tens columns of 525 are smaller than the numbers in the ones and tens columns of 189. This means you will need to use regrouping to perform subtraction.
```
  5 2 5
- 1 8 9
```

To subtract 9 from 5 in the ones column you will need to borrow from the 2 in the tens columns:
```
  5 1 15
- 1 8  9
       6
```

Next, to subtract 8 from 1 in the tens column you will need to borrow from the 5 in the hundreds column:
```
  4 11 15
- 1  8  9
     3  6
```

Last, subtract the 1 from the 4 in the hundreds column:
```
  4 11 15
- 1  8  9
  3  3  6
```

Example 2
Demonstrate how to subtract 477 from 620 using regrouping.

First, set up the subtraction problem:
```
  620
- 477
```

Notice that the numbers in the ones and tens columns of 620 are smaller than the numbers in the ones and tens columns of 477. This means you will need to use regrouping to perform subtraction.

```
  6 2 0
- 4 7 7
```

To subtract 7 from 0 in the ones column you will need to borrow from the 2 in the tens column.

```
  6 1 10
- 4 7  7
       3
```

Next, to subtract 7 from the 1 that's still in the tens column you will need to borrow from the 6 in the hundreds column.

```
  5 11 10
- 4  7  7
     4  3
```

Lastly, subtract 4 from the 5 remaining in the hundreds column to get:

```
  5 11 10
- 4  7  7
  1  4  3
```

Multiplication

Multiplication can be thought of as repeated addition. One number tells how many times to add the other number to itself. Example: 3×2 (three times two) $= 2 + 2 + 2 = 6$. With multiplication, the order does not matter. $2 \times 3 = 3 \times 2$ or $3 + 3 = 2 + 2 + 2$.

Division

Division is the opposite operation to multiplication; one number tells us how many parts to divide the other number into. Example: $20 \div 4 = 5$; if 20 is split into 4 equal parts, each part is 5. With division, the order of the numbers does matter. $20 \div 4 \neq 4 \div 20$.

Decimals

Adding and Subtracting Decimals

When adding and subtracting decimals, the decimal points must always be aligned. Adding decimals is just like adding regular whole numbers.
Example: 4.5 + 2 = 6.5.

If the problem-solver does not properly align the decimal points, an incorrect answer of 4.7 may result. An easy way to add decimals is to align all of the decimal points in a vertical column visually. This will allow one to see exactly where the decimal should be placed in the final answer. Begin adding from right to left. Add each column in turn, making sure to carry the number to the left if a column adds up to more than 9. The same rules apply to the subtraction of decimals.

> ➢ **Review Video: Adding and Subtracting Decimals**
> Visit *mometrix.com/academy* and enter *Code:* **381101**

Multiplying Decimals

A simple multiplication problem has two components: a multiplicand and a multiplier. When multiplying decimals, work as though the numbers were whole rather than decimals. Once the final product is calculated, count the number of places to the right of the decimal in both the multiplicand and the multiplier. Then, count that number of places from the right of the product and place the decimal in that position. For example, 12.3 x 2.56 has three places to the right of the respective decimals. Multiply 123 x 256 to get 31488. Now, beginning on the right, count three places to the left and insert the decimal. The final product will be 31.488.

> ➢ **Review Video: Multiplying Decimals**
> Visit *mometrix.com/academy* and enter *Code:* **731574**

Dividing Decimals

Every division problem has a divisor and a dividend. The dividend is the number that is being divided. In the problem 14 ÷ 7, 14 is the dividend and 7 is the divisor. In a division problem with decimals, the divisor must be converted into a whole number. Begin by moving the decimal in the divisor to the right until a whole number is created. Next, move the decimal in the dividend the same number of spaces to the right. For example, 4.9 into 24.5 would become 49 into 245. The decimal was moved one space to the right to create a whole number in the divisor, and then the same was done for the dividend. Once the whole numbers are created, the problem is carried out normally: 245 ÷ 49 = 5.

> ➢ **Review Video: Dividing Decimals**
> Visit *mometrix.com/academy* and enter *Code:* **560690**

Fractions

A fraction is a number that is expressed as one integer written above another integer, with a dividing line between them $\left(\frac{x}{y}\right)$. It represents the quotient of the two numbers "*x* divided by *y*." It can also be thought of as *x* out of *y* equal parts.

The top number of a fraction is called the numerator, and it represents the number of parts under consideration. The 1 in $\frac{1}{4}$ means that 1 part out of the whole is being considered in the calculation. The bottom number of a fraction is called the denominator, and it represents the total number of equal parts. The 4 in $\frac{1}{4}$ means that the whole consists of 4 equal parts. A fraction cannot have a denominator of zero; this is referred to as "undefined."

Fractions can be manipulated, without changing the value of the fraction, by multiplying or dividing (but not adding or subtracting) both the numerator and denominator by the same number. If you divide both numbers by a common factor, you are reducing or simplifying the fraction. Two fractions that have the same value, but are expressed differently are known as equivalent fractions. For example, $\frac{2}{10}, \frac{3}{15}, \frac{4}{20}$, and $\frac{5}{25}$ are all equivalent fractions. They can also all be reduced or simplified to $\frac{1}{5}$.

When two fractions are manipulated so that they have the same denominator, this is known as finding a common denominator. The number chosen to be that common denominator should be the least common multiple of the two original denominators. Example: $\frac{3}{4}$ and $\frac{5}{6}$; the least common multiple of 4 and 6 is 12. Manipulating to achieve the common denominator: $\frac{3}{4} = \frac{9}{12}; \frac{5}{6} = \frac{10}{12}$.

If two fractions have a common denominator, they can be added or subtracted simply by adding or subtracting the two numerators and retaining the same denominator. Example: $\frac{1}{2} + \frac{1}{4} = \frac{2}{4} + \frac{1}{4} = \frac{3}{4}$. If the two fractions do not already have the same denominator, one or both of them must be manipulated to achieve a common denominator before they can be added or subtracted.

Two fractions can be multiplied by multiplying the two numerators to find the new numerator and the two denominators to find the new denominator. Example: $\frac{1}{3} \times \frac{2}{3} = \frac{1 \times 2}{3 \times 3} = \frac{2}{9}$.

Two fractions can be divided by flipping the numerator and denominator of the second fraction and then proceeding as though it were a multiplication. Example: $\frac{2}{3} \div \frac{3}{4} = \frac{2}{3} \times \frac{4}{3} = \frac{8}{9}$.

A fraction whose denominator is greater than its numerator is known as a proper fraction, while a fraction whose numerator is greater than its denominator is known as an improper fraction. Proper fractions have values less than one and improper fractions have values greater than one.

A mixed number is a number that contains both an integer and a fraction. Any improper fraction can be rewritten as a mixed number. Example: $\frac{8}{3} = \frac{6}{3} + \frac{2}{3} = 2 + \frac{2}{3} = 2\frac{2}{3}$. Similarly, any mixed number can be rewritten as an improper fraction. Example: $1\frac{3}{5} = 1 + \frac{3}{5} = \frac{5}{5} + \frac{3}{5} = \frac{8}{5}$.

> ➢ **Review Video: Fractions**
> Visit **mometrix.com/academy** and enter **Code: 262335**

Factors and Multiples

Factors are numbers that are multiplied together to obtain a product. For example, in the equation $2 \times 3 = 6$, the numbers 2 and 3 are factors. A prime number has only two factors (1 and itself), but other numbers can have many factors.

A common factor is a number that divides exactly into two or more other numbers. For example, the factors of 12 are 1, 2, 3, 4, 6, and 12, while the factors of 15 are 1, 3, 5, and 15. The common factors of 12 and 15 are 1 and 3.

A prime factor is also a prime number. Therefore, the prime factors of 12 are 2 and 3. For 15, the prime factors are 3 and 5.

> ➤ **Review Video:** Factors
> *Visit **mometrix.com/academy** and enter **Code: 920086***

The greatest common factor (GCF) is the largest number that is a factor of two or more numbers. For example, the factors of 15 are 1, 3, 5, and 15; the factors of 35 are 1, 5, 7, and 35. Therefore, the greatest common factor of 15 and 35 is 5.

The least common multiple (LCM) is the smallest number that is a multiple of two or more numbers. For example, the multiples of 3 include 3, 6, 9, 12, 15, etc.; the multiples of 5 include 5, 10, 15, 20, etc. Therefore, the least common multiple of 3 and 5 is 15.

> ➤ **Review Video:** Multiples
> *Visit **mometrix.com/academy** and enter **Code: 626738***

Converting Decimals to Fractions

A fraction can be turned into a decimal and vice versa. In order to convert a fraction into a decimal, simply divide the numerator by the denominator. For example, the fraction $\frac{5}{4}$ becomes 1.25. This is done by dividing 5 by 4. The fraction $\frac{4}{8}$ becomes 0.5 when 4 is divided by 8. This remains true even if the fraction $\frac{4}{8}$ is first reduced to $\frac{1}{2}$. The decimal conversion will still be 0.5. In order to convert a decimal into a fraction, count the number of places to the right of the decimal. This will be the number of zeros in the denominator. The numbers to the right of the decimal will become the whole number in the numerator.

Example 1:

$0.45 = \frac{45}{100}$

$\frac{45}{100}$ reduces to $\frac{9}{20}$

Example 2:

$0.237 = \frac{237}{1000}$

Example 3:

$0.2121 = \frac{2121}{10000}$

> ➤ **Review Video:** Converting Decimals to Fractions and Percentages
> *Visit **mometrix.com/academy** and enter **Code: 986765***

Ratios and Proportions

A ratio is a comparison of two quantities in a particular order. Example: If there are 14 computers in a lab, and the class has 20 students, there is a student to computer ratio of 20 to 14, commonly written as 20:14. Ratios are normally reduced to their smallest whole number representation, so 20:14 would be reduced to 10:7 by dividing both sides by 2.

A proportion is a relationship between two quantities that dictates how one changes when the other changes. A direct proportion describes a relationship in which a quantity increases by a set amount for every increase in the other quantity, or decreases by that same amount for every decrease in the other quantity. Example: Assuming a constant driving speed, the time required for a car trip increases as the distance of the trip increases. The distance to be traveled and the time required to travel are directly proportional.

Inverse proportion is a relationship in which an increase in one quantity is accompanied by a decrease in the other, or vice versa. Example: the time required for a car trip decreases as the speed increases, and increases as the speed decreases, so the time required is inversely proportional to the speed of the car.

Solving for x in a Proportion

Solve for x in this proportion: $\frac{10}{15} = \frac{x}{30}$.

There are two ways to solve for x.

Method 1: Cross multiply; then, solve for x.

$$\frac{10}{15} = \frac{x}{30}$$

10(30) = 15(x)
300 = 15x
300 ÷ 15 = 15x ÷ 15
x = 20

Method 2: Notice that 30 is twice as much as 15, so x should be twice as much as 10. Therefore, x = 10 × 2 = 20.

Percentages

Percentages can be thought of as fractions that are based on a whole of 100; that is, one whole is equal to 100%. The word percent means "per hundred." Fractions can be expressed as percents by finding equivalent fractions with a denomination of 100. Example: $\frac{7}{10} = \frac{70}{100} = 70\%; \frac{1}{4} = \frac{25}{100} = 25\%$.

To express a percentage as a fraction, divide the percentage number by 100 and reduce the fraction to its simplest possible terms. Example: $60\% = \frac{60}{100} = \frac{3}{5}; 96\% = \frac{96}{100} = \frac{24}{25}$.

Converting decimals to percentages and percentages to decimals is as simple as moving the decimal point. To convert from a decimal to a percent, move the decimal point two places to the right. To convert from a percent to a decimal, move it two places to the left. Example: 0.23 = 23%; 5.34 = 534%; 0.007 = 0.7%; 700% = 7.00; 86% = 0.86; 0.15% = 0.0015.

It may be helpful to remember that the percentage number will always be larger than the equivalent decimal number.

A percentage problem can be presented three main ways: (1) Find what percentage of some number another number is. Example: What percentage of 40 is 8? (2) Find what number is some percentage of a given number. Example: What number is 20% of 40? (3) Find what number another number is a given percentage of.

Example: What number is 8 20% of? The three components in all of these cases are the same: a whole (W), a part (P), and a percentage (%). These are related by the equation: $P = W \times \%$. This is the form of the equation you would use to solve problems of type (2). To solve types (1) and (3), you would use these two forms:

$$\% = \frac{P}{W} \text{ and } W = \frac{P}{\%}$$

The thing that frequently makes percentage problems difficult is that they are most often also word problems, so a large part of solving them is figuring out which quantities are what. Example: In a school cafeteria, 7 students choose pizza, 9 choose hamburgers, and 4 choose tacos. Find the percentage that chooses tacos. To find the whole, you must first add all of the parts: 7 + 9 + 4 = 20. The percentage can then be found by dividing the part by the whole ($\% = \frac{P}{W}$): $\frac{4}{20} = \frac{20}{100} = 20\%$.

> ➢ **Review Video: Percentages**
> Visit *mometrix.com/academy* and enter **Code: 141911**

Converting Decimals, Fractions, and Percentages
Percentages are a type of fraction. In a percentage, the denominator, represented by a % sign, is always 100. The sign % stands for per hundred. So, 25% can be read as 25 per hundred. In order to convert a decimal to a percent, move the decimal point two spaces to the right. The decimal 0.45 becomes 45%. In order to convert a percentage into a decimal, move the decimal point two places to the left. The percentage 16% becomes 0.16.

> ➢ **Review Video: Converting Percentages to Decimals and Fractions**
> Visit *mometrix.com/academy* and enter **Code: 287297**

Fractions can also be converted into percentages. The first step is to convert the fraction into a decimal. Next, convert the decimal into a percentage. For example, consider the fraction 3/4. Dividing 3 by 4 yields 0.75, which can be converted into a percentage by shifting the decimal two places to the right (75%).

Decimal and Fraction Equivalents

Fraction	Decimal	Percentage
1/4	0.25	25%
1/2	0.50	50%
3/4	0.75	75%
1/3	$0.\overline{3}$ *	$33.\overline{3}$%
2/3	$0.\overline{6}$ *	$66.\overline{6}$%
1/5	0.20	20%
3/5	0.60	60%
4/5	0.80	80%
1/6	$0.1\overline{6}$ *	$16.\overline{6}$%
5/6	$0.8\overline{3}$ *	$83.\overline{3}$%
1/8	0.125	12.5%
3/8	0.375	37.5%
5/8	0.625	62.5%
7/8	0.875	87.5%

* the symbol ¯ above a number indicates that the number to the right is repeated infinitely.

Military Time

The 24-hour clock is a time system used by the military and on some digital clocks. On the 24-hour clock, minutes and seconds are the same as the standard 12-hour clock. However, time is expressed in 4 figures, and the hours run from 0000 hour (12 a.m.) to 2359 hours (11:59 p.m.).

To convert from 12-hour to 24-hour time, remove the colon and:
1) for a.m. times, if the time has 3 digits, add a 0 to the beginning (e.g., 8:12 a.m. becomes 0812 hours). For times between 12 a.m. and 1 a. m., replace the 12 with a pair of zeros (e.g., 12:41 a.m. becomes 0041 hours).

2) for p.m. times, add 12 to the hour number (e.g., 3:40 p.m. = 1540 hours), except for times between 12 p.m. and 1 p.m., which do not require any further change.

To convert from 24-hour to 12-hour time, add a colon between the second and third digits. If the first two digits are less than 12, the time is a.m.; otherwise it is p.m. If the first two digits are zeros, the hour becomes 12 a.m. (e.g., 0020 becomes 12:20 a.m.) If only the first digit is zero, remove it (e.g., 0730 becomes 7:30 a.m.). If the first two digits are greater than 12, subtract 12 (e.g., 2325 becomes 11:25 p.m.).

Algebra

An exponent is a superscript number placed next to another number at the top right. It indicates how many times the base number is to be multiplied by itself. Exponents provide a shorthand way to write what would be a longer mathematical expression. Example: $a^2 = a \times a$; $2^4 = 2 \times 2 \times 2 \times 2$. A number with an exponent of 2 is said to be "squared," while a number with an exponent of 3 is said to be "cubed." The value of a number raised to an exponent is called its power. So, 8^4 is read as "8 to the 4th power," or "8 raised to the power of 4." A negative exponent is the same as the reciprocal of a positive exponent. Example: $a^{-2} = \frac{1}{a^2}$.

Parentheses are used to designate which operations should be done first when there are multiple operations. Example: 4 − (2 + 1) = 1; the parentheses tell us that we must add 2 and 1, and then subtract the sum from 4, rather than subtracting 2 from 4 and then adding 1 (this would give us an answer of 3).

Order of Operations is a set of rules that dictates the order in which we must perform each operation in an expression so that we will evaluate it accurately. If we have an expression that includes multiple different operations, Order of Operations tells us which operations to do first. The most common mnemonic for Order of Operations is PEMDAS, or "Please Excuse My Dear Aunt Sally." PEMDAS stands for Parentheses, Exponents, Multiplication, Division, Addition, Subtraction. It is important to understand that multiplication and division have equal precedence, as do addition and subtraction, so those pairs of operations are simply worked from left to right in order.

Example: Evaluate the expression $5 + 20 \div 4 \times (2 + 3)^2 - 6$ using the correct order of operations.
P: Perform the operations inside the parentheses, $(2 + 3) = 5$.
E: Simplify the exponents, $(5)^2 = 25$.
The equation now looks like this: $5 + 20 \div 4 \times 25 - 6$.
MD: Perform multiplication and division from left to right, $20 \div 4 = 5$; then $5 \times 25 = 125$.
The equation now looks like this: $5 + 125 - 6$.
AS: Perform addition and subtraction from left to right, $5 + 125 = 130$; then $130 - 6 = 124$.

> ➤ **Review Video: Order of Operations**
> Visit **mometrix.com/academy** and enter **Code: 259675**

Solving for a Variable

Similar to order of operation rules, algebraic rules must be obeyed to ensure a correct answer. Begin by locating all parentheses and brackets, and then solving the equations within them. Then, perform the operations necessary to remove all parentheses and brackets. Next, convert all fractions into whole numbers and combine common terms on each side of the equation.

Beginning on the left side of the expression, solve operations involving multiplication and division. Then, work left to right solving operations involving addition and subtraction. Finally, cross-multiply if necessary to reach the final solution.

Example 1:
> $4a-10=10$

Constants are the numbers in equations that do not change. The variable in this equation is *a*. Variables are most commonly presented as either *x* or *y*, but they can be any letter. Every variable is equal to a number; one must solve the equation to determine what that number is. In an algebraic expression, the answer will usually be the number represented by the variable. In order to solve this equation, keep in mind that what is done to one side must be done to the other side as well. The first step will be to remove 10 from the left side by adding 10 to both sides. This will be expressed as $4a-10+10=10+10$, which simplifies to $4a=20$. Next, remove the 4 by dividing both sides by 4. This step will be expressed as $4a \div 4 = 20 \div 4$. The expression now becomes $a=5$.

Since variables are the letters that represent an unknown number, you must solve for that unknown number in single variable problems. The main thing to remember is that you can do anything to one side of an equation as long as you do it to the other.

Example 2:
> Solve for x in the equation $2x + 3 = 5$.

Answer: First you want to get the "2x" isolated by itself on one side. To do that, first get rid of the 3. Subtract 3 from both sides of the equation $2x + 3 - 3 = 5 - 3$ or $2x = 2$. Now since the x is being multiplied by the 2 in "2x", you must divide by 2 to get rid of it. So, divide both sides by 2, which gives $2x / 2 = 2 / 2$ or $x = 1$.

Evaluate the Expression

In the expression $18{,}000(1 + r)^{20}$, what is the base of the exponent 20? Evaluate the expression for $r = 0.1, 0.4$, and 0.7 and round to the nearest integer.

In the expression $18{,}000(1 + r)^{20}$, the base of the exponent 20 is $(1 + r)$, not 1 or *r*. This is because by the order of operations, the sum in parentheses is calculated first. Then, this sum is raised to the power of 20. The last step is to multiply this result by the coefficient (i.e., 18,000). For $r = 0.1, 0.4$, and 0.7, the expression is equal to the following values (to the nearest integer):

$$8{,}000(1 + r)^{20} = 18{,}000(1.1)^{20} \approx 121{,}095$$
$$18{,}000(1 + r)^{20} = 18{,}000(1.4)^{20} \approx 15{,}060{,}286$$
$$18{,}000(1 + r)^{20} = 18{,}000(1.7)^{20} \approx 731{,}561{,}653$$

The symbol ($\approx$) means that it is approximately equally to the number.

Final Notes

Roman Numerals

Roman numerals are numbers represented by a combination of the letters I, V, X, L, C, D, and M. These letters individually represent the numbers 1, 5, 10, 50, 100, 500, and 1000. When there is a string of letters together, as long as they are written in order of value from greatest to smallest, they represent the sum of the individual letters. For instance, LVI represents 50 + 5 + 1 = 56 because they are written in order 50, 5, 1. If the symbol for a smaller number comes before the symbol for a larger number, the smaller number is subtracted from the larger number. For instance, LIV represents 50 + (5-1) = 54 since I represents a smaller number than V. The only letter pairs that will be used in this way are IV, IX, XL, XC, CD, and CM. For the test, you can either memorize and be on the lookout for these six letter pairs or check the entire string to make sure it is written in order of value.

Whole number	Roman numeral	Whole number	Roman numeral
1	I	6	VI
2	II	7	VII
3	III	8	VIII
4	IV	9	IX
5	V	10	X

> **Review Video: Roman Numerals**
> Visit *mometrix.com/academy* and enter **Code: 530931**

Conversion Units

Metric Conversions

1000 mcg (microgram)	1 mg
1000 mg (milligram)	1 g
1000 g (gram)	1 kg
1000 kg (kilogram)	1 metric ton
1000 ml (milliliter)	1 L
1000 um (micrometer)	1 mm
1000 mm (millimeter)	1 m
100 cm (centimeter)	1 m
1000 m (meter)	1 km

U.S. and Metric Equivalents

Unit	U.S. equivalent	Metric equivalent
Inch	1 inch	2.54 centimeters
Foot	12 inches	0.305 meters
Yard	3 feet	0.914 meters
Mile	5280 feet	1.609 kilometers

Capacity Measurements

Unit	U.S. equivalent	Metric equivalent
Ounce	8 drams	29.573 milliliters
Cup	8 ounces	0.237 liter
Pint	16 ounces	0.473 liter
Quart	2 pints	0.946 liter
Gallon	4 quarts	3.785 liters

Weight Measurements

Unit	U.S. equivalent	Metric equivalent
Ounce	16 drams	28.35 grams
Pound	16 ounces	453.6 grams
Ton	2,000 pounds	907.2 kilograms

Nursing Measurements

Unit	English equivalent	Metric equivalent
1 gtt (drop)	1 m (minum)	.06 milliliter
1 tsp	1 fluid dram	5 milliliters
3 tsp	4 fluid drams	15 or 16 milliliters
2 tbsp	1 fluid ounce	30 milliliters
1 glass	8 fluid ounces	240 milliliters

Mathematics Application

Converting Percents, Fractions, and Decimals

Example 1
15% can be written as a fraction and as a decimal. 15% written as a fraction is $\frac{15}{100}$ which equals $\frac{3}{20}$. 15% written as a decimal is 0.15.

To convert a percent to a fraction, follow these steps:
1) Write the percent over 100 because percent means "per one hundred." So, 15% can be written as $\frac{15}{100}$.
2) Fractions should be written in simplest form, which means that the numbers in the numerator and denominator should be reduced if possible. Both 15 and 100 can be divided by 5.
3) Therefore, $\frac{15 \div 5}{100 \div 5} = \frac{3}{20}$.

To convert a percent to a decimal, follow these steps:
1) Write the percent over 100 because percent means "per one hundred." So, 15% can be written as $\frac{15}{100}$.
2) 15 divided by 100 equals 0.15, so 15% = 0.15. In other words, when converting from a percent to a decimal, drop the percent sign and move the decimal two places to the left.

Example 2
Write 24.36% as a fraction and then as a decimal. Explain how you made these conversions.

24.36% written as a fraction is $\frac{24.36}{100}$, or $\frac{2436}{10,000}$, which reduces to $\frac{609}{2500}$. 24.36% written as a decimal is 0.2436. Recall that dividing by 100 moves the decimal two places to the left.

Example 3
Convert $\frac{4}{5}$ to a decimal and to a percent.

To convert a fraction to a decimal, simply divide the numerator by the denominator in the fraction. The numerator is the top number in the fraction and the denominator is the bottom number in a fraction. So $\frac{4}{5} = 4 \div 5 = 0.80 = 0.8$.
Percent means "per hundred." $\frac{4 \cdot 20}{5 \cdot 20} = \frac{80}{100} = 80\%$.

Example 4
Convert $3\frac{2}{5}$ to a decimal and to a percent.

The mixed number $3\frac{2}{5}$ has a whole number and a fractional part. The fractional part, namely $\frac{2}{5}$, can be written as a decimal by dividing 5 into 2, which gives 0.4. Adding the whole to the part gives 3.4. Alternatively, note that $3\frac{2}{5} = 3\frac{4}{10} = 3.4$

To change a decimal to a percent, multiply it by 100.
3.4(100) = 340%. Notice that this percentage is greater than 100%. This makes sense because the original mixed number $3\frac{2}{5}$ is greater than 1.

> ➤ **Review Video: Converting Fractions to Percentages and Decimals**
> Visit *mometrix.com/academy* and enter **Code: 306233**

Percentage

Example 1
What is 30% of 120?

The word "of" indicates multiplication, so 30% of 120 is found by multiplying 30% by 120. First, change 30% to a fraction or decimal. Recall that "percent" means per hundred, so 30% = $\frac{30}{100} = 0.30$. 120 times 0.3 is 36.

Example 2
What is 150% of 20?

150% of 20 is found by multiplying 150% by 20. First, change 150% to a fraction or decimal. Recall that "percent" means per hundred, so 150% = $\frac{150}{100} = 1.50$. So, (1.50)(20) = 30. Notice that 30 is greater than the original number of 20. This makes sense because you are finding a number that is more than 100% of the original number.

Example 3
According to a hospital survey, 82% of nurses were highly satisfied at their job. Of 145 nurses, how many were highly satisfied?

82% of 145 = 0.82 · 145 = 118.9. Because you can't have 0.9 of a person, the answer is "about 119 nurses are highly satisfied with their jobs."

Example 4
What is 14.5% of 96?

Change 14.5% to a decimal before multiplying. 0.145 · 96 = 13.92. Notice that 13.92 is much smaller than the original number of 96. This makes sense because you are finding a small percentage of the original number.

Example 5
Find 275% of 33.

Change 275% to a decimal before multiplying: 275% of 33 = (275%)(33) = (2.75)(33) = 90.75. Notice that 90.75 is greater than the original number of 33. This makes sense because you are finding a number that is more than 100% of the original number.

Mathematical Reasoning and Computational Procedures

Example 1
By what percentage does $\frac{3}{4}$ exceed $\frac{1}{3}$?

$\frac{\text{new fraction} - \text{original fraction}}{\text{original fraction}} \cdot 100\% = $ percent increase.

$\frac{\frac{3}{4} - \frac{1}{3}}{\frac{1}{3}} \cdot 100\% = \frac{\frac{5}{12}}{\frac{1}{3}} \cdot 100\% = \frac{5}{12} \cdot \frac{3}{1} \cdot 100\% = \frac{15}{12} \cdot 100\% = 125\%$.

Example 2
A patient's age is thirteen more than half of 60. How old is the patient?

"More than" indicates addition, and "of" indicates multiplication. The expression can be written as "1/2(60) + 13". So, the patient's age is equal to $\frac{1}{2}(60) + 13 = 30 + 13 = 43$. The patient is 43 years old.

Simplifying

Example 1
How to simplify:

$$\frac{\frac{2}{5}}{\frac{4}{7}}$$

Dividing a fraction by a fraction may appear tricky, but it's not if you write out your steps carefully. Follow these steps to divide a fraction by a fraction.

Step 1: Rewrite the problem as a multiplication problem. Dividing by a fraction is the same as multiplying by its reciprocal, also known as its multiplicative inverse. The product of a number and its reciprocal is 1. Because $\frac{4}{7}$ times $\frac{7}{4}$ is 1, these numbers are reciprocals. Note that reciprocals can be found by simply interchanging the numerators and denominators. So, rewriting the problem as a multiplication problem gives $\frac{2}{5} \times \frac{7}{4}$.

Step 2: Perform multiplication of the fractions by multiplying the numerators by each other and the denominators by each other. In other words, multiply across the top and then multiply across the bottom.

$$\frac{2}{5} \times \frac{7}{4} = \frac{2 \times 7}{5 \times 4} = \frac{14}{20}$$

Step 3: Make sure the fraction is reduced to lowest terms. Both 14 and 20 can be divided by 2.
$\frac{14}{20} = \frac{14 \div 2}{20 \div 2} = \frac{7}{10}$
The answer is $\frac{7}{10}$.

Example 2
How to simplify:

$$\frac{1}{4} + \frac{3}{6}$$

Fractions with common denominators can be easily added or subtracted. Recall that the denominator is the bottom number in the fraction and that the numerator is the top number in the fraction.

The denominators of $\frac{1}{4}$ and $\frac{3}{6}$ are 4 and 6, respectively. The lowest common denominator of 4 and 6 is 12 because 12 is the least common multiple of 4 (multiples 4, 8, 12, 16, ...) and 6 (multiples 6, 12, 18, 24, ...). Convert each fraction to its equivalent with the newly found common denominator of 12.
$\frac{1 \times 3}{4 \times 3} = \frac{3}{12}; \frac{3 \times 2}{6 \times 2} = \frac{6}{12}$.

Now that the fractions have the same denominator, you can add them.
$\frac{3}{12} + \frac{6}{12} = \frac{9}{12}$.

Be sure to write your answer in lowest terms. Both 9 and 12 can be divided by 3, so the answer is $\frac{3}{4}$.

Example 3
How to simplify:

$$\frac{7}{8} - \frac{8}{16}$$

Fractions with common denominators can be easily added or subtracted. Recall that the denominator is the bottom number in the fraction and that the numerator is the top number in the fraction.

The denominators of $\frac{7}{8}$ and $\frac{8}{16}$ are 8 and 16, respectively. The lowest common denominator of 8 and 16 is 16 because 16 is the least common multiple of 8 (multiples 8, 16, 24 ...) and 16 (multiples 16, 32, 48, ...). Convert each fraction to its equivalent with the newly found common denominator of 16.

$$\frac{7 \times 2}{8 \times 2} = \frac{14}{16} \qquad \frac{8 \times 1}{16 \times 1} = \frac{8}{16}$$

Now that the fractions have the same denominator, you can subtract them.

$$\frac{14}{16} - \frac{8}{16} = \frac{6}{16}$$

Be sure to write your answer in lowest terms. Both 6 and 16 can be divided by 2, so the answer is $\frac{3}{8}$.

Example 4
How to simplify:
$$\frac{1}{2} + \left(3\left(\frac{3}{4}\right) - 2\right) + 4^2$$

When simplifying expressions, first perform operations within groups. Within the set of parentheses are multiplication and subtraction operations. Perform the multiplication first to get $\frac{1}{2} + \left(\frac{9}{4} - 2\right) + 4^2$. Then, subtract two to obtain $\frac{1}{2} + \frac{1}{4} + 4^2$.

Next, evaluate the exponent: $\frac{1}{2} + \frac{1}{4} + 16$. Finally, perform addition from left to right.
$\frac{1}{2} + \frac{1}{4} + 16 = \frac{2}{4} + \frac{1}{4} + \frac{64}{4} = \frac{67}{4}$.

Example 5
How to simplify:
$$0.22 + 0.5^2 - (5.5 + 3.3 \div 3)$$

First, evaluate the terms in the parentheses $(5.5 + 3.3 \div 3)$ using order of operations. $3.3 \div 3 = 1.1$, and $5.5 + 1.1 = 6.6$. Rewrite the problem: $0.22 + 0.5^2 - 6.6$. Next, evaluate the exponent of $0.5^2 = 0.5 \times 0.5 = 0.25$.

Rewrite the problem: $0.22 + 0.25 - 6.6$. Finally, add and subtract from left to right. $0.22 + 0.25 = 0.47$; $0.47 - 6.6 = -6.13$. The answer is -6.13.

Example 6
How to simplify:
$$\frac{3}{2} + (4(0.5) - 0.75) + 2^2$$

First, simplify within the parentheses:
$$\frac{3}{2} + (2 - 0.75) + 2^2$$
$$\frac{3}{2} + 1.25 + 2^2$$

Next, evaluate the exponent:
$$\frac{3}{2} + 1.25 + 4$$

Finally, change the fraction to a decimal and perform addition from left to right:
$$1.5 + 1.25 + 4 = 6.75$$

Example 7
How to simplify:
$$1.45 + 1.5^2 + (6 - 9 \div 2) + 45$$

First, evaluate the terms in the parentheses using proper order of operations.
$$1.45 + 1.5^2 + (6 - 4.5) + 45$$
$$1.45 + 1.5^2 + 1.5 + 45$$

Next, evaluate the exponent.
$$1.45 + 2.25 + 1.5 + 45$$

Finally, add from left to right.
$$1.45 + 2.25 + 1.5 + 45 = 50.2$$

Word Problems

<u>Example 1</u>
A patient was given pain medicine at a dosage of 0.22 grams. The patient's dosage was then increased to 0.80 grams. By how much was the patient's dosage increased?

The first step is to determine what operation (addition, subtraction, multiplication, or division) the problem requires. Notice the key words and phrases "by how much" and "increased." "Increased" means that you go from a smaller amount to a larger amount. This change can be found by subtracting the smaller amount from the larger amount: 0.80 grams – 0.22 grams = 0.58 grams.

Remember to line up the decimal when subtracting.
```
  0.80
- 0.22
  0.58
```

<u>Example 2</u>
At a hospital, $\frac{3}{4}$ of the 100 beds are occupied today. Yesterday, $\frac{4}{5}$ of the 100 beds were occupied. On which day were more of the hospital beds occupied and by how much more?

First, find the actual number of beds that were occupied each day. To do so, multiply the fraction of beds occupied by the number of beds available:
Actual number of beds occupied = fraction of beds occupied × number of beds available
Today: Actual number of beds occupied = $\frac{3}{4}$ × 100.
$$\frac{3}{4} \times \frac{100}{1} = \frac{3 \times 100}{4 \times 1} = \frac{300}{4}$$

Then, write the fraction in lowest terms. $\frac{300}{4} \div \frac{4}{4} = \frac{75}{1} = 75$.
Today, 75 beds are occupied.
Yesterday: Actual number of beds occupied = $\frac{4}{5}$ × 100.
$$\frac{4}{5} \times \frac{100}{1} = \frac{4 \times 100}{5 \times 1} = \frac{400}{5}$$

Then, write the fraction in lowest terms. $\frac{400}{5} \div \frac{5}{5} = \frac{80}{1} = 80$.
Yesterday, 80 beds were occupied.
The difference in the number of beds occupied is 80 – 75 = 5 beds.
Therefore, five more beds were occupied yesterday than today.

Example 3
A patient complaining of fatigue and weight gain was diagnosed with hypothyroidism and was prescribed 125 mcg of medication. Three months later, her symptoms had improved, and her thyroid stimulation hormone (TSH) level was found to be 0.5 mIU/L. The doctor reduced the patient's thyroid medication dosage to 100 mcg, after which the patient's TSH level was found to be 1.5 mIU/L, which is within the normal range. By what percentage did the doctor reduce the patient's thyroid medication?

In this problem you must determine which information is necessary to answer the question. The question asks by what percentage the doctor reduced the patient's thyroid medication dosage. Find the two dosage amounts and perform subtraction to find their difference. The first dosage amount is 125 mcg. The second dosage amount is 100 mcg. Therefore, the difference is 125 mcg – 100 mcg = 25 mcg. The percentage reduction can then be calculated as $\frac{\text{change}}{\text{original}} = \frac{25 \text{ mcg}}{125 \text{ mcg}} = \frac{1}{5} = 20\%$.

Example 4
In a hospital emergency room, there are 4 nurses for every 12 patients. What is the ratio of nurses to patients? If the nurse-to-patient ratio remains constant, how many nurses must be present to care for 24 patients?

The ratio of nurses to patients can be written as 4 to 12, 4:12, or $\frac{4}{12}$. Because four and twelve have a common factor of four, the ratio should be reduced to 1:3, which means that there is one nurse present for every three patients. If this ratio remains constant, there must be eight nurses present to care for 24 patients.

Example 5
In an intensive care unit, the nurse-to-patient ratio is 1:2. If seven nurses are on duty, how many patients are currently in the ICU?

Use proportional reasoning or set up a proportion to solve. Because there are twice as many patients as nurses, there must be fourteen patients when seven nurses are on duty. Setting up and solving a proportion gives the same result:

$$\frac{\text{number of nurses}}{\text{number of patients}} = \frac{1}{2} = \frac{7}{\text{number of patients}}$$

Represent the unknown number of patients as the variable x.

$$\frac{1}{2} = \frac{7}{x}$$

To solve for x, cross multiply:
$1 \cdot x = 7 \cdot 2$, so x = 14.

Example 6
During a shift, a new nurse spent five hours of her time observing procedures, three hours working in the oncology department, and four hours doing paperwork. During the next shift, she spent four hours observing procedures, six hours in the oncology department, and two hours doing paperwork. What was the percent change for each task between the two shifts?

The three tasks are observing procedures, working in the oncology department, and doing paperwork. To find the amount of change, compare the first amount with the second amount for each task. Then, write this difference as a percentage compared to the initial amount.

Amount of change for observing procedures: 5 hours – 4 hours = 1 hour.

The percent of change is $\frac{\text{amount of change}}{\text{original amount}} \cdot 100\%$. $\frac{1 \text{ hour}}{5 \text{ hours}} \cdot 100\% = 20\%$. The nurse spent 20% less time observing procedures on her second shift than on her first.

Amount of change for working in the oncology department: 6 hours – 3 hours = 3 hours.

The percent of change is $\frac{\text{amount of change}}{\text{original amount}} \cdot 100\%$. $\frac{3 \text{ hours}}{3 \text{ hours}} \cdot 100\% = 100\%$. The nurse spent 100% more time (or twice as much time) working in the oncology department during her second shift than she did in her first.

Amount of change for doing paperwork: 4 hours – 2 hours = 2 hours.

The percent of change is $\frac{\text{amount of change}}{\text{original amount}} \cdot 100\%$. $\frac{2 \text{ hours}}{4 \text{ hours}} \cdot 100\% = 50\%$. The nurse spent 50% less time (or half as much time) working on paperwork during her second shift than she did in her first.

Example 7
A patient's heart beat 422 times over the course of six minutes. About how many times did the patient's heart beat during each minute?

"About how many" indicates that you need to estimate the solution. In this case, look at the numbers you are given. 422 can be rounded down to 420, which is easily divisible by 6. A good estimate is 420 ÷ 6 = 70 beats per minute. More accurately, the patient's heart rate was just over 70 beats per minute since his heart actually beat a little more than 420 times in six minutes.

Example 8
At a hospital, 40% of the nurses work in labor and delivery. If 20 nurses work in labor and delivery, how many nurses work at the hospital?

To answer this problem, first think about the number of nurses that work at the hospital. Will it be more or less than the number of nurses who work in a specific department such as labor and delivery? More nurses work at the hospital, so the number you find to answer this question will be greater than 20.

40% of the nurses are labor and delivery nurses. "Of" indicates multiplication, and words like "is" and "are" indicate equivalence. Translating the problem into a mathematical sentence gives 40% · n = 20, where n represents the total number of nurses. Solving for n gives

n = $\frac{20}{40\%} = \frac{20}{0.40} = 50$.

Fifty nurses work at the hospital.

Example 9
A patient was given 40 mg of a certain medicine. Later, the patient's dosage was increased to 45 mg. What was the percent increase in his medication?

To find the percent increase, first compare the original and increased amounts. The original amount was 40 mg, and the increased amount is 45 mg, so the dosage of medication was increased by 5 mg (45 − 40 = 5). Note, however, that the question asks not by how much the dosage increased but by what percentage it increased. Percent increase = $\frac{\text{new amount} - \text{original amount}}{\text{original amount}} \cdot 100\%$.

So, $\frac{45 \text{ mg} - 40 \text{ mg}}{40 \text{ mg}} \cdot 100\% = \frac{5}{40} \cdot 100\% = 0.125 \cdot 100\% \approx 12.5\%$

The percent increase is approximately 12.5%.

Example 10
A patient was given 100 mg of a medicine every two hours. How much medication will the patient receive in four hours?

Using proportional reasoning, since four hours is twice as long as two hours, the patient will receive twice as much medication, 2·100 mg = 200 mg, within that time period.

To write an equation, first, write the amount of medicine per 2 hours as a ratio.
$$\frac{100 \text{ mg}}{2 \text{ hours}}$$

Next create a proportion to relate the different time increments of 2 hours and 4 hours.

$\frac{100 \text{ mg}}{2 \text{ hours}} = \frac{x \text{ mg}}{4 \text{ hours}}$, where x is the amount of medicine the patient receives in four hours. Make sure to keep the same units in either the numerator or denominator. In this case the numerator units must be mg for both ratios and the denominator units must be hours for both ratios.

Use cross multiplication and division to solve for x.
$\frac{100 \text{ mg}}{2 \text{ hours}} = \frac{x \text{ mg}}{4 \text{ hours}}$

100(4) = 2(x)
400 = 2x
400 ÷ 2 = 2x ÷ 2
200 = x

Therefore, the patient receives 200 mg every four hours.

Example 11
Jane ate lunch at a local restaurant. She ordered a $4.99 appetizer, a $12.50 entrée, and a $1.25 soda. If she wants to tip her server 20%, how much money will she spend in all?

To find total amount, first find the sum of the items she ordered from the menu and then add 20% of this sum to the total.

In other words:
$4.99 + $12.50 + $1.25 = $18.74.
Then 20% of $18.74 is (20%)($18.74) = (0.20)($18.74) = $3.75.
So, the total she spends is cost of the meal plus the tip or $18.74 + $3.75 = $22.49.

Another way to find this sum is to multiply 120% by the cost of the meal.
$18.74(120%) = $18.74(1.20) = $22.49.

Example 12
A patient was given 100 mg of a certain medicine. The patient's dosage was later decreased to 88mg. What was the percent decrease?

The medication was decreased by 12 mg (100 mg - 88 mg = 12 mg). To find by what percent the medication was decreased, this change must be written as a percentage when compared to the original amount.

In other words, $\frac{\text{original amount} - \text{new amount}}{\text{original amount}} \cdot 100\% = \text{percent decrease}$

So $\frac{12 \text{ mg}}{100 \text{ mg}} \cdot 100\% = 0.12 \cdot 100\% = 12\%$.

The percent decrease is 12%.

Example 13
A patient was given blood pressure medicine at a dosage of 2 grams. The patient's dosage was then decreased to 0.45 grams. By how much was the patient's dosage decreased?

The decrease is represented by the difference between the two amounts:
2 grams – 0.45 grams = 1.55 grams.
Remember to line up the decimal point before subtracting.
  2.00
- 0.45
  1.55

Example 14
Two weeks ago, $\frac{2}{3}$ of the 60 patients at a hospital were male. Last week, $\frac{3}{6}$ of the 80 patients were male. During which week were there more male patients?

First, you need to find the number of male patients that were in the hospital each week. You are given this amount in terms of fractions. To find the actual number of male patients, multiply the fraction of male patients by the number of patients in the hospital.

Actual number of male patients = fraction of male patients × total number of patients.
Two weeks ago: Actual number of male patients = $\frac{2}{3}$ × 60.
$\frac{2}{3} \times \frac{60}{1} = \frac{2 \times 60}{3 \times 1} = \frac{120}{3} = 40$.

Two weeks ago, 40 of the patients were male.
Last week: Actual number of male patients = $\frac{3}{6}$ × 80.
$\frac{3}{6} \times \frac{80}{1} = \frac{3 \times 80}{6 \times 1} = \frac{240}{6} = 40$.

Last week, 40 of the patients were male.
The number of male patients was the same both weeks.

Example 15
At a hospital, for every 20 female patients there are 15 male patients. This same patient ratio happens to exist at another hospital. If there are 100 female patients at the second hospital, how many male patients are there?

One way to find the number of male patients is to set up and solve a proportion.
$\frac{\text{number of female patients}}{\text{number of male patients}} = \frac{20}{15} = \frac{100}{\text{number of male patients}}$.

Represent the unknown number of male patients as the variable x.
$\frac{20}{15} = \frac{100}{x}$.
Follow these steps to solve for x:
1) Cross multiply. 20 × x = 15 × 100.
20x = 1500
2) Divide each side of the equation by 20.
x = 75

Or, notice that
$\frac{20 \cdot 5}{15 \cdot 5} = \frac{100}{75}$, so x = 75.

Example 16
In a performance review, an employee received a score of 70 out of 100 for efficiency and 90 out of 100 for meeting project deadlines. Six months later, the employee received a score of 65 out of 100 for efficiency and 96 out of 100 for meeting project deadlines. What was the percent change for each score on the performance review?

To find the percent change, compare the first amount with the second amount for each score; then, write this difference as a percentage compared to the initial amount. Or, write the original amounts as percentages and then subtract.
Percent change for efficiency score:
70% – 65% = 5%.
The employee's efficiency decreased by 5%.

Percent change for meeting project deadlines score:
96% – 90% = 6%
The employee increased his ability to meet project deadlines by 6%.

Example 17
A patient's total bill is about $128 for the same procedure repeated each month for 5 months. About how much does the procedure cost?

"About how much" indicates that you need to estimate the solution. In this case, look at the numbers you are given which are $128 and 5. 128 can be rounded up to130 which is easily divisible by 5. So a good estimate is 130 ÷ 5 = $26 per procedure. More accurately, the procedure costs a little less than $26.

Calculation of Salary after Deductions

Example 1
Before taxes, a monthly paycheck was $2,160. However, the following deductions were taken from the paycheck: Federal Withholding, $154; Social Security, $90.72; Medicare $31.22; and State Withholding, $126.20. What is actual amount of the paycheck after these deductions?

Notice the key words in the problem: the words "deduction" and "from" indicate subtraction. To determine the amount of the paycheck after the deductions, or expenses, use either of these methods.

Method 1: Add all the deductions. Then, subtract this amount from the original amount.
Total Deductions = $154 + $90.72 + $31.22 + $126.20 = $402.14
Subtract this total amount from the original amount. $2,160 - $402.14 = $1,757.86.

Method 2: Subtract each amount from the original amount.
$2,160 - $154 - $90.72 - $31.22 - $126.20 = $1,757.86

Example 2
Before taxes, a monthly paycheck was $787.57. However, the following deductions were taken from the paycheck: Federal Withholding, $78.42; Social Security, $36.99; Medicare, $7.04; and State Withholding, $45.86. What is amount of the paycheck after these deductions?

Deductions, or expenses, are subtracted from the original amount. There are two ways to answer this problem.
Method 1: Add all the deductions. Then subtract this amount from the original amount.
Total Deductions = $78.42 + $36.99 + $7.04 + $45.86 = $168.31
Subtract this total amount from the original amount. $787.57 - $168.31 = $619.26.

Method 2: Subtract each amount from the original amount.
$787.57 - $78.42 - $36.99 - $7.04 - $45.86 = $619.26

Calculation of Balance after Transactions

Example 1
Two weeks ago, a checking account had a balance of $7,809.45. The transactions for the last two weeks are shown in table below.

Water Bill	$36.78	Expense
Paycheck	$2,891.45	Income
Cell Phone Bill	$98.99	Expense
Credit Card Bill	$375.17	Expense
Refund for returned clothing items	$45.28	Refund

What is the new account balance after these transactions?

When reconciling a checking account balance, you need to know what operation (addition or subtraction) to use for each transaction. An expense is a deduction from the account balance. Therefore, you subtract the expense amount from the account balance. A transaction labeled "income" means that you are adding the amount to your account balance. Lastly, a refund means that you are receiving, or adding money back, to your account

To find the new account balance, perform the following operations:
$7,809.45 - $36.78 + $2,891.45 - $98.99 - $375.17 + $45.28 = $10,235.24

Example 2
Two months ago, a checking account had a balance of $4,009.67. The transactions for the last two months are shown in table below.

Electric Bill	$189.45	Expense
Paycheck	$1,000.31	Income
Internet Bill	$68.77	Expense
Paycheck	$1,000.31	Income
Sold items on Ebay	$201.55	Income

What is the new account balance after these transactions?

When reconciling a checking account balance, you need to know what operation (addition or subtraction) to use for each transaction. An expense is a deduction from the account balance. Therefore, you would subtract the expense amount from the account balance. An income is added to the account balance.

To find the new account balance, perform the following operations:
$4,009.67 - $189.45 + $1,000.31 - $68.77 + $1,000.31 + $201.55 = $5953.62

Algebraic Applications

Equations with One Unknown

<u>Example 1</u>

$\frac{45\%}{12\%} = \frac{15\%}{x}$. Solve for x.

First, cross multiply; then, solve for x: $\frac{45\%}{12\%} = \frac{15\%}{x}$
$\frac{0.45}{0.12} = \frac{0.15}{x}$.
0.45(x) = 0.12(0.15)
0.45 x = 0.0180
0.45x ÷ 0.45 = 0.0180 ÷ 0.45
x = 0.04 = 4%

Alternatively, notice that $\frac{45\% \div 3}{12\% \div 3} = \frac{15\%}{4\%}$. So, x = 4%.

<u>Example 2</u>

How do you solve for x in the proportion $\frac{0.50}{2} = \frac{1.50}{x}$?

First, cross multiply; then, solve for x.
$\frac{0.50}{2} = \frac{1.50}{x}$.
0.50(x) = 2(1.50)
0.50x = 3
0.50x ÷ 0.50 = 3 ÷ 0.50
x = 6

Or, notice that $\frac{0.50 \cdot 3}{2 \cdot 3} = \frac{1.50}{6}$, so x = 6.

<u>Example 3</u>

$\frac{40}{8} = \frac{x}{24}$. Find x.

One way to solve for x is to first cross multiply.
$\frac{40}{8} = \frac{x}{24}$.
40(24) = 8(x)
960 = 8x
960 ÷ 8 = 8x ÷ 8
x = 120

Or, notice that:
$\frac{40 \cdot 3}{8 \cdot 3} = \frac{120}{24}$, so x = 120

Example 4

$x = \frac{1}{4} + 70\%$. Write your answer as a percent and as a fraction in lowest terms.

The key is to write the two values in the same format. You can write both of them as percents and then perform addition, or you can write both of them as fractions and then perform addition.

Method 1: Write both numbers as percents and then perform addition.
To convert $\frac{1}{4}$ to a percent simply divide the numerator by the denominator in the fraction and then multiply by 100%. $\frac{1}{4}$ = 0.25. Then 0.25(100%) = 25%.
Then perform addition: x = 25% + 70% = 95%.
$95\% = \frac{95}{100} = \frac{19}{20}$.

Method 2: Write both numbers as fractions and then perform addition.
$70\% = \frac{70}{100} = \frac{7}{10}$.
$x = \frac{7}{10} + \frac{1}{4} = \frac{14}{20} + \frac{5}{20} = \frac{19}{20}$.
$\frac{19}{20} = \frac{95}{100} = 95\%$.

Biology

General Knowledge

Classification

The groupings in the five kingdom classification system are kingdom, phylum/division, class, order, family, genus, and species. A memory aid for this is: King Phillip Came Over For Good Soup. The five kingdoms are Monera, Protista, Fungi, Plantae, and Animalia. The kingdom is the top level classification in this system. Below that are the following groupings: phylum, class, order, family, genus, and species. The Monera kingdom includes about 10,000 known species of prokaryotes, such as bacteria and cyanobacteria. Members of this kingdom can be unicellular organisms or colonies. The next four kingdoms consist of eukaryotes. The Protista kingdom includes about 250,000 species of unicellular protozoans and unicellular and multicellular algae. The Fungi kingdom includes about 100,000 species. A recently introduced system of classification includes a three domain grouping above kingdom. The domain groupings are Archaea, Bacteria (which both consist of prokaryotes), and Eukarya, which include eukaryotes. According to the five kingdom classification system, humans are: kingdom Animalia, phylum Chordata, subphylum Vertebrata, class Mammalia, order Primate, family Hominidae, genus Homo, and species Sapiens.

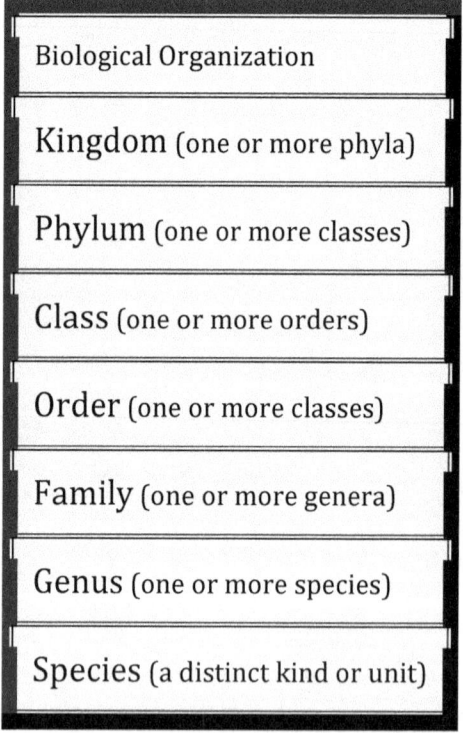

> **Review Video: Biological Classifications**
> Visit *mometrix.com/academy* and enter **Code: 736052**

Evoulution: Natural Selection, Gradualism, and Punctuated Equilibrium

Natural selection: This theory developed by Darwin states that traits that help give a species a survival advantage are passed on to subsequent generations. Members of a species that do not have the advantageous trait die before they reproduce. Darwin's four principles are: from generation to generation, there are various individuals within a species; genes determine variations; more individuals are born than survive to maturation; and specific genes enable an organism to better survive.

Gradualism: This can be contrasted with punctuationism. It is an idea that evolution proceeds at a steady pace and does not include sudden developments of new species or features from one generation to the next.

Punctuated equilibrium: This can be contrasted with gradualism. It is the idea in evolutionary biology that states that evolution involves long time periods of no change (stasis) accompanied by relatively brief periods (hundreds of thousands of years) of rapid change.

Scientific Knowledge and the Scientific Method

One could argue that scientific knowledge is the sum of all scientific inquiries for truths about the natural world carried out throughout the history of human kind. More simply put, it is thanks to scientific inquiry that we know what we do about the world. Scientists use a number of generally accepted techniques collectively known as the scientific method. The scientific method generally involves carrying out the following steps:
1. Identifying a problem or posing a question
2. Formulating a hypothesis or an educated guess
3. Conducting experiments or tests that will provide a basis to solve the problem or answer the question
4. Observing the results of the test
5. Drawing conclusions

An important part of the scientific method is using acceptable experimentation techniques to ensure results are not skewed. Objectivity is also important if valid results are to be obtained. Another important part of the scientific method is peer review. It is essential that experiments be performed and data be recorded in such a way that experiments can be reproduced to verify results.

Water

The important properties of water (H_2O) are high polarity, hydrogen bonding, cohesiveness, adhesiveness, high specific heat, high latent heat, and high heat of vaporization. It is essential to life as we know it, as water is one of the main if not the main constituent of many living things. Water is a liquid at room temperature. The high specific heat of water means it resists the breaking of its hydrogen bonds and resists heat and motion, which is why it has a relatively high boiling point and high vaporization point. It also resists temperature change. Water is peculiar in that its solid state floats in its liquid state. Most substances are denser in their solid forms. Water is cohesive, which means it is attracted to itself. It is also adhesive, which means it readily attracts other molecules. If water tends to adhere to another substance, the substance is said to be hydrophilic. Water makes a good solvent. Substances, particularly those with polar ions and molecules, readily dissolve in water.

Metabolism

Metabolism is all of the chemical reactions that take place within a living organism. These chemical changes convert nutrients to energy and macromolecules. Macromolecules are large and complex, and play an important role in cell structure and function. Metabolic pathways refer to a series of reactions in which the product of one reaction is the substrate for the next. These pathways are dependent upon enzymes that act as catalysts. An anabolic reaction is one that builds larger and more complex molecules (macromolecules) from smaller ones. Catabolic reactions are the opposite. Larger molecules are broken down into smaller, simpler molecules. Catabolic reactions release energy, while anabolic ones require energy. The four basic organic macromolecules produced by anabolic reactions are carbohydrates (polysaccharides), nucleic acids, proteins, and lipids. The four basic building blocks involved in catabolic reactions are monosaccharides (glucose), amino acids, fatty acids (glycerol), and nucleotides.

The Cell

Function and Structure of Cells in Living Organisms

The functions of plant and animal cells vary greatly, and the functions of different cells within a single organism can also be vastly different. Animal and plant cells are similar in structure in that they are eukaryotic, which means they contain a nucleus. The nucleus is a round structure that controls the activities of the cell and contains chromosomes. Both types of cells have cell membranes, cytoplasm, vacuoles, and other structures. The main difference between the two is that plant cells have a cell wall made of cellulose that can handle high levels of pressure within the cell, which can occur when liquid enters a plant cell. Plant cells have chloroplasts that are used during the process of photosynthesis, which is the conversion of sunlight into food. Plant cells usually have one large vacuole, whereas animal cells can have many smaller ones. Plant cells have a regular shape, while the shapes of animal cell can vary.

Nuclear Parts of a Eukaryotic Cell

Nucleus (pl. nuclei): This is a small structure that contains the chromosomes and regulates the DNA of a cell. The nucleus is the defining structure of eukaryotic cells, and all eukaryotic cells have a nucleus. The nucleus is responsible for the passing on of genetic traits between generations. The nucleus contains a nuclear envelope, nucleoplasm, a nucleolus, nuclear pores, chromatin, and ribosomes.

Chromosomes: These are highly condensed, threadlike rods of DNA. Short for deoxyribonucleic acid, DNA is the genetic material that stores information about the plant or animal.

Chromatin: This consists of the DNA and protein that make up chromosomes.

Nucleolus (nucleole): This structure contained within the nucleus consists of protein. It is small, round, does not have a membrane, is involved in protein synthesis, and synthesizes and stores RNA (ribonucleic acid).

Nuclear envelope: This encloses the structures of the nucleus. It consists of inner and outer membranes made of lipids.

Nuclear pores: These are involved in the exchange of material between the nucleus and the cytoplasm.

Nucleoplasm: This is the liquid within the nucleus, and is similar to cytoplasm.

Other Parts of a Cell

Ribosomes: Ribosomes are involved in synthesizing proteins from amino acids. They are numerous, making up about one quarter of the cell. Some cells contain thousands of ribosome. Some are mobile and some are embedded in the rough endoplasmic reticulum.

Golgi complex (Golgi apparatus): This is involved in synthesizing materials such as proteins that are transported out of the cell. It is located near the nucleus and consists of layers of membranes.

Vacuoles: These are sacs used for storage, digestion, and waste removal. There is one large vacuole in plant cells. Animal cells have small, sometimes numerous vacuoles.

Vesicle: This is a small organelle within a cell. It has a membrane and performs varying functions, including moving materials within a cell.

Cytoskeleton: This consists of microtubules that help shape and support the cell.

Microtubules: These are part of the cytoskeleton and help support the cell. They are made of protein.

Cytosol: This is the liquid material in the cell. It is mostly water, but also contains some floating molecules.

Cytoplasm: This is a general term that refers to cytosol and the substructures (organelles) found within the plasma membrane, but not within the nucleus.

Cell membrane (plasma membrane): This defines the cell by acting as a barrier. It helps keeps cytoplasm in and substances located outside the cell out. It also determines what is allowed to enter and exit the cell.

> ➢ **Review Video: Plasma Membrane**
> *Visit* **mometrix.com/academy** *and enter* **Code: 943095**

Endoplasmic reticulum: The two types of endoplasmic reticulum are rough (has ribosomes on the surface) and smooth (does not have ribosomes on the surface). It is a tubular network that comprises the transport system of a cell. It is fused to the nuclear membrane and extends through the cytoplasm to the cell membrane.

Mitochondrion (pl. mitochondria): These cell structures vary in terms of size and quantity. Some cells may have one mitochondrion, while others have thousands. This structure performs various functions such as generating ATP, and is also involved in cell growth and death. Mitochondria contain their own DNA that is separate from that contained in the nucleus.

Mitochondria
Four functions of mitochondria are: the production of cell energy, cell signaling (how communications are carried out within a cell, cellular differentiation (the process whereby a non-differentiated cell becomes transformed into a cell with a more specialized purpose), and cell cycle and growth regulation (the process whereby the cell gets ready to reproduce and reproduces). Mitochondria are numerous in eukaryotic cells. There may be hundreds or even thousands of mitochondria in a single cell.

Mitochondria can be involved in many functions, their main one being supplying the cell with energy. Mitochondria consist of an inner and outer membrane. The inner membrane encloses the matrix, which contains the mitochondrial DNA (mtDNA) and ribosomes. Between the inner and outer membranes are folds (cristae). Chemical reactions occur here that release energy, control water levels in cells, and recycle and create proteins and fats. Aerobic respiration also occurs in the mitochondria.

> **Review Video:** Mitochondria
> Visit *mometrix.com/academy* and enter **Code: 444287**

Eukaryotic and Prokaryotic Cells

The main difference between eukaryotic and prokaryotic cells is that eukaryotic cells have a nucleus and prokaryotic cells do not. Eukaryotic cells are considered more complex, while prokaryotic cells are smaller and simpler. Eukaryotic cells have membrane-bound organelles that perform various functions and contribute to the complexity of these types of cells. Prokaryotic cells do not contain membrane-bound organelles. In prokaryotic cells, the genetic material (DNA) is not contained within a membrane-bound nucleus. Instead, it aggregates in the cytoplasm in a nucleoid. In eukaryotic cells, DNA is mostly contained in chromosomes in the nucleus, although there is some DNA in mitochondria and chloroplasts. Prokaryotic cells usually divide by binary fission and are haploid. Eukaryotic cells divide by mitosis and are diploid. Prokaryotic structures include plasmids, ribosomes, cytoplasm, a cytoskeleton, granules of nutritional substances, a plasma membrane, flagella, and a few others. They are single-celled organisms. Bacteria are prokaryotic cells.

> **Review Video:** Eukaryotic and Prokaryotic
> Visit *mometrix.com/academy* and enter **Code: 231438**

Structures Unique to Animal Cells

Centrosome: This is comprised of the pair of centrioles located at right angles to each other and surrounded by protein. The centrosome is involved in mitosis and the cell cycle.

Centriole: These are cylinder-shaped structures near the nucleus that are involved in cellular division. Each cylinder consists of nine groups of three microtubules. Centrioles occur in pairs.

Lysosome: This digests proteins, lipids, and carbohydrates, and also transports undigested substances to the cell membrane so they can be removed. The shape of a lysosome depends on the material being transported.

Cilia (singular: cilium): These are appendages extending from the surface of the cell, the movement of which causes the cell to move. They can also result in fluid being moved by the cell.

Flagella: These are tail-like structures on cells that use whip-like movements to help the cell move. They are similar to cilia, but are usually longer and not as numerous. A cell usually only has one or a few flagella.

Structures Unique to Plant Cells

Cell wall: Made of cellulose and composed of numerous layers, the cell wall provides plants with a sturdy barrier that can hold fluid within the cell. The cell wall surrounds the cell membrane.

Chloroplast: This is a specialized organelle that plant cells use for photosynthesis, which is the process plants use to create food energy from sunlight. Chloroplasts contain chlorophyll, which has a green color.

Plastid: This is a membrane-bound organelle found in plant cells that is used to make chemical compounds and store food. It can also contain pigments used during photosynthesis. Plastids can develop into more specialized structures such as chloroplasts, chromoplasts (make and hold yellow and orange pigments), amyloplasts (store starch), and leucoplasts (lack pigments, but can become differentiated).

Plasmodesmata (sing. plasmodesma): These are channels between the cell walls of plant cells that allow for transport between cells.

Cell Theory

The basic tenets of cell theory are that all living things are made up of cells and that cell are the basic units of life. Cell theory has evolved over time and is subject to interpretation. The development of cell theory is attributed to Matthias Schleiden and Theodor Schwann, who developed the theory in the early 1800s. Early cell theory was comprised of four statements: all organisms (living things) are made of cells; new cells are formed from pre-existing cells; all cells are similar; and cells are the most basic units of life. Other concepts related to classic and modern cell theory include statements such as: cells provide the basic units of functionality and structure in living things; cells are both distinct stand-alone units and basic building blocks; energy flow occurs within cells; cells contain genetic information in the form of DNA; and all cells consist of mostly the same chemicals.

Passive and Active Transport Mechanisms

Transport mechanisms allow for the movement of substances through membranes. Passive transport mechanisms include simple and facilitated diffusion and osmosis. They do not require energy from the cell. Diffusion is when particles are transported from areas of higher concentration to areas of lower concentration. When equilibrium is reached, diffusion stops. Examples are gas exchange (carbon dioxide and oxygen) during photosynthesis and the transport of oxygen from air to blood and from blood to tissue. Facilitated diffusion is when specific molecules are transported by a specific carrier protein. Carrier proteins vary in terms of size, shape, and charge. Glucose and amino acids are examples of substances transported by carrier proteins. Osmosis is the diffusion of water through a semi-permeable membrane from an area of higher concentration to one of lower concentration. Examples of osmosis include the absorption of water by plant roots and the alimentary canal. Plants lose and gain water through osmosis. A plant cell that swells because of water retention is said to be turgid.

Active transport mechanisms include exocytosis and endocytosis. Active transport involves transferring substances from areas of lower concentration to areas of higher concentration. Active transport requires energy in the form of ATP. Endocytosis is the ingestion of large particles into a cell, and can be categorized as phagocytosis (ingestion of a particle), pinocytosis (ingestion of a liquid), or receptor mediated. Endocytosis occurs when a substance is too large to cross a cell membrane. Endocytosis is a process by which eukaryotes ingest food particles. During phagocytosis, cell eating vesicles used during ingestion are quickly formed and unformed. Pinocytosis is also known as cell drinking. Exocytosis is the opposite of endocytosis. It is the expulsion or discharge of substances from a cell. A lysosome digests particles with enzymes, and can be expelled through exocytosis. A vacuole containing the substance to be expelled attaches to the cell membrane and expels the substance.

Cellular Respiration

Cellular respiration refers to a set of metabolic reactions that convert chemical bonds into energy stored in the form of ATP. Respiration includes many oxidation and reduction reactions that occur thanks to the electron transport system within the cell. Oxidation is a loss of electrons and reduction is a gain of electrons. Electrons in C-H (carbon/hydrogen) and C-C (carbon/carbon) bonds are donated to oxygen atoms. Processes involved in cellular respiration include glycolysis, the Krebs cycle, the electron transport chain, and chemiosmosis. The two forms of respiration are aerobic and anaerobic. Aerobic respiration is very common, and oxygen is the final electron acceptor. In anaerobic respiration, the final electron acceptor is not oxygen. Aerobic respiration results in more ATP than anaerobic respiration. Fermentation is another process by which energy is converted.

Photosynthesis

Photosynthesis is the conversion of sunlight into energy in plant cells, and also occurs in some types of bacteria and protists. Carbon dioxide and water are converted into glucose during photosynthesis, and light is required during this process. Cyanobacteria are thought to be the descendants of the first organisms to use photosynthesis about 3.5 billion years ago. Photosynthesis is a form of cellular respiration. It occurs in chloroplasts that use thylakoids, which are structures in the membrane that contain light reaction chemicals. Chlorophyll is a pigment that absorbs light. During the process, water is used and oxygen is released. The equation for the chemical reaction that occurs during photosynthesis is $6H_2O + 6CO_2 \rightarrow C_6H_{12}O_6 + 6O_2$. During photosynthesis, six molecules of water and six molecules of carbon dioxide react to form one molecule of sugar and six molecules of oxygen.

Cellular Reproduction

The term cell cycle refers to the process by which a cell reproduces, which involves cell growth, the duplication of genetic material, and cell division. Complex organisms with many cells use the cell cycle to replace cells as they lose their functionality and wear out. The entire cell cycle in animal cells can take 24 hours. The time required varies among different cell types. Human skin cells, for example, are constantly reproducing. Some other cells only divide infrequently. Once neurons are mature, they do not grow or divide. The two ways that cells can reproduce are through meiosis and mitosis. When cells replicate through mitosis, the "daughter cell" is an exact replica of the parent cell. When cells divide through meiosis, the daughter cells have different genetic coding than the parent cell. Meiosis only happens in specialized reproductive cells called gametes.

Cell division is performed in organisms so they can grow and replace cells that are old, worn out, or damaged.

Chromatids: During cell division, the DNA is replicated, and chromatids are the two identical replicated pieces of chromosome that are joined at the centromere to form an "X."

Gametes: These are cells used by organisms to reproduce sexually. Gametes in humans are haploid, meaning they contain only half of the organism's genetic information (23 chromosomes). Other human cells contain all 46 chromosomes.

Haploid/diploid: Haploid means there is one set of chromosomes. Diploid means there are two sets of chromosomes (one set from each parent).

Genetics

Mendel's Laws and Punnett Squares

Mendel's laws are the law of segregation (the first law) and the law of independent assortment (the second law). The law of segregation states that there are two alleles and that half of the total number of alleles are contributed by each parent organism. The law of independent assortment states that traits are passed on randomly and are not influenced by other traits. The exception to this is linked traits. A Punnett square can illustrate how alleles combine from the contributing genes to form various phenotypes. One set of a parent's genes are put in columns, while the genes from the other parent are placed in rows. The allele combinations are shown in each cell. When two different alleles are present in a pair, the dominant one is expressed. A Punnett square can be used to predict the outcome of crosses.

Gene, Genotype, Phenotype, and Allele

A gene is a portion of DNA that identifies how traits are expressed and passed on in an organism. A gene is part of the genetic code. Collectively, all genes form the genotype of an individual. The genotype includes genes that may not be expressed, such as recessive genes. The phenotype is the physical, visual manifestation of genes. It is determined by the basic genetic information and how genes have been affected by their environment. An allele is a variation of a gene. Also known as a trait, it determines the manifestation of a gene. This manifestation results in a specific physical appearance of some facet of an organism, such as eye color or height. For example the genetic information for eye color is a gene. The gene variations responsible for blue, green, brown, or black eyes are called alleles. Locus (pl. loci) refers to the location of a gene or alleles.

Dominant and Recessive Traits

Gene traits are represented in pairs with an upper case letter for the dominant trait (A) and a lower case letter for the recessive trait (a). Genes occur in pairs (AA, Aa, or aa). There is one gene on each chromosome half supplied by each parent organism. Since half the genetic material is from each parent, the offspring's traits are represented as a combination of these. A dominant trait only requires one gene of a gene pair for it to be expressed in a phenotype, whereas a recessive requires both genes in order to be manifested. For example, if the mother's genotype is Dd and the father's is dd, the possible combinations are Dd and dd. The dominant trait will be manifested if the genotype is DD or Dd. The recessive trait will be manifested if the genotype is dd. Both DD and dd are homozygous pairs. Dd is heterozygous.

Monohybrid and Hybrid Crosses

Genetic crosses are the possible combinations of alleles, and can be represented using Punnett squares. A monohybrid cross refers to a cross involving only one trait. Typically, the ratio is 3:1 (DD, Dd, Dd, dd), which is the ratio of dominant gene manifestation to recessive gene manifestation. This ratio occurs when both parents have a pair of dominant and recessive genes. If one parent has a pair of dominant genes (DD) and the other has a pair of recessive (dd) genes, the recessive trait can not be expressed in the next generation because the resulting crosses all have the Dd genotype.

A dihybrid cross refers to one involving more than one trait, which means more combinations are possible. The ratio of genotypes for a dihybrid cross is 9:3:3:1 when the traits are not linked. The ratio for incomplete dominance is 1:3:1:, which corresponds to dominant, mixed, and recessive phenotypes.

Co-Dominance and Incomplete Dominance

Co-dominance refers to the expression of both alleles so that both traits are shown. Cows, for example, can have hair colors of red, white, or red and white (not pink). In the latter color, both traits are fully expressed. The ABO human blood typing system is also co-dominant. Incomplete dominance is when both the dominant and recessive genes are expressed, resulting in a phenotype that is a mixture of the two. The fact that snapdragons can be red, white, or pink is a good example. The dominant red gene (RR) results in a red flower because of large amounts of red pigment. White (rr) occurs because both genes call for no pigment. Pink (Rr) occurs because one gene is for red and one is for no pigment. The colors blend to produce pink flowers. A cross of pink flowers (Rr) can result in red (RR), white (rr), or pink (Rr) flowers.

Crossing Over, Gametes, Pedigree Analysis, and Probability Analysis

Crossing over: This refers to the swapping of genetic material between homologous chromosomes. This leads to different combinations of genes showing up in a phenotype. This is part of gene recombination, which is when DNA breaks down and is then reassembled.

Gametes: These are the sex cells in organisms that reproduce sexually. Each gamete contains half the genetic information of the parent. They are haploid (having 23 chromosome pairs in humans). The resulting zygote, which is formed when the two gametes become one cell, is diploid (46 chromosome pairs in humans).

Pedigree analysis: This involves isolating a trait in an organism and tracing its manifestation. Pedigree charts are often used for this type of analysis. A family pedigree shows how a trait can be seen throughout generations.

Probability analysis: This calculates the chances of a particular trait or combination of traits being expressed in an organism.

Different Types of Mutations

Gene disorders are the result of DNA mutations. DNA mutations lead to unfavorable gene disorders, but also provide genetic variability. This diversity can lead to increased survivability of a species. Mutations can be neutral, beneficial, or harmful. Mutations can be hereditary, meaning they are passed from parent to child. Polymorphism refers to differences in humans, such as eye and hair color, that may have originally been the result of gene mutations, but are now part of the normal variation of the species. Mutations can be de novo, meaning they happen either only in sex cells or shortly after fertilization. They can also be acquired, or somatic. These are the kinds that happen as a result of DNA changes due to environmental factors or replication errors. Mosaicism is when a mutation happens in a cell during an early embryonic stage. The result is that some cells will have the mutation and some will not.

Mutation at the DNA Level

A DNA mutation occurs when the normal gene sequence is altered. Mutations can happen when DNA is damaged as a result of environmental factors, such as chemicals, radiation, or ultraviolet rays from the sun. It can also happen when errors are made during DNA replication. The phosphate-sugar side rail of DNA can be damaged if the bonds between oxygen and phosphate groups are disassociated. Translocation happens when the broken bonds attempt to bond with other DNA. This repair can cause a mutation. The nucleotide itself can be altered. A C, for example, might look like a T. During replication, the damaged C is replicated as a T and paired with a G, which is incorrect base pairing. Another way mutations can occur is if an error is made by the DNA polymerase while replicating a base. This happens about once for every 100,000,000 bases. A repair protein proofreads the code, however, so the mistake is usually repaired.

Random Mutations, Nonrandom Mating, and Gene Migration

Random mutations: These are genetic changes caused by DNA errors or environmental factors such as chemicals and radiation. Mutations can be beneficial or harmful.

Nonrandom mating: This refers to the fact that the probability of two individuals mating in a population is not the same for all pairs. Nonrandom mating can be caused by geographical isolation, small populations, and other factors. Nonrandom mating can lead to inbreeding (mating with a relative), which can lead to a decline in physical fitness as seen in a phenotype and the reduction of allele frequency and occurrence.

Gene migration: Also known as gene flow, gene migration is the movement of alleles to another population. This can occur through immigration, when individuals of a species move into an area, or through emigration, when individuals of a species move out of an area.

Non-Mendelian Terms

Polygenic inheritance: This goes beyond the simplistic Mendelian concept that one gene influences one trait. It refers to traits that are influenced by more than one gene, and takes into account environmental influences on development.

Multiple alleles: Only two alleles make up a gene, but when there are three or more possible alleles, it is known as a multiple allele. A gene where only two alleles are possible is termed polymorphic.

Complete dominance: This refers the situation in which a homozygous pair of dominant alleles (AA) and a heterozygous pair of alleles (Aa) result in the same phenotype. Dominate genes have the following characteristics: they are expressed in each generation; they are passed on to roughly half the offspring; and a parent that does not express the trait can not pass it on to offspring. The Mendelian complete dominance concept states that one gene consisting of two alleles is the only factor involved in the creation of a phenotype. Most traits, however, are more complex.

Linkage

Linkage involves characteristics that are on the same chromosome. This leads to two different traits being seen together more often than not. Linkage is the exception to independent assortment. Sex-linked traits are those that occur on a sex chromosome. Autosomal refers to non-sex chromosomes. In humans, there are 22 autosomal pairs of chromosomes and a pair of sex chromosomes. Depending on the sex, pairs are either XX (female) or XY (male). Since females don't have Y chromosomes, alleles on this gene are only manifested in males. Males can only pass on sex-linked traits on the X chromosome to their daughters since sons would not receive an X from them. Hemizygous means there is only one copy of a gene. Color blindness occurs more in males than females because it is a sex-linked trait on the X chromosome. Since it is recessive, females have a better chance of expressing the dominant characteristic of non-color blindness.

Lethal Allele, Pleiotropy, Epistasis, and Karyotype

Lethal allele: This is when a mutation in an essential gene results in the death of the organism. Cystic fibrosis and Tay-Sachs disease are examples of lethal recessive alleles.

Pleiotropy: This refers to a gene that affects more than one trait.

Epistasis: This refers to the situation in which two or more genes determine a single phenotype.
Karyotype: This is a picture of genes based on a sample of blood or skin.

Interaction between Heredity and Environment

The non-Mendelian concept of polygenetic inheritance takes into account environmental factors on phenotypes. For example, an individual inherits genes that help determine height, but a diet lacking in certain nutrients could limit that individual's ability to reach that height. Another example is the concept of genetic disposition, which is a propensity for a certain disease that is genetically inherited, but not necessarily manifested. For example, individuals with certain skin types are more likely to develop skin cancer. If they limit their exposure to solar radiation, however, this will not necessarily occur.

Allele Frequency

The gene pool refers to all alleles of a gene and their combinations. The Hardy-Weinberg principle (or Castle-Hardy Weinberg principle) postulates that the allele frequency for dominant and recessive alleles will remain the same in a population through successive generations if certain conditions exist. These conditions are: no mutations, large populations, random mating, no migration, and equal genotypes. This is an ideal and not how most population's function. Changes in the frequency and types of alleles in a gene pool can be caused by gene flow, random mutation, nonrandom mating, and genetic drift. In organisms that reproduce by sexual reproduction, reproduction isolation is defined as something that acts as a barrier to two species reproducing. These barriers are classified as prezygotic and postzygotic.

DNA

Chromosomes consist of genes, which are single units of genetic information. Genes are made up of deoxyribonucleic acid (DNA). DNA is a nucleic acid located in the cell nucleus. There is also DNA in the mitochondria. DNA replicates to pass on genetic information. The DNA in almost all cells is the same. It is also involved in the biosynthesis of proteins. The model or structure of DNA is described as a double helix. A helix is a curve, and a double helix is two congruent curves connected by horizontal members. The model can be likened to a spiral staircase. It is right-handed. The British scientist Rosalind Elsie Franklin is credited with taking the x-ray diffraction image in 1952 that was used by Francis Crick and James Watson to formulate the double-helix model of DNA and speculate about its important role in carrying and transferring genetic information.

DNA has a double helix shape, resembles a twisted ladder, and is compact. It consists of nucleotides. Nucleotides consist of a five-carbon sugar (pentose), a phosphate group, and a nitrogenous base. Two bases pair up to form the rungs of the ladder. The "side rails" or backbone consists of the covalently bonded sugar and phosphate. The bases are attached to each other with hydrogen bonds, which are easily dismantled so replication can occur. Each base is attached to a phosphate and to a sugar. There are four types of nitrogenous bases: adenine (A), guanine (G), cytosine (C), and thymine (T). There are about 3 billion bases in human DNA. The bases are mostly the same in everybody, but their order is different. It is the order of these bases that creates diversity in people. Adenine (A) pairs with thymine (T), and cytosine (C) pairs with guanine (G).

DNA Replication

Pairs of chromosomes are composed of DNA, which is tightly wound to conserve space. When replication starts, it unwinds. The steps in DNA replication are controlled by enzymes. The enzyme helicase instigates the deforming of hydrogen bonds between the bases to split the two strands. The splitting starts at the A-T bases (adenine and thymine) as there are only two hydrogen bonds. The cytosine-guanine base pair has three bonds. The term "origin of replication" is used to refer to where the splitting starts. The portion of the DNA that is unwound to be replicated is called the replication fork. Each strand of DNA is transcribed by an mRNA. It copies the DNA onto itself, base by base, in a complementary manner. The exception is that uracil replaces thymine.

Semiconservative, Antiparallel Replication, and Base Pairing

Semiconservative: DNA replication is considered semiconservative because the two replicated copies of DNA each have one strand of the original parent DNA, or half of the original genetic material.

Antiparallel replication: This refers to the fact that during DNA replication, the nucleotides (A, C, G, T, and U) on leading and lagging strands run in opposite directions. RNA synthesis is said to occur in a $5' \rightarrow 3'$ (five prime to three prime) direction. That means that the phosphate group of the nucleotide that is being added to the chain, which is $5'$, is attached to the end of the chain at the end of a hydroxyl group, which is $3'$.

Base pairing: This explains how RNA transcribes DNA in an inverted fashion. C on DNA is inserted as a G on RNA, and A on DNA becomes U on RNA.

Functions of Proteins in DNA Replication

Many proteins are involved in the replication of DNA, and each has a specific function. Helicase is a protein that facilitates the unwinding of the double helix structure of DNA. Single strand binding (SSB) proteins attach themselves to each strand to prevent the DNA strands from joining back together. After DNA is unwound, there are leading and lagging strands. The leading strand is synthesized continuously and the lagging strand is synthesized in Okazaki fragments. Primase, an RNA polymerase (catalyzing enzyme), acts as a starting point for replication by forming short strands, or primers, of RNA. The DNA clamp, or sliding clamp, helps prevent DNA polymerase from coming apart from the strand. DNA polymerase helps form the DNA strand by linking nucleotides. As the process progresses, RNase H removes the primers. DNA ligase then links the existing shorter strands into a longer strand.

Chemistry

Scientific Notation, Metric System, and Temperature

Scientific Notation

Scientific notation is a way of writing large numbers in a shorter form. The form $a \times 10^n$ is used in scientific notation, where a is greater than or equal to 1, but less than 10, and n is the number of places the decimal must move to get from the original number to a.

Example: The number 230,400,000 is cumbersome to write. To write the value in scientific notation, place a decimal point between the first and second numbers, and include all digits through the last non-zero digit (a = 2.304). To find the appropriate power of 10, count the number of places the decimal point had to move (n = 8). The number is positive if the decimal moved to the left, and negative if it moved to the right. We can then write 230,400,000 as 2.304×10^8.

If we look instead at the number 0.00002304, we have the same value for a, but this time the decimal moved 5 places to the right (n = -5). Thus, 0.00002304 can be written as 2.304×10^{-5}. Using this notation makes it simple to compare very large or very small numbers. By comparing exponents, it is easy to see that 3.28×10^4 is smaller than 1.51×10^5, because 4 is less than 5.

Decimal Notation to Scientific Notation
Scientific notation is used because values in science can be very large or very small, which makes them unwieldy. A number in decimal notation is 93,000,000. In scientific notation, it is 9.3×10^7. The first number, 9.3, is the coefficient. It is always greater than or equal to 1 and less than 10. This number is followed by a multiplication sign. The base is always 10 in scientific notation. If the number is greater than zero, the exponent is a positive number. If it is less than zero, the exponent is negative. The first digit of the number is followed by a decimal point and then the rest of the number. In this case, the number is 9.3. To get that number, the decimal point was moved seven places from the end of the number, 93,000,000. The number of places, seven, is the exponent.

Metric System

Metric Prefixes for Multiples and Subdivisions
The prefixes for multiples are as follows: deka (da), 10^1 (deka is the American spelling, but deca is also used); hecto (h), 10^2; kilo (k), 10^3; mega (M), 10^6; giga (G), 10^9; tera (T), 10^{12}; peta (P), 10^{15}; exa (E), 10^{18}; zetta (Z), 10^{21}; and yotta (Y), 10^{24}. The prefixes for subdivisions are as follows: deci (d), 10^{-1}; centi (c), 10^{-2}; milli (m), 10^{-3}; micro (μ), 10^{-6}; nano (n), 10^{-9}; pico (p), 10^{-12}; femto (f), 10^{-15}; atto (a), 10^{-18}; zepto (z), 10^{-21}; and yocto (y), 10^{-24}. The rule of thumb is that prefixes greater than 10^3 are capitalized. These abbreviations do not need a period after them. A decimeter is a tenth of a meter, a deciliter is a tenth of a liter, and a decigram is a tenth of a gram. Pluralization is understood. For example, when referring to 5 mL of water, no "s" needs to be added to the abbreviation.

Basic Units of Measurement in the Metric System
Using the metric system is generally accepted as the preferred method for taking measurements. Having a universal standard allows individuals to interpret measurements more easily, regardless of where they are located. The basic units of measurement are: the meter, which measures length; the liter, which measures volume; and the gram, which measures mass. The metric system starts with a base unit and increases or decreases in units of 10. The prefix and the base unit combined

are used to indicate an amount. For example, deka is 10 times the base unit. A dekameter is 10 meters; a dekaliter is 10 liters; and a dekagram is 10 grams. The prefix hecto refers to 100 times the base amount; kilo is 1,000 times the base amount. The prefixes that indicate a fraction of the base unit are deci, which is 1/10 of the base unit; centi, which is 1/100 of the base unit; and milli, which is 1/1000 of the base unit.

SI Units of Measurement

SI uses second(s) to measure time. Fractions of seconds are usually measured in metric terms using prefixes such as millisecond (1/1,000 of a second) or nanosecond (1/1,000,000,000 of a second). Increments of time larger than a second are measured in minutes and hours, which are multiples of 60 and 24. An example of this is a swimmer's time in the 800-meter freestyle being described as 7:32.67, meaning 7 minutes, 32 seconds, and 67 one-hundredths of a second. One second is equal to 1/60 of a minute, 1/3,600 of an hour, and 1/86,400 of a day. Other SI base units are the ampere (A) (used to measure electric current), the kelvin (K) (used to measure thermodynamic temperature), the candela (cd) (used to measure luminous intensity), and the mole (mol) (used to measure the amount of a substance at a molecular level). Meter (m) is used to measure length and kilogram (kg) is used to measure mass.

Temperature

There are three main scales for measuring temperature. Celsius uses the base reference points of water freezing at 0 degrees and boiling at 100 degrees. Fahrenheit uses the base reference points of water freezing at 32 degrees and boiling at 212 degrees. Celsius and Fahrenheit are both relative temperature scales since they use water as their reference point. The Kelvin temperature scale is an absolute temperature scale. Its zero mark corresponds to absolute zero. Water's freezing and boiling points are 273.15 Kelvin and 373.15 Kelvin, respectively. Where Celsius and Fahrenheit are measured is degrees, Kelvin does not use degree terminology.

- Converting Celsius to Fahrenheit: $°F = \frac{9}{5}°C + 32$
- Converting Fahrenheit to Celsius: $°C = \frac{5}{9}(°F - 32)$
- Converting Celsius to Kelvin: $K = °C + 273.15$
- Converting Kelvin to Celsius: $°C = K - 273.15$

The Atom

Atom: The atom is one of the most basic units of matter. An atom consists of a central nucleus surrounded by electrons.

Nucleus: The nucleus of an atom consists of protons and neutrons. It is positively charged, dense, and heavier than the surrounding electrons. The plural form of nucleus is nuclei.

Electrons: These are atomic particles that are negatively charged and orbit the nucleus of an atom.

Protons: Along with neutrons, protons make up the nucleus of an atom. The number of protons in the nucleus determines the atomic number of an element. Carbon atoms, for example, have six protons. The atomic number of carbon is 6. The number of protons also indicates the charge of an atom. The number of protons minus the number of electrons indicates the charge of an atom.

Structure of Atoms

All matter consists of atoms. Atoms consist of a nucleus and electrons. The nucleus consists of protons and neutrons. The properties of these are measurable; they have mass and an electrical charge. The nucleus is positively charged due to the presence of protons. Electrons are negatively charged and orbit the nucleus. The nucleus has considerably more mass than the surrounding electrons. Atoms can bond together to make molecules. Atoms that have an equal number of protons and electrons are electrically neutral. If the number of protons and electrons in an atom is not equal, the atom has a positive or negative charge and is an ion.

Models of Atoms

Atoms are extremely small. A hydrogen atom is about 5×10^{-8} mm in diameter. According to some estimates, five trillion hydrogen atoms could fit on the head of a pin. Atomic radius refers to the average distance between the nucleus and the outermost electron. Models of atoms that include the proton, nucleus, and electrons typically show the electrons very close to the nucleus and revolving around it, similar to how the Earth orbits the sun. However, another model relates the Earth as the nucleus and its atmosphere as electrons, which is the basis of the term "electron cloud." Another description is that electrons swarm around the nucleus. It should be noted that these atomic models are not to scale. A more accurate representation would be a nucleus with a diameter of about 2 cm in a stadium. The electrons would be in the bleachers. This model is similar to the not-to-scale solar system model.

Periodic Table

The periodic table groups elements with similar chemical properties together. The grouping of elements is based on atomic structure. It shows periodic trends of physical and chemical properties and identifies families of elements with similar properties. It is a common model for organizing and understanding elements. In the periodic table, each element has its own cell that includes varying amounts of information presented in symbol form about the properties of the element. Cells in the table are arranged in rows (periods) and columns (groups or families). At minimum, a cell includes the symbol for the element and its atomic number. The cell for hydrogen, for example, which appears first in the upper left corner, includes an "H" and a "1" above the letter. Elements are ordered by atomic number, left to right, top to bottom.

Groups in the Periodic Table

In the periodic table, the groups are the columns numbered 1 through 18 that group elements with similar outer electron shell configurations. Since the configuration of the outer electron shell is one of the primary factors affecting an element's chemical properties, elements within the same group have similar chemical properties. Previous naming conventions for groups have included the use of Roman numerals and upper-case letters. Currently, the periodic table groups are: Group 1, alkali metals; Group 2, alkaline earth metals; Groups 3-12, transition metals; Group 13, boron family; Group 14; carbon family; Group 15, pnictogens; Group 16, chalcogens; Group 17, halogens; Group 18, noble gases.

Additional Information on the Periodic Table

Other information that can be included in each elemental cell includes the atomic weight below the symbol, the element name, colors to organize elements into categories (such as the light pink used for transitional elements and the light blue used for noble gases), colors to indicate the phase of elements (such as red for gas and green for liquid), and line styles around cells to indicate an element's origins (a solid line around the cell indicates a primordial element, a dotted indicates an element created from decay, and no line indicates that the origins have not yet been discovered). Atomic weight is also known as standard atomic weight or relative atomic mass (not atomic mass), and is defined as the ratio of an average mass of atoms of a specific source of an element to 1/12 of the mass of an atom of carbon-12. Uncertainty may also be included in parenthesis after the atomic weight. Instead of atomic weight, artificial elements may list the most stable isotope in brackets.

Periodic Table Periods and Electrons

In the periodic table, there are seven periods (rows), and within each period there are blocks that group elements with the same outer electron subshell. The number of electrons in that outer shell determines which group an element belongs to within a given block. Each row's number (1, 2, 3, etc.) corresponds to the highest number electron shell that is in use. For example, row 2 uses only electron shells 1 and 2, while row 7 uses all shells from 1-7.

Periodic Table and Atomic Radii, Ionic Radii, Electronegativity

Atomic radii will decrease from left to right across a period (row) on the periodic table. In a group (column), there is an increase in the atomic radii of elements from top to bottom. Ionic radii will be smaller than the atomic radii for metals, but the opposite is true for non-metals. From left to right, electronegativity, or an atom's likeliness of taking another atom's electrons, increases. In a group, electronegativity decreases from top to bottom. Ionization energy or the amount of energy needed to get rid of an atom's outermost electron, increases across a period and decreases down a group. Electron affinity will become more negative across a period but will not change much within a group. The melting point decreases from top to bottom in the metal groups and increases from top to bottom in the non-metal groups.

Chemical Equations

Chemical equations describe chemical reactions. The reactants are on the left side before the arrow and the products are on the right side after the arrow. The arrow indicates the reaction or change. The coefficient, or stoichiometric coefficient, is the number before the element, and indicates the ratio of reactants to products in terms of moles. The equation for the formation of water from hydrogen and oxygen, for example, is $2H_2$ (g) + O_2 (g) → $2H_2O$ (l). The 2 preceding hydrogen and water is the coefficient, which means there are 2 moles of hydrogen and 2 of water. There is 1 mole of oxygen, which does not have to be indicated with the number 1. In parentheses, g stands for gas, l stands for liquid, s stands for solid, and aq stands for aqueous solution (a substance dissolved in water). Charges are shown in superscript for individual ions, but not for ionic compounds. Polyatomic ions are separated by parentheses so the ion will not be confused with the number of ions.

Balancing Chemical Equations

An unbalanced equation is one that does not follow the law of conservation of mass, which states that matter can only be changed, not created. If an equation is unbalanced, the numbers of atoms indicated by the stoichiometric coefficients on each side of the arrow will not be equal. Start by writing the formulas for each species in the reaction. Count the atoms on each side and determine if the number is equal. Coefficients must be whole numbers. Fractional amounts, such as half a molecule, are not possible. Equations can be balanced by multiplying the coefficients by a constant that will produce the smallest possible whole number coefficient. $H_2 + O_2 \rightarrow H_2O$ is an example of an unbalanced equation. The balanced equation is $2H_2 + O_2 \rightarrow 2H_2O$, which indicates that it takes two moles of hydrogen and one of oxygen to produce two moles of water.

Solutions

A solution is a homogeneous mixture. A mixture is two or more different substances that are mixed together, but not combined chemically. Homogeneous mixtures are those that are uniform in their composition. Solutions consist of a solute (the substance that is dissolved) and a solvent (the substance that does the dissolving). An example is sugar water. The solvent is the water and the solute is the sugar. The intermolecular attraction between the solvent and the solute is called solvation. Hydration refers to solutions in which water is the solvent. Solutions are formed when the forces of the molecules of the solute and the solvent are as strong as the individual molecular forces of the solute and the solvent. An example is that salt (NaCl) dissolves in water to create a solution. The Na^+ and the Cl^- ions in salt interact with the molecules of water and vice versa to overcome the individual molecular forces of the solute and the solvent.

Percent Concentrations

Concentrations can be measured in mole fractions, parts per million or billion, and percent by mass or volume. Percent concentrations can be calculated by mass or by volume by dividing the mass or volume of the solute by the mass or volume of the solution. This quotient is a decimal that can be converted to a percent by multiplying by 100. Many percent concentrations are given as mg/100mL or mg/dL. Other concentrations can be given as mL/mL or mL/dL.

Molarity

The concentration of a solution is measured in terms of molarity. One molar (M) is equal to a quantity of moles of solute per liter of solution. Adding one mole of a substance to one liter of solution would most likely result in a molarity greater than one. The amount of substance should be measured into a small amount of solution, and then more solution should be added to reach a volume of one liter to ensure accuracy.

The Mole and Avogadro's Number

Atomic mass unit (amu) is the smallest unit of mass, and is equal to 1/12 of the mass of the carbon isotope carbon-12. A mole (mol) is a measurement of molecular weight that is equal to the molecule's amu in grams. For example, carbon has an amu of 12, so a mole of carbon weighs 12 grams. One mole is equal to about 6.0221415×10^{23} elementary entities, which are usually atoms or molecules. This amount is also known as the Avogadro constant or Avogadro's number (NA). Another way to say this is that one mole of a substance is the same as one Avogadro's number of that substance. One mole of chlorine, for example, is 6.0221415 × 10^{23} chlorine atoms. The charge on one mole of electrons is referred to as a Faraday.

Common Solutions and Dilute v. Concentrated Solutions

A syrup is a solution of water and sugar. A brine is a solution of table salt, or sodium chloride (NaCl), and water. A saline solution is a sterilized concentration of sodium chloride in water. A seltzer is a solution of carbon dioxide in water.

The term dilute is used when there is less solute. Adding more solvent is known as diluting a solution, as is removing a portion of the solute. Concentrated is the term used when there is more solute. Adding more solute makes a solution more concentrated, as does removing a portion of the solvent.

Properties of Solutions

Properties of solutions include: they have a maximum particle size of one nm, they do not separate when allowed to stand or when poured through a fiber filter, they are clear and do not scatter light, and their boiling points increase while their melting points decrease when the amount of solute is increased.

Effects of Temperature and Pressure on Solubility

Solids tend to dissolve faster when the temperature is increased. Higher temperatures help break bonds through an increase in kinetic energy. Solubility tends to increase for solids being dissolved in water as the temperature approaches 100 °C, but at higher temperatures ionic solutes tend to become less soluble. Gases tend to be less soluble at higher temperatures. When solutions are saturated at high temperatures, the solute will precipitate (return to solid form) and "fall out of the solution" as the solution cools. Melting points can be lowered by using a solvent such as salt on icy roads, which lowers the freezing point of ice. Adding salt to water when making ice cream also lowers the melting point of the water. A solution's melting point is usually lower than the melting point of the solvent alone. Pressure has little effect on the solubility of liquid solutions. In gas solutions, an increase in pressure increases solubility, and vice versa.

Polar vs. Nonpolar Solutes and Solvents

For solvation to occur, bonds of similar strength must be broken and formed. Nonpolar substances are usually soluble in nonpolar solvents. Ionic and polar matter is usually soluble in polar solvents. Water is a polar solvent. Oil is nonpolar. Therefore, the saying "oil and water don't mix" is quite true. Heptane (C_7H_{16}) is another nonpolar liquid that is said to be immiscible in water, meaning it can't combine with water. The hydrogen bonds of the water molecules are stronger than the London dispersion forces of the heptane. Polar molecules such as NH_3 (ammonia), SO_2 (sulfur dioxide), and H_2S (hydrogen sulfide) are termed hydrophilic, meaning they readily combine with water. Nonpolar molecules, including the noble gases and other gases such as He (helium), Ne (neon), and CO_2 (carbon dioxide) are termed hydrophobic, meaning they repel or do not readily combine with water. One way to remember this is that "like dissolves like." Polar solvents dissolve polar solutes, while nonpolar solvents dissolve nonpolar solutes.

Chemical Reactions

Chemical reactions measured in human time can take place quickly or slowly. They can take fractions of a second or billions of years. The rates of chemical reactions are determined by how frequently reacting atoms and molecules interact. Rates are also influenced by the temperature and various properties (such as shape) of the reacting materials. Catalysts accelerate chemical reactions, while inhibitors decrease reaction rates. Some types of reactions release energy in the form of heat and light. Some types of reactions involve the transfer of either electrons or hydrogen ions between reacting ions, molecules, or atoms. In other reactions, chemical bonds are broken down by heat or light to form reactive radicals with electrons that will readily form new bonds. Processes such as the formation of ozone and greenhouse gases in the atmosphere and the burning and processing of fossil fuels are controlled by radical reactions.

Effect of Temperature on Reaction Rate

The collision theory states that for a chemical reaction to occur, atoms or molecules have to collide with each other with a certain amount of energy. A certain amount of energy is required to breach the activation barrier. Heating a mixture will raise the energy levels of the molecules and the rate of reaction (the time it takes for a reaction to complete). Generally, the rate of reaction is doubled for every 10 degrees Celsius temperature increase. However, the increase needed to double a reaction rate increases as the temperature climbs. This is due to the increase in collision frequency that occurs as the temperature increases. Other factors that can affect the rate of reaction are surface area, concentration, pressure, and the presence of a catalyst.

Catalysts and the Maxwell-Boltzmann Distribution

Catalysts, substances that help change the rate of reaction without changing their form, can increase reaction rate by decreasing the number of steps it takes to form products. The mass of the catalyst should be the same at the beginning of the reaction as it is at the end. The activation energy is the minimum amount required to get a reaction started. Activation energy causes particles to collide with sufficient energy to start the reaction. A catalyst enables more particles to react, which lowers the activation energy. Examples of catalysts in reactions are manganese oxide (MnO_2) in the decomposition of hydrogen peroxide, iron in the manufacture of ammonia using the Haber process, and concentrate of sulfuric acid in the nitration of benzene.

Maxwell-Boltzmann distribution: This refers to a graph or plot showing the energies or speeds of particles or gas molecules in a system.

Combination and Decomposition Reactions

Combination, or synthesis, reactions: In a combination reaction, two or more reactants combine to form a single product (A + B → C). These reactions are also called synthesis or addition reactions. An example is burning hydrogen in air to produce water. The equation is $2H_2$ (g) + O_2 (g) → $2H_2O$ (l). Another example is when water and sulfur trioxide react to form sulfuric acid. The equation is $H_2O + SO_3$ → H_2SO_4.

Decomposition (or desynthesis, decombination, or deconstruction) reactions: In a decomposition reaction, a reactant is broken down into two or more products (A → B + C). These reactions are also called analysis reactions. Thermal decomposition is caused by heat. Electrolytic decomposition is due to electricity. An example of this type of reaction is the decomposition of water into hydrogen and oxygen gas. The equation is $2H_2O \rightarrow 2H_2 + O_2$.

Combustion

Combustion, or burning, is a sequence of chemical reactions involving fuel and an oxidant that produces heat and sometimes light. There are many types of combustion, such as rapid, slow, complete, turbulent, microgravity, and incomplete. Fuels and oxidants determine the compounds formed by a combustion reaction. For example, when rocket fuel consisting of hydrogen and oxygen combusts, it results in the formation of water vapor. When air and wood burn, resulting compounds include nitrogen, unburned carbon, and carbon compounds. Combustion is an exothermic process, meaning it releases energy. Exothermic energy is commonly released as heat, but can take other forms, such as light, electricity, or sound.

Single and Double Substitution Reactions

Single substitution, displacement, or replacement reactions are when one reactant is displaced by another to form the final product (A + BC → AB + C). Single substitution reactions can be cationic or anionic. When a piece of copper (Cu) is placed into a solution of silver nitrate ($AgNO_3$), the solution turns blue. The copper appears to be replaced with a silvery-white material. The equation is $2AgNO_3 + Cu \rightarrow Cu(NO_3)_2 + 2Ag$. When this reaction takes place, the copper dissolves and the silver in the silver nitrate solution precipitates (becomes a solid), resulting in copper nitrate and silver. Copper and silver have switched places in the nitrate.

Double displacement, double replacement, substitution, metathesis, or ion exchange reactions are when ions or bonds are exchanged by two compounds to form different compounds (AC + BD → AD + BC). An example of this is that silver nitrate and sodium chloride form two different products (silver chloride and sodium nitrate) when they react. The formula for this reaction is $AgNO_3 + NaCl \rightarrow AgCl + NaNO_3$.

Covalent and Ionic Bonding

Covalent bonding results from the sharing of electrons between atoms. Atoms seek to fill their valence shell and will share electrons with another atom in order to have a full octet (except hydrogen and helium, which only hold two electrons in their valence shells). Molecular compounds have covalent bonds. Organic compounds such as proteins, carbohydrates, lipids, and nucleic acids are molecular compounds formed by covalent bonds. Methane (CH_4) is a molecular compound in which one carbon atom is covalently bonded to four hydrogen atoms as shown below.

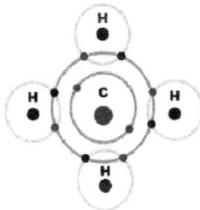

Ionic bonding results from the transfer of electrons between atoms. A cation or positive ion is formed when an atom loses one or more electrons. An anion or negative ion is formed when an atom gains one or more electrons. An ionic bond results from the electrostatic attraction between a cation and an anion. One example of a compound formed by ionic bonds is sodium chloride or NaCl.

Sodium (Na) is an alkali metal and tends to form Na+ ions. Chlorine is a halogen and tends to form Cl- ions. The Na+ ion and the Cl- ion are attracted to each other. This electrostatic attraction between these oppositely charged ions is what results in the ionic bond between them.

$$Na\cdot + \overset{\times\times}{\underset{\times\times}{:Cl:}}_\times \longrightarrow [Na]^+ [\overset{\times\times}{\underset{\times\times}{:Cl:}}_\times]^-$$

electron transfer from sodium to chlorine

Hydrogen Bonds

Hydrogen bonds are weaker than covalent and ionic bonds, and refer to the type of attraction in an electronegative atom such as oxygen, fluorine, or nitrogen. Hydrogen bonds can form within a single molecule or between molecules. A water molecule is polar, meaning it is partially positively charged on one end (the hydrogen end) and partially negatively charged on the other (the oxygen end). This is because the hydrogen atoms are arranged around the oxygen atom in a close tetrahedron. Hydrogen is oxidized (its number of electrons is reduced) when it bonds with oxygen to form water. Hydrogen bonds tend not only to be weak, but also short-lived. They also tend to be numerous. Hydrogen bonds give water many of its important properties, including its high specific heat and high heat of vaporization, its solvent qualities, its adhesiveness and cohesiveness, its hydrophobic qualities, and its ability to float in its solid form. Hydrogen bonds are also an important component of proteins, nucleic acids, and DNA.

Intermolecular Forces

Intermolecular forces are weaker than ionic and covalent bonds. They occur between stable molecules or functional groups of macromolecules. Macromolecules are large molecules that are usually created by polymerization and sometimes distinguished by their lack of covalent bonds. London dispersion force, dipole-dipole interactions, and hydrogen bonding are all examples of intermolecular forces. London dispersion force is also known as instantaneous dipole-induced dipole force because the force is caused by a change in dipole (a separation of the positive and negative charges in an atom). These forces are weak and the attractions are quickly formed and broken. An electron from one atom affects another atom, resulting in a force that dissipates as soon as an electron moves. Dipole-dipole (Keesom) interactions occur within atoms that are already covalently bonded and have permanent dipoles. These atoms have a different amount of electronegativity (attraction of electrons). One atom attracts another, electrostatic forces are generated, and molecules align to increase this attraction.

Oxidation-Reduction Reactions

One way to organize chemical reactions is to sort them into two categories: oxidation/reduction reactions (also called redox reactions) and metathesis reactions (which include acid/base reactions). Oxidation/reduction reactions can involve the transfer of one or more electrons, or they can occur as a result of the transfer of oxygen, hydrogen, or halogen atoms. The species that loses electrons is oxidized and is referred to as the reducing agent. The species that gains electrons is reduced and is referred to as the oxidizing agent. The element undergoing oxidation experiences an increase in its oxidation number, while the element undergoing reduction experiences a decrease in its oxidation number. Single replacement reactions are types of oxidation/reduction reactions. In a single replacement reaction, electrons are transferred from one chemical species to another. The transfer of electrons results in changes in the nature and charge of the species.

Oxidation State and Oxidation Number

Oxidation state and oxidation number are usually the same number. Even though they have different meanings, they are frequently used interchangeably. Oxidation numbers are Roman numerals in parentheses that are used as part of the naming scheme for inorganic compounds. Oxidation state refers to the hypothetical charge on an atom if all of its bonds are 100 percent ionic. They are integers that can occasionally be fractional numbers. Oxidation state is increased through oxidation (loss of electrons) and decreased through reduction (gain of electrons). The number for an oxidation state refers to a single atom or ion, and is a way to keep track of electrons. When using Lewis diagrams, shared electrons are generally assigned to the more electronegative element. In bonds involving two atoms of the same element, electrons are split between them. Lone pairs of electrons are assigned to the atom they are with.

Rules for Determining Oxidation State

Rules for calculating oxidation state include the one that states that the oxidation state is 0 for atoms in elemental form (only one kind of atom is present and its charge is 0). For example, both S_8 and Fe have an oxidation state of 0. For a monatomic ion, the oxidation state is equal to its charge. For example, the oxidation state is -2 for S^{2-} and +3 for Al^{3+}. For all Group 1A (alkali) metals, the oxidation state is +1. It is +2 for all Group 2A (alkaline earth) metals unless they are in elemental form. Hydrogen has an oxidation state of +1 when it is bonded to a nonmetal. It can be -1 when bonded to a metal. Oxygen almost always has an oxidation state of -2, but in peroxides it is -1. There are other exceptions as well. The oxidation state for fluorine is always -1. In a neutral compound, the sum of all atoms or ions must equal zero. In a polyatomic ion, its charge is equal to the sum of all oxidation state numbers.

Acids and Bases

Acids

When they are dissolved in aqueous solutions, some properties of acids are that they conduct electricity, change blue litmus paper to red, have a sour taste, react with bases to neutralize them, and react with active metals to free hydrogen. A weak acid is one that does not donate all of its protons or disassociate completely. Strong acids include hydrochloric, hydriodic, hydrobromic, perchloric, nitric, and sulfuric. They ionize completely. Superacids are those that are stronger than 100 percent sulfuric acid. They include fluoroantimonic, magic, and perchloric acids. Acids can be used in pickling, a process used to remove rust and corrosion from metals. They are also used as catalysts in the processing of minerals and the production of salts and fertilizers. Phosphoric acid (H_3PO_4) is added to sodas and other acids are added to foods as preservatives or to add taste.

Bases

When they are dissolved in aqueous solutions, some properties of bases are that they conduct electricity, change red litmus paper to blue, feel slippery, and react with acids to neutralize their properties. A weak base is one that does not completely ionize in an aqueous solution, and usually has a low pH. Strong bases can free protons in very weak acids. Examples of strong bases are hydroxide compounds such as potassium, barium, and lithium hydroxides. Most are in the first and second groups of the periodic table. A superbase is extremely strong compared to sodium hydroxide and cannot be kept in an aqueous solution. Superbases are organized into organic, organometallic, and inorganic classes. Bases are used as insoluble catalysts in heterogeneous reactions and as catalysts in hydrogenation.

pH

The potential of hydrogen (pH) is a measurement of the concentration of hydrogen ions in a substance in terms of the number of moles of H^+ per liter of solution. A lower pH indicates a higher H^+ concentration, while a higher pH indicates a lower H^+ concentration. Pure water has a neutral pH, which is 7. Anything with a pH lower than water (less than 7) is considered acidic. Anything with a pH higher than water (greater than 7) is a base. Drain cleaner, soap, baking soda, ammonia, egg whites, and sea water are common bases. Urine, stomach acid, citric acid, vinegar, hydrochloric acid, and battery acid are acids. A pH indicator is a substance that acts as a detector of hydrogen or hydronium ions. It is halochromic, meaning it changes color to indicate that hydrogen or hydronium ions have been detected.

Nuclear Chemistry

Nuclear Reactions

The particles of an atom's nucleus (the protons and neutrons) are bound together by nuclear force, also known as residual strong force. Unlike chemical reactions, which involve electrons, nuclear reactions occur when two nuclei or nuclear particles collide. This results in the release or absorption of energy and products that are different from the initial particles. The energy released in a nuclear reaction can take various forms, including the release of kinetic energy of the product particles and the emission of very high energy photons known as gamma rays. Some energy may also remain in the nucleus. Radioactivity refers to the particles emitted from nuclei as a result of nuclear instability. There are many nuclear isotopes that are unstable and can spontaneously emit some kind of radiation. The most common types of radiation are alpha, beta, and gamma radiation, but there are several other varieties of radioactive decay.

Radioactive Half-Life and Radiation

Radioactive half-life is the time it takes for half of the radioactive nuclei in a sample to undergo radioactive decay. Radioactive decay rates are usually expressed in terms of half-lives. The different types of radioactivity lead to different decay paths, which transmute the nuclei into other chemical elements. Decay products (or daughter nuclides) make radioactive dating possible. Decay chains are a series of decays that result in different products. For example, uranium-238 is often found in granite. Its decay chain includes 14 daughter products. It eventually becomes a stable isotope of lead, which is why lead is often found with deposits of uranium ore. Its first half-life is equivalent to the approximate age of the earth, about 4.5 billion years. One of its products is radon, a radioactive gas. Radiation is when energy is emitted by one body and absorbed by another. Nuclear weapons, nuclear reactors, and radioactive substances are all examples of things that involve ionizing radiation. Acoustic and electromagnetic radiation are other types of radiation.

Isotopes

The number of protons in an atom determines the element of that atom. For instance, all helium atoms have exactly two protons, and all oxygen atoms have exactly eight protons. If two atoms have the same number of protons, then they are the same element. However, the number of neutrons in two atoms can be different without the atoms being different elements. Isotope is the term used to distinguish between atoms that have the same number of protons but a different number of neutrons. The names of isotopes have the element name with the mass number. Recall that the mass number is the number of protons plus the number of neutrons. For example, carbon-12 refers to an atom that has 6 protons, which makes it carbon, and 6 neutrons. In other words, 6 protons + 6 neutrons = 12. Carbon-13 has six protons and seven neutrons, and carbon-14 has six protons and eight neutrons. Isotopes can also be written with the mass number in superscript before the element symbol. For example, carbon-12 can be written as ^{12}C.

Radioisotopes, Radioactive Decay, Radioactivity

Radioisotopes: Also known as radionuclides or radioactive isotopes, radioisotopes are atoms that have an unstable nucleus. This is a nucleus that has excess energy and the potential to make radiation particles within the nucleus (subatomic particles) or undergo radioactive decay, which can result in the emission of gamma rays. Radionuclides may occur naturally, but can also be artificially produced.

Radioactive decay: This occurs when an unstable atomic nucleus spontaneously loses energy by emitting ionizing particles and radiation. Decay is a form of energy transfer, as energy is lost. It also results in different products. Before decay there is one type of atom, called the parent nuclide. After decay there are one or more different products, called the daughter nuclide(s).

Radioactivity: This refers to particles that are emitted from nuclei as a result of nuclear instability.

Stable and Radioactive Isotopes

Stable isotopes: Isotopes that have not been observed to decay are stable, or non-radioactive, isotopes. It is not known whether some stable isotopes may have such long decay times that observing decay is not possible. Currently, 80 elements have one or more stable isotopes. There are 256 known stable isotopes in total. Carbon, for example, has three isotopes. Two (carbon-12 and carbon-13) are stable and one (carbon-14) is radioactive.

Radioactive isotopes: These have unstable nuclei and can undergo spontaneous nuclear reactions, which results in particles or radiation being emitted. It can not be predicted when a specific nucleus will decay, but large groups of identical nuclei decay at predictable rates. Knowledge about rates of decay can be used to estimate the age of materials that contain radioactive isotopes.

Alpha, Beta, and Gamma Rays

Ionizing radiation is that which can cause an electron to detach from an atom. It occurs in radioactive reactions and comes in three types: alpha (α), beta (β), and gamma (γ). Alpha rays are positive, beta rays are negative, and gamma rays are neutral. Alpha particles are larger than beta particles and can cause severe damage if ingested. Because of their large mass, however, they can be stopped easily. Even paper can protect against this type of radiation. Beta particles can be beta-minus or beta-plus. Beta-minus particles contain an energetic electron, while beta-plus particles are emitted by positrons and can result in gamma photons. Beta particles can be stopped with thin metal. Gamma rays are a type of high energy electromagnetic radiation consisting of photons. Gamma radiation rids the decaying nucleus of excess energy after it has emitted either alpha or beta radiation. Gamma rays can cause serious damage when absorbed by living tissue, and it takes thick lead to stop them. Alpha, beta, and gamma radiation can also have positive applications.

Biochemistry

Carbohydrates

The simple sugars can be grouped into monosaccharides (glucose, fructose, and sucrose) and disaccharides. These are both types of carbohydrates. Monosaccharides have one monomer of sugar and disaccharides have two. Monosaccharides (CH_2O) have one carbon for every water molecule. Aldose and ketose are monosaccharides with a carbonyl (=O, double bonded oxygen to carbon) functional group. The difference between aldose and ketose is that the carbonyl group in aldose is connected at an end carbon and the carbonyl group in ketose is connected at a middle carbon. Glucose is a monosaccharide containing six carbons, making it a hexose and an aldose. A disaccharide is formed from two monosaccharides with a glycosidic link. Examples include two glucoses forming a maltose, a glucose and a galactose forming a lactose, and a glucose and a fructose forming a sucrose. A starch is a polysaccharide consisting only of glucose monomers. Examples are amylose, amylopectin, and glycogen.

In glycolysis, glucose is converted into pyruvate and energy stored in ATP bonds is released. Glycolysis can involve various pathways. Various intermediates are produced that are used in other processes, and the pyruvic acid produced by glycolysis can be further used for respiration by the Krebs cycle or in fermentation. Glycolysis occurs in both aerobic and anaerobic organisms. Oxidation of molecules produces reduced coenzymes, such as NADH. The coenzymes relocate hydrogens to the electron transport chain. The proton is transported through the cell membrane and the electron is transported down the chain by proteins. At the end of the chain, water is formed when the final acceptor releases two electrons that combine with oxygen. The protons are pumped back into the cell or organelle by the ATP synthase enzyme, which uses energy produced to add a phosphate to ADP to form ATP. The proton motive force is produced by the protons being moved across the membrane.

Glycolysis can involve different metabolic pathways. The following 10 steps are based on the Embden-Meyerhof pathway, in which glucose is the starting product and pyruvic acid is the final product. Two molecules of ATP and two of NADH are the products of this process. To start, enzymes utilize ATP to form glucose-6-phosphate. The glucose-6 is converted to fructose-6-phosphate. Another ATP molecule and an enzyme are used to convert fructose-6-phosphate to fructose-1,6-disphosphate. Both dihydroxyacetone phosphate (DHAP) and glyceraldehyde-3-phosphate are formed from fructose-1,6-disphosphate. It is during the preceding reactions that energy is conserved or gained. NAD conversions to NADH molecules and phosphate influx result in 1,3-diphosphoglceric acid. Then, two ADP molecules are phosphorized into ATP molecules, resulting in 3-phosphoglyceric acid, which reforms into 2-phosphoglyceric acid. At this point, water is produced as a product and phosphoenolpyruvic acid is formed. Another set of ADP molecules are phosphorized into ATP molecules. Pyruvic acid is the end result.

Glycolysis is a general term for the conversion of glucose into pyruvate.

Embden-Meyerhof pathway: This is a type of glycolysis in which one molecule of glucose becomes two ATP and two NADH molecules. Pyruvic acid (two pyruvate molecules) is the end product.

Entner-Doudoroff pathway: This is a type of glycolysis in which one glucose molecule forms into one molecule of ATP and two of NADPH, which are used for other reactions. The end product is two pyruvate molecules.

Pentose Phosphate pathway: Also known as the hexose monophosphate shunt, this is a type of glycolysis in which one glucose molecule produces one ATP and two NADPH molecules. Five carbon sugars are metabolized during this reaction. Glucose is broken down into ribose, ribulose, and xylose, which are used during glycolysis and during the Calvin (or Calvin-Benson) cycle to create nucleotides, nucleic acids, and amino acids.

Proteins

Proteins are macromolecules formed from amino acids. They are polypeptides, which consist of many (10 to 100) peptides linked together. The peptide connections are the result of condensation reactions. A condensation reaction results in a loss of water when two molecules are joined together. A hydrolysis reaction is the opposite of a condensation reaction. During hydrolysis, water is added. -H is added to one of the smaller molecules and OH is added to another molecule being formed. A peptide is a compound of two or more amino acids. Amino acids are formed by the partial hydrolysis of protein, which forms an amide bond. This partial hydrolysis involves an amine group and a carboxylic acid. In the carbon chain of amino acids, there is a carboxylic acid group (-COOH), an amine group ($-NH_2$), a central carbon atom between them with an attached hydrogen, and an attached "R" group (side chain), which is different for different amino acids. It is the "R" group that determines the properties of the protein.

Alkyl: This is a nonpolar group that forms hydrophobic amino acids. Amino acids include glycine with a single hydrogen atom R group, alanine with a methyl R group, and valine with an isopropyl R group. Leucine and isoleucine also have alkyl side chains.

Hydroxyl: This is a polar group that forms hydrophilic amino acids such as serine and threonine.

Sulfur: Amino acids in this group include cysteine and methionine.

Carboxylic acid: In proteins belonging to this group, a second carboxylic acid group is attached as the R group. This acid group is polar and can be negatively charged when the acidic proton attaches to a water molecule, which leaves a negatively charged carboxylate ion. Proteins that belong to this group include aspartic acid and glutamic acid.

Amide: The formula for amides is $-CONH_2$. Proteins belonging to this group include glutamine and asparagine.

Amino: This group includes lysine, arginine, and histidine. The double-bonded nitrogen atom can take a proton to become positively charged.

Aromatic: This group has a ring structure, and includes the proteins phenylalanine, tyrosine, and tryptophan. Tyrosine is polar, while tryptophan and phenylalanine are nonpolar.

Looped: This group includes praline. Because it is nonpolar, it forms a ring rather than a chain.

Lipids

Carbohydrates, proteins, and nucleic acids are groups of macromolecules that are polymers. Lipids are not long polymers with high molecular weights. They are hydrophobic, meaning they do not bond well with water or mix well with water solutions. Lipids have numerous C-H bonds. In this way, they are similar to hydrocarbons (substances consisting only of carbon and hydrogen). The major roles of lipids include energy storage and structural functions. Examples of lipids include fats, phospholipids, steroids, and waxes. Fats are made of long chains of fatty acids (three fatty acids bound to a glycerol). Fatty acids are chains with reduced carbon at one end and a carboxylic acid group at the other. An example is soap, which contains the sodium salts of free fatty acids.

Phospholipids are lipids that have a phosphate group rather than a fatty acid. Glycerides are another type of lipid. Examples of glycerides are fat and oil. Glycerides are formed from fatty acids and glycerol (a type of alcohol).

Nucleic Acids

Nucleic acids are macromolecules that are composed of nucleotides. Hydrolysis is a reaction in which water is broken down into hydrogen cations (H or H$^+$) and hydroxide anions (OH or OH$^-$). This is part of the process by which nucleic acids are broken down by enzymes to produce shorter strings of RNA and DNA (oligonucleotides). Oligonucleotides are broken down into smaller sugar nitrogenous units called nucleosides. These can be digested by cells since the sugar is divided from the nitrogenous base. This, in turn, leads to the formation of the five types of nitrogenous bases, sugars, and the preliminary substances involved in the synthesis of new RNA and DNA. DNA and RNA have a double helix shape.

Macromolecular nucleic acid polymers, such as RNA and DNA, are formed from nucleotides, which are monomeric units joined by phosphodiester bonds. Cells require energy in the form of ATP to synthesize proteins from amino acids and replicate DNA. Nitrogen fixation is used to synthesize nucleotides for DNA and amino acids for proteins. Nitrogen fixation uses the enzyme nitrogenase in the reduction of dinitrogen gas (N_2) to ammonia (NH_3). Nucleic acids store information and energy and are also important catalysts. It is the RNA that catalyzes the transfer of DNA genetic information into protein coded information. ATP is an RNA nucleotide. Nucleotides are used to form the nucleic acids. Nucleotides are made of a five carbon sugar, such as ribose or deoxyribose, a nitrogenous base, and one or more phosphates. Nucleotides consisting of more than one phosphate can also store energy in their bonds.

Anatomy and Physiology

Anatomical Planes and Direction

The Three Primary Body Planes

The **Transverse (or horizontal) plane** divides the patient's body into imaginary upper (superior) and lower (inferior or caudal) halves.

The **Sagittal plane** divides the body, or any body part, vertically into right and left sections. The sagittal plane runs parallel to the midline of the body.

The **Coronal (or frontal) plane** divides the body, or any body structure, vertically into front and back (anterior and posterior) sections. The coronal plane runs vertically through the body at right angles to the midline.

Terms of Direction

Medial means nearer to the midline of the body. In anatomical position, the little finger is medial to the thumb.

Lateral is the opposite of medial. It refers to structures further away from the body's midline, at the sides. In anatomical position, the thumb is lateral to the little finger.

Proximal refers to structures closer to the center of the body. The hip is proximal to the knee.

Distal refers to structures further away from the center of the body. The knee is distal to the hip.

Anterior refers to structures in front.

Posterior refers to structures behind.

Cephalad and cephalic are adverbs meaning towards the head. Cranial is the adjective, meaning of the skull.

Caudad is an adverb meaning towards the tail or posterior. Caudal is the adjective, meaning of the hindquarters.

Superior means above, or closer to the head.

Inferior means below, or closer to the feet.

Histology

Importance of Cells and Structural Organization

All organisms, whether plants, animals, fungi, protists, or bacteria, exhibit structural organization on the cellular and organism level. All cells contain DNA and RNA and can synthesize proteins. Cells are the basic structural units of all organisms. All organisms have a highly organized cellular structure. Each cell consists of nucleic acids, cytoplasm, and a cell membrane. Specialized organelles such as mitochondria and chloroplasts have specific functions within the cell. In single-celled organisms, that single cell contains all of the components necessary for life. In multicellular organisms, cells can become specialized. Different types of cells can have different functions. Life begins as a single cell whether by asexual or sexual reproduction. Cells are grouped together in tissues. Tissues are grouped together in organs. Organs are grouped together in systems. An organism is a complete individual.

Tissues

Tissues are groups of cells that work together to perform a specific function. Tissues can be grouped into four broad categories: muscle tissue, nerve tissue, epithelial tissue, and connective tissue. Muscle tissue is involved in body movement. Muscle tissues can be composed of skeletal muscle cells, cardiac muscle cells, or smooth muscle cells. Skeletal muscles include the muscles commonly called biceps, triceps, hamstrings, and quadriceps. Cardiac muscle tissue is found only in the heart. Smooth muscle tissue provides tension in the blood vessels, control pupil dilation, and aid in peristalsis. Nerve tissue is located in the brain, spinal cord, and nerves. Epithelial tissue makes up the layers of the skin and various membranes. Connective tissues include bone tissue, cartilage, tendons, ligaments, fat, blood, and lymph. Tissues are grouped together as organs to form specific functions.

Mitosis and Meiosis

Mitosis

Interphase: The cell prepares for division by replicating its genetic and cytoplasmic material. Interphase can be further divided into G_1, S, and G_2.

Prophase: The chromatin thickens into chromosomes and the nuclear membrane begins to disintegrate. Pairs of centrioles move to opposite sides of the cell and spindle fibers begin to form. The mitotic spindle, formed from cytoskeleton parts, moves chromosomes around within the cell.

Metaphase: The spindle moves to the center of the cell and chromosome pairs align along the center of the spindle structure.

Anaphase: The pairs of chromosomes, called sisters, begin to pull apart, and may bend. When they are separated, they are called daughter chromosomes. Grooves appear in the cell membrane.

Telophase: The spindle disintegrates, the nuclear membranes reform, and the chromosomes revert to chromatin. In animal cells, the membrane is pinched. In plant cells, a new cell wall begins to form.

Cytokinesis: This is the physical splitting of the cell (including the cytoplasm) into two cells. Cytokinesis begins during anaphase, as the cell begins to furrow, and is completed following telophase.

Meiosis

Meiosis has the same phases as mitosis, but they happen twice. In addition, different events occur during some phases of meiosis than mitosis. The events that occur during the first phase of meiosis are interphase (I), prophase (I), metaphase (I), anaphase (I), telophase (I), and cytokinesis (I). During this first phase of meiosis, chromosomes cross over, genetic material is exchanged, and tetrads of four chromatids are formed. The nuclear membrane dissolves. Homologous pairs of chromatids are separated and travel to different poles. At this point, there has been one cell division resulting in two cells. Each cell goes through a second cell division, which consists of prophase (II), metaphase (II), anaphase (II), telophase (II), and cytokinesis (II). The result is four daughter cells with different sets of chromosomes. The daughter cells are haploid, which means they contain half the genetic material of the parent cell. The second phase of meiosis is similar to the process of mitosis. Meiosis encourages genetic diversity.

Body Systems

The Integumentary System

The integumentary system, which consists of the skin including the sebaceous glands sweat glands, hair, and nails, serves a variety of functions associated with protection, secretion, and communication. In the functions associated with protection, the integumentary system protects the body from pathogens including bacteria, viruses, and various chemicals from entering the body. In the functions associated with secretion, sebaceous glands secrete sebum (oil) that waterproofs the skin, and sweat glands are associated with the body's homeostatic relationship of thermoregulation. Sweat glands also serve as excretory organs and help rid the body of metabolic wastes. In the functions associated with communication, sensory receptors distributed throughout the skin send information to the brain regarding pain, touch, pressure, and temperature. In addition to protection, secretion, and communication, the skin manufactures vitamin D and can absorb certain chemicals such as specific medications.

Layers of the Skin

The layers of the skin from the surface of the skin inward are the epidermis and dermis. The subcutaneous layer lying below the dermis is also part of the integumentary system. The epidermis is the most superficial layer of the skin. The epidermis, which consists entirely of epithelial cells, does not contain any blood vessels. The deepest portion of the epidermis is the stratum basale, which is a single layer of cells that continually undergo division. As more and more cells are produced, older cells are pushed toward the surface. Most epidermal cells are keratinized. Keratin is a waxy protein that helps to waterproof the skin. As the cells die, they are sloughed off. The dermis lies directly beneath the epidermis. The dermis consists mostly of connective tissue. The dermis contains blood vessels, sensory receptors, hair follicles, sebaceous glands, and sweat glands. The dermis also contains elastin and collagen fibers. The subcutaneous layer or hypodermis is actually not a layer of the skin. The subcutaneous layer consists of connective tissue, which binds the skin to the underlying muscles. Fat deposits in the subcutaneous layer help to cushion and insulate the body.

Skin and Thermoregulation

The skin is involved in temperature homeostasis or thermoregulation through the activation of the sweat glands. By thermoregulation, the body maintains a stable body temperature as one component of a stable internal environment. The temperature of the body is controlled by a negative feedback system consisting of a receptor, control center, and effector. The receptors are sensory cells located in the dermis of the skin. The control center is the hypothalamus, which is located in the brain. The effectors include the sweat glands, blood vessels, and muscles (shivering). The evaporation of sweat across the surface of the skin cools the body to maintain its tolerance range. Vasodilation of the blood vessels near the surface of the skin also releases heat into the environment to lower body temperature. Shivering is associated with the muscular system.

Sebaceous Glands and Sweat Glands

Sebaceous glands and sweat glands are exocrine glands found in the skin. Exocrine glands secrete substances into ducts. In this case, the secretions are through the ducts to the surface of the skin. Sebaceous glands are holocrine glands, which secrete sebum. Sebum is an oily mixture of lipids and proteins. Sebaceous glands are connected to hair follicles and secrete sebum through the hair pore. Sebum inhibits water loss from the skin and protects against bacterial and fungal infections. Sweat glands are either eccrine glands or apocrine glands. Eccrine glands are not connected to hair follicles. They are activated by elevated body temperature. Eccrine glands are located throughout the body and can be found on the forehead, neck, and back. Eccrine glands secrete a salty solution of electrolytes and water containing sodium chloride, potassium, bicarbonate, glucose, and antimicrobial peptides. Eccrine glands are activated as part of the body's thermoregulation. Apocrine glands secrete an oily solution containing fatty acids, triglycerides, and proteins. Apocrine glands are located in the armpits, groin, palms, and soles of the feet. Apocrine glands secrete this oily sweat when a person experiences stress or anxiety. Bacteria feed on apocrine sweat and expel aromatic fatty acids, producing body odor.

The Skeletal System

The human skeletal system, which consists of 206 bones along with numerous tendons, ligaments, and cartilage, is divided into the axial skeleton and the appendicular skeleton. The axial skeleton consists of 80 bones and includes the vertebral column, rib cage, sternum, skull, and hyoid bone. The vertebral column consists of 33 vertebrae classified as cervical vertebrae, thoracic vertebrae, lumbar vertebrae, and sacral vertebrae. The rib cage includes 12 paired ribs, 10 pairs of true ribs and 2 pairs of floating ribs, and the sternum, which consists of the manubrium, corpus sterni, and xiphoid process. The skull includes the cranium and facial bones. The ossicles are bones in the middle ear. The hyoid bone provides an attachment point for the tongue muscles. The axial skeleton protects vital organs including the brain, heart, and lungs. The appendicular skeleton consists of 126 bones including the pectoral girdle, pelvic girdle, and appendages. The pectoral girdle consists of the scapulae (shoulders) and clavicles (collarbones). The pelvic girdle consists of two pelvic (hip) bones, which attach to the sacrum. The upper appendages (arms) include the humerus, radius, ulna, carpals, metacarpals, and phalanges. The lower appendages (legs) include the femur, patella, fibula, tibia, tarsals, metatarsals, and phalanges.

<u>Compact and Spongy Bone</u>
Two types of connective bone tissue include compact bone and spongy bone. Compact, or cortical, bone, which consists of tightly packed cells, is strong, dense, and rigid. Running vertically throughout compact bone are the Haversian canals, which are surrounded by concentric circles of bone tissue called lamellae. The spaces between the lamellae are called the lacunae. These lamellae and canals along with their associated arteries, veins, lymph vessels, and nerve endings are referred to collectively as the Haversian system. The Haversian system provides a reservoir for calcium and phosphorus for the blood. Also, bones have a thin outside layer of compact bone, which gives them their characteristic smooth, white appearance. Spongy, or cancellous, bone consists of trabeculae, which are a network of girders with open spaces filled with red bone marrow. Compared to compact bone, spongy bone is lightweight and porous, which helps reduce the bone's overall weight. The red marrow manufactures red and white blood cells. In long bones, the diaphysis consists of compact bone surrounding the marrow cavity and spongy bone containing red marrow in the epiphyses. Bones have varying amounts of compact bone and spongy bone depending on their classification.

<u>Functions of the Skeletal System</u>
The skeletal system serves many functions including providing structural support, providing movement, providing protection, producing blood cells, and storing substances such as fat and minerals. The skeletal system provides the body with structure and support for the muscles and organs. The axial skeleton transfers the weight from the upper body to the lower appendages. The skeletal system provides movement with joints and the muscular system. Bones provide attachment points for muscles. Joints including hinge joints, ball-and-socket joints, pivot joints, ellipsoid joints, gliding joints, and saddle joints. Each muscle is attached to two bones: the origin

and the insertion. The origin remains immobile, and the insertion is the bone that moves as the muscle contracts and relaxes. The skeletal system serves to protect the body. The cranium protects the brain. The vertebrae protect the spinal cord. The rib cage protects the heart and lungs. The pelvis protects the reproductive organs. The red marrow manufactures red and white blood cells. All bone marrow is red at birth, but adults have approximately one-half red bone marrow and one-half yellow bone marrow. Yellow bone marrow stores fat. Also, the skeletal system provides a reservoir to store the minerals calcium and phosphorus.

The Muscular System

The human body has more than 650 skeletal muscles than account for approximately half of a person's weight. Starting with the head and face, the temporalis and masseter move the mandible. The orbicularis oculi closes the eye. The orbicularis oris draws the lips together. The sternocleidomastoids move the head. The trapezius moves the shoulder, and the pectoralis major, deltoid, and latissimus dorsi move the upper arm. The biceps brachii and the triceps brachii move the lower arm. The rectus abdominus, external oblique, and erector spine move the trunk. The external and internal obliques elevate and depress the ribs. The gluteus maximus moves the upper leg. The quadriceps femoris, hamstrings, and sartorius move the lower leg. The gastrocnemius and the soleus extend the foot.

Types of Muscular Tissue
The three types of muscular tissue are skeletal muscle, smooth muscle, and cardiac muscle. Skeletal muscles are voluntary muscles that work in pairs to move various parts of the skeleton. Skeletal muscles are composed of muscle fibers (cells) that are bound together in parallel bundles. Skeletal muscles are also known as striated muscle due to their striped appearance under a microscope. Smooth muscle tissues are involuntary muscles that are found in the walls of internal organs such as the stomach, intestines, and blood vessels. Smooth muscle tissues or visceral tissue is nonstriated. Smooth muscle cells are shorter and wider than skeletal muscle fibers. Smooth muscle tissue is also found in sphincters or valves that control various openings throughout the body. Cardiac muscle tissue is involuntary muscle that is found only in the heart. Like skeletal muscle cells, cardiac muscle cells are also striated.

Skeletal Muscle Contraction
Skeletal muscles consist of numerous muscle fibers. Each muscle fiber contains a bundle of myofibrils, which are composed of multiple repeating contractile units called sarcomeres. Myofibrils contain two protein microfilaments: a thick filament and a thin filament. The thick filament is composed of the protein myosin. The thin filament is composed of the protein actin. The dark bands (striations) in skeletal muscles are formed when thick and thin filaments overlap. Light bands occur where the thin filament is overlapped. Skeletal muscle attraction occurs when the thin filaments slide over the thick filaments shortening the sarcomere. When an action potential (electrical signal) reaches a muscle fiber, calcium ions are released. According to the sliding filament model of muscle contraction, these calcium ions bind to the myosin and actin, which assists in the binding of the myosin heads of the thick filaments to the actin molecules of the thin filaments. Adenosine triphosphate released from glucose provides the energy necessary for the contraction.

Muscular System and Thermoregulation
Thermoregulation or temperature regulation is a homeostatic relationship involving the muscular system. Skeletal muscles and smooth muscles are involved in thermoregulation. If the body temperature drops below acceptable levels, the hypothalamus signals the body's warming

mechanisms to initiate. Smooth muscles in the walls of blood vessels in the skin cause the blood vessels to constrict and divert blood into deeper tissues. Skeletal muscles are triggered, and shivering generates heat. When the body temperature increases back to acceptable levels, the hypothalamus signals the body's warming mechanisms to stop. Similarly, if the body temperature rises above acceptable levels, the blood vessels in the skin dilate by means of their smooth muscle tissue. As blood fills the skin's capillaries, heat is radiated away from the body.

The Nervous System

The nervous system consists of two major divisions: the central nervous system (CNS) and the peripheral nervous system (PNS). The CNS includes the brain and spinal cord. The brain is the major organ of the nervous system. The brain, which is divided into the cerebrum, cerebellum, and brain stem, controls the entire body including thinking, coordination of skeletal muscle movement, and involuntary actions such as breathing and heart rate. The brain communicates with the rest of the body via the spinal cord. The PNS includes the nerves that branch from the brain and spinal cord. As part of the PNS, 12 pairs of cranial nerves branch off the brain stem. Also extending from the spinal cord are 31 pairs of branching spinal nerves. The PNS includes the somatic nervous system and the autonomic nervous system. The somatic nervous system controls the five senses and the movement of skeletal muscles. The autonomic nervous system includes the sympathetic and parasympathetic nervous system. The sympathetic nervous system deals with stressful or emergency situations, and the parasympathetic nervous system returns the body to normal after stressful or emergency situations and maintains normal functioning.

<u>Reflex Arc and Stimulus</u>
A reflex, the simplest act of the nervous system, is an automatic response without any conscious thought to a stimulus via the reflex arc. The reflex arc is the simplest nerve pathway, which bypasses the brain and is controlled by the spinal cord. For example, in the classic knee-jerk response (patellar tendon reflex), the stimulus is the reflex hammer hitting the tendon, and the response is the muscle contracting, which jerks the foot upward. The stimulus is detected by sensory receptors, and a message is sent along a sensory (afferent) neuron to one or more interneurons in the spinal cord. The interneuron(s) transmit this message to a motor (efferent) neuron, which carries the message to the correct effector (muscle).

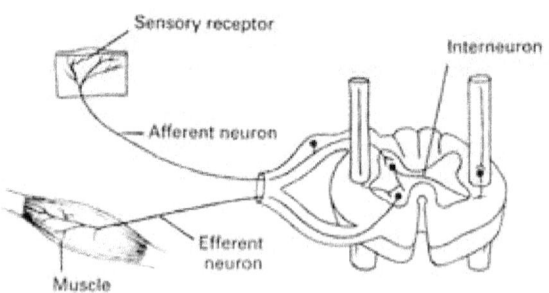

<u>Autonomic Nervous System and Homeostasis</u>
The autonomic nervous system (ANS) maintains homeostasis within the body. In general, the ANS controls the functions of the internal organs, blood vessels, smooth muscle tissues, and glands. This is accomplished through the direction of the hypothalamus, which is located above the midbrain. The hypothalamus controls the ANS through the brain stem. With this direction from the hypothalamus, the ANS helps maintain a stable body environment (homeostasis) by regulating numerous factors including heart rate, breathing rate, body temperature, and blood pH. The ANS

consists of two divisions: the sympathetic nervous system and the parasympathetic nervous system. The sympathetic nervous system controls the body's reaction to extreme, stressful, and emergency situations. For example, the sympathetic nervous system increases the heart rate, signals the adrenal glands to secrete adrenaline, triggers the dilation of the pupils, and slows digestion. The parasympathetic nervous system counteracts the effects of the sympathetic nervous system. For example, the parasympathetic nervous system decreases heart rate, signals the adrenal glands to stop secreting adrenaline, constricts the pupils, and returns the digestion process to normal.

Neurons

The three general functional types of neurons are the sensory neurons, motor neurons, and interneurons. Sensory neurons transmit signals to the central nervous system (CNS) from the sensory receptors associated with touch, pain, temperature, hearing, sight, smell, and taste. Motor neurons transmit signals from the CNS to the rest of the body such as by signaling muscles or glands to respond. Interneurons transmit signals between neurons; for example, interneurons receive transmitted signals between sensory neurons and motor neurons. In general, a neuron consists of three basic parts: the cell body, the axon, and many dendrites. The dendrites receive impulses from sensory receptors or interneurons and transmit them toward the cell body. The cell body (soma) contains the nucleus of the neuron. The axon transmits the impulses away from the cell body. The axon is insulated by oligodendrocytes and the myelin sheath with gaps known as the nodes of Ranvier. The axon terminates at the synapse.

The Endocrine System

The endocrine system is responsible for secreting the hormones and other molecules that help regulate the entire body in both the short and the long term. There is a close working relationship between the endocrine system and the nervous system. The hypothalamus and the pituitary gland coordinate to serve as a neuroendrocrine control center.

Hormone secretion is triggered by a variety of signals, including hormonal signs, chemical reactions, and environmental cues. Only cells with particular receptors can benefit from hormonal influence. This is the "key in the lock" model for hormonal action. Steroid hormones trigger gene activation and protein synthesis in some target cells. Protein hormones change the activity of existing enzymes in target cells. Hormones such as insulin work quickly when the body signals an urgent need. Slower acting hormones afford longer, gradual, and sometimes permanent changes in the body.

Major Endocrine Glands
1. **Adrenal cortex** - Monitors blood sugar level; helps in lipid and protein metabolism.
2. **Adrenal medulla** - Controls cardiac function; raises blood sugar and controls the size of blood vessels.
3. **Thyroid gland** - Helps regulate metabolism and functions in growth and development.
4. **Parathyroid** - Regulates calcium levels in the blood.
5. **Pancreas islets** - Raises and lowers blood sugar; active in carbohydrate metabolism.
6. **Thymus gland** - Plays a role in immune responses.
7. **Pineal gland** - Has an influence on daily biorhythms and sexual activity.
8. **Pituitary gland** - Plays an important role in growth and development.

Endocrine glands are intimately involved in a myriad of reactions, functions, and secretions that are crucial to the well-being of the body.

The Circulatory System

The circulatory system is responsible for the internal transport of substances to and from the cells. The circulatory system usually consists of the following three parts:
1. **Blood** - Blood is composed of water, solutes, and other elements in a fluid connective tissue.
2. **Blood Vessels** - Tubules of different sizes that transport blood.
3. **Heart** - The heart is a muscular pump providing the pressure necessary to keep blood flowing.

Circulatory systems can be either open or closed. Most animals have closed systems, where the heart and blood vessels are continually connected. As the blood moves through the system from larger tubules through smaller ones, the rate slows down. The flow of blood in the capillary beds, the smallest tubules, is quite slow. A supplementary system, the lymph vascular system, cleans up excess fluids and proteins and returns them to the circulatory system.

Blood
Blood helps maintain a healthy internal environment in animals by carrying raw materials to cells and removing waste products. It helps stabilize internal pH and hosts various kinds of infection fighters.

An adult human has about five quarts of blood. Blood is composed of red and white blood cells, platelets, and plasma. Plasma constitutes over half of the blood volume. It is mostly water and serves as a solvent. Plasma contains plasma proteins, ions, glucose, amino acids, hormones, and dissolved gases.

Red blood cells transport oxygen to cells. Red blood cells form in the bone marrow and can live for about two months. These cells are constantly being replaced by fresh ones, keeping the total number relatively stable.

White blood cells defend the body against infection and remove various wastes. The types of white blood cells include lymphocytes, neutrophils, monocytes, eosinophils, and basophils.

Platelets are fragments of stem cells thatwhich serve an important function in blood clotting.

The Heart
The heart is a muscular pump made of cardiac muscle tissue. It has four chambers; each half contains both an atrium and a ventricle, and the halves are separated by an AV valve. The valve is located between the ventricle and the artery leading away from the heart. Valves keep blood moving in a single direction and prevent any backwash into the chambers.

The heart has its own circulatory system with its own coronary arteries. The heart functions by contracting and relaxing. Atrial contraction fills the ventricles and ventricular contraction empties them, forcing circulation. This sequence is called the cardiac cycle. Cardiac muscles are attached to each other and signals for contractions spread rapidly. A complex electrical system controls the heartbeat as cardiac muscle cells produce and conduct electric signals. These muscles are said to be self-exciting, needing no external stimuli.

Blood Pressure
Blood pressure is the fluid pressure generated by the cardiac cycle.

Arterial blood pressure functions by transporting oxygen-poor blood into the lungs and oxygen-rich blood to the body tissues. Arteries branch into smaller arterioles which contract and expand based on signals from the body. Arterioles are where adjustments are made in blood delivery to specific areas based on complex communication from body systems.

Capillary beds are diffusion sites for exchanges between blood and interstitial fluid. A capillary has the thinnest wall of any blood vessel, consisting of a single layer of endothelial cells.

Capillaries merge into venues which in turn merge with larger diameter tubules called veins. Veins transport blood from body tissues back to the heart. Valves inside the veins facilitate this transport. The walls of veins are thin and contain smooth muscle and also function as blood volume reserves.

The Respiratory System

The respiratory system can be divided into the upper and lower respiratory system. The upper respiratory system includes the nose, nasal cavity, mouth, pharynx, and larynx. The lower respiratory system includes the trachea, lungs, and bronchial tree. Alternatively, the components of the respiratory system can be categorized as part of the airway, the lungs, or the respiratory muscles. The airway includes the nose, nasal cavity, mouth, pharynx, (throat), larynx (voice box), trachea (windpipe), bronchi, and bronchial network. The airway is lined with cilia that trap microbes and debris and sweep them back toward the mouth. The lungs are structures that house the bronchi and bronchial network, which extend into the lungs and terminate in millions of alveoli (air sacs). The walls of the alveoli are only one cell thick, allowing for the exchange of gases with the blood capillaries that surround them. The right lung has three lobes. The left lung only has two lobes, leaving room for the heart on the left side of the body. The lungs are surrounded by a pleural membrane, which reduces friction between surfaces when breathing. The respiratory muscles include the diaphragm and the intercostal muscles. The diaphragm is a dome-shaped muscle that separates the thoracic and abdominal cavities. The intercostal muscles are located between the ribs.

Functions of the Respiratory System
The main function of the respiratory system is to supply the body with oxygen and rid the body of carbon dioxide. This exchange of gases occurs in millions of tiny alveoli, which are surrounded by blood capillaries. The respiratory system also filters air. Air is warmed, moistened, and filtered as it passes through the nasal passages before it reaches the lungs. The respiratory system is responsible for speech. As air passes through the throat, it moves through the larynx (voice box), which vibrates and produces sound, before it enters the trachea (windpipe). The respiratory system is vital in cough production. Foreign particles entering the nasal passages or airways are expelled from the body by the respiratory system. The respiratory system functions in the sense of smell. Chemoreceptors that are located in the nasal cavity respond to airborne chemicals. The respiratory system also helps the body maintain acid-base homeostasis. Hyperventilation can increase blood pH during acidosis (low pH). Slowing breathing during alkalosis (high pH) helps to lower blood pH.

Breathing Process
During the breathing process, the diaphragm and the intercostal muscles contract to expand the lungs. During inspiration or inhalation, the diaphragm contracts and moves down, increasing the size of the chest cavity. During expiration or exhalation, the intercostal muscles contract and the ribs expand, increasing the size of the chest cavity. As the volume of the chest cavity increases, the

pressure inside the chest cavity decreases (Boyle's law). Because the outside air is under a greater amount of pressure than the air inside the lungs, air rushes into the lungs. When the diaphragm and intercostal muscles relax, the size of the chest cavity decreases, forcing air out of the lungs. The breathing process is controlled by the portion of the brain stem called the medulla oblongata. The medulla oblongata monitors the level of carbon dioxide in the blood and signals the breathing rate to increase when these levels are too high.

The Digestive System

Most digestive systems function by the following means:
1. **Movement** - Movement mixes and passes nutrients through the system and eliminates waste.
2. **Secretion** - Enzymes, hormones, and other substances necessary for digestion are secreted into the digestive tract.
3. **Digestion** - Includes the chemical breakdown of nutrients into smaller units that enter the internal environment.
4. **Absorption** - The passage of nutrients through plasma membranes into the blood or lymph and then to the body.

The human digestive system consists of the mouth, pharynx, esophagus, stomach, small and large intestine, rectum, and anus. Enzymes and other secretions are infused into the digestive system to assist the absorption and processing of nutrients. The nervous and endocrine systems control the digestive system. Smooth muscle moves the food by peristalsis, contracting and relaxing to move nutrients along.

Role of Mouth and Stomach in Digestion
Digestion begins in the mouth with the chewing and mixing of nutrients with saliva. Only humans and other mammals actually chew their food. Salivary glands are stimulated and secrete saliva. Saliva contains enzymes that initiate the breakdown of starch in digestion. Once swallowed, the food moves down the pharynx into the esophagus en route to the stomach.

The stomach is a flexible, muscular sac. It has three main functions:
1. Mixing and storing food
2. Dissolving and degrading food via secretions
3. Controlling passage of food into the small intestine

Protein digestion begins in the stomach. Stomach acidity helps break down the food and make nutrients available for absorption. Smooth muscle contractions move nutrients into the small intestine where the absorption process begins.

Digestion and the Small Intestine
In the digestive process, most nutrients are absorbed in the small intestine. Enzymes from the pancreas, liver, and stomach are transported to the small intestine to aid digestion. These enzymes act on fats, carbohydrates, nucleic acids, and proteins. Bile is a secretion of the liver and is particularly useful in breaking down fats. It is stored in the gall bladder between meals.

By the time food reaches the lining of the small intestine, it has been reduced to small molecules. The lining of the small intestine is covered with villi, tiny absorptive structures that greatly increase the surface area for interaction with chyme. Epithelial cells at the surface of the villi, called microvilli, further increase the ability of the small intestine to serve as the main absorption organ of the digestive tract.

Digestion and the Large Intestine
Also called the colon, the large intestine concentrates, mixes, and stores waste material. A little over a meter in length, the colon ascends on the right side of the abdominal cavity, cuts across transversely to the left side, then descends and attaches to the rectum, a short tube for waste disposal.

When the rectal wall is distended by waste material, the nervous system triggers an impulse in the body to expel the waste from the rectum. A muscle sphincter at the end of the anus is stimulated to facilitate the expelling of waste matter.

The speed at which waste moves through the colon is influenced by the volume of fiber and other undigested material present. Without adequate bulk in the diet, it takes longer to move waste along, sometimes with negative effects. Lack of bulk in the diet has been linked to a number of disorders.

Digestion and the Alimentary Canal
Digestion occurs in the alimentary canal (gastrointestinal tract), which consists of the mouth, throat (pharynx), esophagus, stomach, small intestine, large intestine, rectum, and anus. Digestion begins in the mouth as food is chewed and mixed with saliva containing enzymes for the digestion of carbohydrates (starches). Peristalsis, involuntary muscle contractions, moves the partially digested food down the esophagus and into the stomach through the lower esophageal sphincter. The stomach, which consists of three layers of smooth muscle lined with a mucous membrane, churns the food with hydrochloric acid (HCl).

The stomach stores the chyme and releases it to the small intestine through the pyloric sphincter. The small intestine consists of three sections: the duodenum, jejunum, and ileum. The duodenum continues breaking down the food with help from the liver, gallbladder, and pancreas. The liver manufactures bile, which is stored in the gallbladder and secreted into the small intestine to aid in the digestion of fats. The pancreas secretes pancreatic juices, which aid in the digestion of carbohydrates, fats, and proteins. The pancreas secretes sodium bicarbonate to neutralize the HCl from the stomach. The jejunum and ileum contain numerous villi for absorption. The large intestine, which houses helpful gut flora, consists of three sections called the ascending colon, transverse colon, and descending colon. The primary function of the large intestine is to absorb water. The rectum stores solid wastes (feces) until they exit the body through the anus.

The Renal System

The renal/urinary system is capable of eliminating excess substances while preserving the substances needed by the body to function. The urinary system consists of the kidneys, urinary ducts, and bladder. The mammalian kidney is a bean-shaped organ attached to the body near the peritoneum. The kidney helps to eliminate water and waste from the body. Within the kidney, there are various tubes and capillaries. Substances exit the bloodstream if they are not needed, and those that are needed are reabsorbed. The unnecessary substances are filtered out into the tubules that form urine. From theses tubes, urine flows into the bladder and then out of the body through the urethra.

The Reproductive System

Male Reproductive System

The functions of the male reproductive system are to produce, maintain, and transfer sperm and semen into the female reproductive tract and to produce and secrete male hormones. The eternal structure includes the penis, scrotum, and testes. The penis, which contains the urethra, can fill with blood and become erect, enabling the deposition of semen and sperm into the female reproductive tract during sexual intercourse. The scrotum is a sac of skin and smooth muscle that houses the testes and keeps the testes at the proper temperature for spermatogenesis. The testes, or testicles, are the male gonads, which produce sperm and testosterone. The internal structure includes the epididymis, vans deferens, ejaculatory ducts, urethra, seminal vesicles, prostate gland, and bulbourethral glands. The epididymis stores the sperm as it matures. Mature sperm moves from the epididymis through the vas deferens to the ejaculatory duct. The seminal vesicles secrete alkaline fluids with proteins and mucus into the ejaculatory duct, also. The prostate gland secretes a milky white fluid with proteins and enzymes as part of the semen. The bulbourethral, or Cowper's, glands secrete a fluid into the urethra to neutralize the acidity in the urethra. Additionally, the hormones associated with the male reproductive system include follicle-stimulating hormone, which stimulates spermatogenesis; luteinizing hormone, which stimulates testosterone production; and testosterone, which is responsible for the male sex characteristics.

Female Reproductive System

The functions of the female reproductive system are to produce ova (oocytes, or egg cells), transfer the ova to the fallopian tubes for fertilization, receive the sperm from the male, and to provide a protective, nourishing environment for the developing embryo. The external portion of the female reproductive system includes the labia major, labia minor, Bartholin's glands and clitoris. The labia major and the labia minor enclose and protect the vagina. The Bartholin's glands secrete a lubricating fluid. The clitoris contains erectile tissue and nerve endings for sensual pleasure. The internal portion of the female reproductive system includes the ovaries, fallopian tubes, uterus, and vagina. The ovaries, which are the female gonads, produce the ova and secrete estrogen and progesterone. The fallopian tubes carry the mature egg toward the uterus. Fertilization typically occurs in the fallopian tubes. If fertilized, the egg travels to the uterus, where it implants in the uterine wall. The uterus protects and nourishes the developing embryo until birth. The vagina is a muscular tube that extends from the cervix of the uterus to the outside of the body. The vagina receives the semen and sperm during sexual intercourse and provides a birth canal when needed.

Professional Practice

Practice Settings

Nurses can work in a variety of industries. The obvious locations where nurses can apply their skills are hospitals, clinics, and doctor's offices. Nurses also practice in community agencies, schools, businesses, military units, summer camps, vacation resorts, and cruise ships. Some nurses put their skills and knowledge to use by teaching others to become nurses in college courses or nursing schools. Nurses can work in nursing homes, retirement communities, ambulatory care agencies, volunteer organizations, private practices, hospices, occupational health facilities, and federal or state agencies.

Nurses' Roles

One of the most basic tasks that a nurse can perform is patient care. Nurses must constantly manage and care for patients. While caring for patients, nurses may perform many other roles, and sometimes they may fill multiple roles at once. Nurses can find themselves in the role of caregiver, comforter, teacher, counselor, role model, protector, advocate, decision maker, case manager, researcher, or communicator. Additionally, it is important to note that nurses do not work exclusively one-on-one with patients; nurses can actually work with groups of patients. In some cases, a nurse will work with a whole family or an entire community.

Career Opportunities

A nursing degree will allow you to pursue a variety of career options within the field. In general, the career opportunities for nurses increase as the education level of the nurse increases. In other words, more education can result in better job opportunities and higher pay. In addition to working as a general duty or staff nurse, a nurse may work as a private practice nurse, home health nurse, midwife, or anesthetist. Nurses can focus their careers on teaching others by becoming educators in nursing programs. They can work as clinical specialists, administrators, practitioners, or consultants. Nurses can also focus their career in the area of research. Nurses can actually pursue career paths that target their own special areas of interest. For example, midwives can visit expectant mothers and help them prepare for childbirth in the comfort of their own home.

Qualities of Successful Nurses

Successful nurses possess certain qualities that help them excel at their jobs. A good nurse is a team player. Nurses should be able to work well with their peers. The best nurses are honest, dependable, responsible, and accountable. They are capable of following directions and managing stressful situations. Nurses must understand that they are responsible for the wellbeing of others, and they should avoid abusing substances that could alter their decision-making ability. In other words, nurses should avoid drugs and alcohol. Nurses must be able to care for all patients, regardless of gender, race, religion, or other individual characteristics. Nurses must also be able to control their temper. Patients can be disagreeable and colleagues can be frustrating, but nurses must manage their emotions to perform their job effectively.

Nursing Technicians vs. Generalists

There are three types of programs that nursing candidates can choose to pursue: diploma programs, associate degree programs, and baccalaureate programs. Students who complete diploma programs or associate degree programs are considered technicians. These types of programs prepare students for the technical practice of nursing. In other words, these nurses will focus almost exclusively on patient care. Graduates of nursing baccalaureate programs are considered generalists. These nurses are equipped to work in a variety of health care environments. Nurses with a baccalaureate degree can fill many roles, including (but not limited to) care givers, educators, and consultants. While technicians care for individual patients in a structured setting, a generalist may care for groups of patients in unstructured settings.

Graduate Education Options

Nurses who hold either a master's degree or doctoral degree will have more professional opportunity, as well as higher paying careers. The first step for nurses who wish to pursue higher education in nursing is to obtain a baccalaureate degree. Obtaining a master's degree prepares a nurse to become an educator in various nursing programs. A master's degree also allows a nurse to become a researcher, manager, nurse practitioner, or administrator. Doctoral training allows a nurse to earn degrees in education, nursing science, nursing, and philosophy. A nurse with a doctoral degree can become an educator in undergraduate or graduate nursing programs. He or she can become an advanced clinical researcher, consultant, or independent practitioner.

Nursing Programs

In the United States, there are three types of programs available for those who want to become a registered nurse. Each program has a unique curriculum, accreditation agency, and professional organization. The three programs are associate degree programs, diploma programs, and baccalaureate degree programs. Associate degree programs are the shortest—usually taking only two years to complete. Diploma programs, which take three years to complete, are generally affiliated with a hospital. Baccalaureate programs are the longest type of nursing program, lasting four years. These programs are typically offered at a college or university.

<u>Admissions Departments</u>
Nursing programs consider many factors when deciding which candidates will be accepted. In general, nursing programs will consider a candidate's GPA, SAT or ACT scores, writing ability, community service, interviews, references, and entrance exam scores. Nursing schools must often set high standards for admission because of the number of students attempting to join the program. Each program can only accept a certain number of students, making it a highly competitive field. High GPAs and test scores are all key factors in the selection process; they indicate that a candidate is studious and dedicated, and will do well in rigorous nursing courses. Candidates should also be able to provide a list of references—usually people to whom they are not related. References should be people with whom the candidates have worked, such as teachers and employers.

<u>Financial Requirements</u>
In addition to the time commitment required when entering a nursing program, there is a large financial investment involved. Baccalaureate programs are more expensive than other programs because they take longer to complete. Each student must decide how he or she will pay for his or her nursing education. Working while in school is an option, but nursing courses require many hours outside of the classroom. If obtaining financial aid is an option, students are advised to

pursue it. Nursing school costs, in addition to the obvious tuition cost, can include many fees, room and board, daily meals at clinical sites, books, uniforms, and malpractice insurance. Students will also have to purchase nursing supplies, such as stethoscopes, bandage scissors, and thermometers. Students must also consider the cost of vehicle maintenance, personal health costs, and the costs of life outside of nursing school.

Financial Assistance Considerations
The first step for students pursuing financial aid is to consult with their nursing program's financial aid department. Before accepting financial aid, students must be sure to understand fully all of the terms of the loan. Financial aid may require students to maintain a certain grade-point average or number of credit hours. While student loans are usually associated with lower interest rates, they must be repaid upon graduation from the nursing program (earlier if the student fails or withdraws from the nursing program). Students who do not repay the loan can be impacted by a negative credit score and, in more severe cases, forfeiture of their license to practice nursing. In some cases, students may be eligible to receive grants or scholarships that do not require repayment.

Sociology

Sociology is the study of humans as they coexist in groups. One of the basic principles of sociology is that humans will behave in the same manner as those around them. Sociologists study the development of society and social behavior among humans, origins, organizations, and institutions. They may study one group or institution as a self-contained entity or as part of a greater whole. Sociology also concerns itself with the question of whether nature or nurture exerts greater influence on the existence of a human. It may be said that a sociologist studies the various processes that create and maintain a system of social structure.

Psychology

Psychology is the study of the mental processes and behavior of an individual. Psychologists may study the general characteristics of individuals or large groups. The field of psychology can be divided into applied and experimental areas. Certain psychologists examine mental processes. Other psychologists examine the elements of consciousness, such as mental activity, free will, and memory. The field of social psychology combines psychology and sociology. It is the study of the interactions that occur between individuals and groups. It also is the study of the effects of groups on the behaviors and attitudes of the individual.

Ethics

Ethical principles should be understood and used by nurses. When applied correctly, ethical principles can facilitate decision making in all facets of life. Nursing especially is a profession in which ethics play a large role. The patients trust that the nurses will always make decisions that are in the best interest of the patient. The study of science and medicine can equip an individual with the skills necessary to save or improve a person's life; however, ethics give the individual the ability to make decisions regarding matters of life and death. Nurses must always be aware of the impact their behavior and actions will have on their patients.

Ethical Principle of Beneficence
Beneficence is the practice of always helping other people. The definition of the word *beneficent* is *doing or producing good, especially through the acts of charity and kindness.* This principle is central to the role of health care providers that it is part of the Hippocratic Oath sworn by medical doctors.

In the field of ethics, the term *beneficence* has an additional component that requires that no intentional harm be done to another person. In other words, nonmaleficence is an essential component of beneficence. There are three theories regarding beneficence: Humes' theory, utilitarian theory, and Kant's theory. Hume's theory is that the motive behind an act of kindness determines the validity of the act. Utilitarian theory states that beneficence is simply the drive to create happiness through kindness or unhappiness through unkindness. Kant's theory states that beneficence is motivated by a sense of duty.

Ethical Principle of Justice
The ethical principle of justice centers on the fair and equal treatment of all individuals. Nurses must constantly evaluate their own motives when treating patients. Each patient should receive the same degree of attention, compassion, and care. Nurses must remember to speak confidentially about patients, as well as to maintain discretion about a patient's condition. In the health care field, questions of ethical justice often arise because of insurance and patient needs. Oftentimes, a patient will need a specific type of care but does not have the financial resources to pay for it. There is also the question of compensatory justice, in which one individual or group of individuals has been harmed by the actions of another.

Ethical Principle of Autonomy
In the most basic sense, the ethical principle of autonomy refers to a patient's right to choose a course of action and follow or change it as they see fit. In order for patients to choose freely, they must be provided with the appropriate information. Medical facilities often attempt to uphold the ethical principle of autonomy by providing patients with informed consent documents. Autonomy requires that patients be allowed to decide and act without pressure or coercion from another party. Medical professionals can aid in the freedom to choose by making sure that patients have adequate information about the choices available to them. Medical professionals can aid in the freedom to act by ensuring that the patient and the patient's family understand the importance of respecting the autonomy of the individual.

Mass Casualties
It seems that the increasing technological capabilities of the modern world are accompanied by the increasing threat of mass devastation. Entire cities can be built of towers that reach hundreds of stories in height. With all of this development comes an increase in the risk of mass injury. Imagine that you are a triage nurse working the emergency room when over 300 seriously injured patients are routed to your hospital. How do you decide who is treated first? Nurses must use the utilitarian principle of ethics, in which the greatest good must be done for the greatest number of people.

Bioethical Issues
The most intense bioethical issues faced by nurses involve the beginning and end of life. Modern technology has introduced in vitro fertilization, contraception, abortion, genetic modification, cloning, and surrogate mothers. All of these are useful tools, but each comes with its own set of ethical dilemmas. This is also the case with issues surrounding the end of life. Ethical concerns include euthanasia, the definition of death, death through outside intervention, and the handling of patients with diseases brought about by avoidable behaviors. For example, imagine that a hospital with a limited staff has two patients suffering from lung cancer. They are the same age with similar backgrounds. Now imagine one patient is a lifelong smoker, while the other has never smoked. If the hospital only has resources to treat one of those patients, which one should they choose?

Testing

Critical Thinking Skills

Critical thinking is a skill that nurses must use on a regular basis. Critical thinking is a combination of scientific knowledge and the logical application of that knowledge. In the course of daily life, people are constantly faced with opportunities to use critical thinking skills. An individual may be presented with a problem for which they must find the best possible solution. In order to do so, the individual must consider a variety of possible solutions. They must understand the consequences associated with each solution and the manner in which the solution will resolve the problem. Students should carefully read and analyze each possible response for each test question. By understanding fully all of the options available, students can select the best solution.

Standardized Testing Tips

In addition to critical thinking, a variety of testing strategies can be utilized in standardized testing. For example, in a timed multiple-choice test, students should answer the questions of which they are certain, skipping over questions that require more time to think. This will allow the student to devote the appropriate amount of time to harder questions, without running the risk of earning a lower score for running out of time. Test-takers should read questions carefully, looking out for words such as *first* or *usually*. These words can be very important when selecting the best response. When faced with a tough question, students should avoid selecting answers that use the terms *always* and *never*. Correct answers are most often worded with less absolute language, such as the phrases *in most cases* or *usually*. Students should also be cautious when answering questions that imply a cause-and-effect relationship. When selecting an answer for this type of question, avoid options that state one thing is causing another. Instead, select a more conservative option that states the two things are somehow connected.

Process of Elimination

Standardized tests are most commonly organized into questions with four possible answer choices. For each question, there is a 1 in 4 chance (25%) that the student will select the correct answer. This also means there is a 3 in 4 chance (75%) that the student will select the wrong answer. The odds seem to favor the student answering incorrectly. By simply eliminating the obviously incorrect answers, students can increase the odds of selecting the correct answer. If there are four possible answer choices, eliminating two of those answers will give the student a 50% chance of answering the question correctly. By the simple process of elimination, a student can increase his chances of answering a question correctly even if he knows very little about the subject.

Multiple-Choice Questions

In standardized multiple-choice tests, there are three levels of test questions: recall, application, and analysis.

Recall Questions
In standardized multiple-choice tests, there are three levels of test questions: recall, application, and analysis. Recall questions require the test-taker simply to remember a piece of information. An example of a recall question is a definition. The question may ask the student to select the best definition of a word that is either contained within a sentence or provided in a more

straightforward form. Recall questions will not require the student to analyze or apply knowledge. Once a student identifies a recall question, she can answer it directly (if she knows the correct answer) or she can begin to eliminate incorrect answers to increase her odds of answering correctly.

When answering a recall-level question, students often either know the answer or do not. When a student does not immediately know the correct answer, he can try a memory trick. Namely, he should move on to another question or think of something else entirely. By giving his mind a distraction, and then returning to the troublesome question, the answer will often become clear. Students may also use visual association when learning material. For example, in order to remember that arteries carry blood away from the heart, a student might picture the heart as a museum filled with art, which is stolen by a thief. By picturing a thief stealing art, the student associates the word *art* with the word *arteries*, thus remembering that arteries carry blood away from the heart. Another method is the comparison strategy. By finding similarities between pieces of information, students can more readily retain knowledge. For example, arteries carry blood away from the heart. Both *artery* and *away* begin with the letter *a*.

Application Questions
Application questions require that students use the knowledge they have learned. Students may be asked to apply the knowledge they have acquired from textbooks and apply it to a real-life situation. For example, a question may provide a brief scenario described in paragraph form. A question will ask the student to use the information presented in the paragraph. In general, the questions will be asked in the form of "if you know this about X, what can be assumed about Y?" These questions will present all of the information students need within the question. By carefully reading the questions and examining the answer choices, students should be able to locate the correct answer.

Analysis Questions
Analysis-level questions are the most complex of the three levels. For this type of problem, students must carefully read the question, dissect it, and then study the interaction between its various parts. Students may find that analysis-level questions require them to identify what piece of information is missing. Students should read each answer choice provided and examine how well that piece fits into the puzzle. The student should consider whether the answer choice actually provides a solution, or whether it simply produces more questions. As with all test questions, students improve their chances of success by eliminating the obviously incorrect choices.

Preparing for Standardized Exams

Standardized testing can be a stressful situation for students. It is crucial that students begin studying material early so that they have plenty of time to prepare. By studying early, students can avoid all-night cram sessions that deprive them of sleep, nutrition, and mental health. Students should avoid overly emotional interactions prior to a test, because this can cause increased anxiety, which could lead to decreased performance. At least ten days prior to the test, the student should begin taking multi-vitamins, eating properly, getting plenty of rest, and exercising. All of these things will give the body what it needs to perform at its highest level on test day.

Personality Profile

The Admission Assessment test will include 15 items designed to gauge your personality type. Although there are no wrong answers to these questions, it is a good idea to learn the conceptual framework underlying the personality profile. The primary distinction made by these questions is between the extroverted and introverted personality types.

Extroverted Personality Type
The extroverted personality type is characterized by a desire to be around other people. Extroverted individuals draw energy from their interaction with others. Extroverts are likely to enjoy social gatherings, and are most successful when working in collaboration with other people. Extroverts are more talkative, gregarious, and assertive of their own desires than are introverts.

Introverted PersonalityType
The introverted personality type is characterized by a desire to be alone and away from other people. Introversion should not be confused with antisocial personality disorder; there is no pathology associated with normal introversion. Introverts tend to be imaginative and thoughtful, and often enjoy activities like reading, distance running, and writing. Introverts tend to be more successful when they are allowed to work independently. For introverts, social interaction can be depleting and exhausting. Introverts often report a need to "recharge" by spending time alone. Introverts prefer to observe activities before participating, and tend to be more analytical than extroverts.

Learning Styles

The Admission Assessment will include 14 items designed to gauge your learning style. As with the personality profile, there are no incorrect answers to these questions. However, it is a good idea to be acquainted with the seven common learning styles: spatial, auditory-musical, linguistic, kinesthetic, mathematical, interpersonal, and intrapersonal.

Spatial Learning Style
Students with the spatial learning style (also known as the visual learning style) learn best by using pictures and images. They find it is easier to retain information that is presented in a table or chart. They prefer to use a map to orient themselves rather than to rely on a set of written directions. Color coding information is a helpful method of teaching for student with this learning style.

Auditory-Musical Learning Style
Students with the auditory-musical learning style (also known as the aural learning style) learn best by using sound, and especially music. These students have a natural sense of rhythm and harmony, and find it easy to remember the words to songs. Often, these students unconsciously drum out a beat on their desk or keep up a constant rhythm of toe taps under their chair. They can improve their retention of new information by placing it into a rhyme or setting it to a familiar tune. These students often have success using mnemonics based on popular songs.

Linguistic Learning Style
Students with the linguistic learning style (also known as the verbal learning style) learn best by using words, whether spoken or written. These students like to express themselves with words, and are very receptive to the language used in texts and by teachers. They will also have a natural facility for wordplay, and will enjoy word-based puzzles and games. Students with a linguistic learning style will find it easy to retain the information they read, and should be able to express themselves clearly in writing. They enjoy reading texts aloud, and benefit from mnemonics based on wordplay and common expressions.

Kinesthetic Learning Style
Students with the kinesthetic learning style (also known as the physical learning style) learn best by using physical movement and gesture. These students retain information that they receive through their sense of touch. Often, students with a kinesthetic style of learning will be able to retain spoken information better when their hands are kept occupied. For instance, studies have shown that kinesthetic learners pick up their multiplication tables faster when they are allowed to bounce a ball while practicing. These students also love to make models and three-dimensional representations of the things they have learned.

Mathematical Learning Style
Students with the mathematical learning style (also known as the logical learning style) learn best by using systems of logic and analytical reasoning. These students are great at recognizing patterns, and are quick to discern the logical system underlying a set of information. These students prefer to work through problems in a systematic manner, and thrive in highly structured learning environments. A student with a mathematical learning style will appreciate being given a list of the tasks to be accomplished over a certain interval. These students excel in the sciences and any other area that calls for rigorous, systematic thinking.

Interpersonal Learning Style
Students with the interpersonal learning style (also known as the social learning style) learn best when working in collaboration with other people. These students are good communicators, and have no problem making their meaning plain to other people. They are also sensitive to the concerns of other people, and have a genuine interest in preserving harmony within the work group. Interpersonal learners work best in groups, and often exhibit strong leadership skills. These students enjoy role-playing exercises and peer-review assignments. They may become frustrated or bored when asked to work alone for a long time.

Intrapersonal Learning Style
Students with the intrapersonal learning style (also known as the solitary learning style) learn best by themselves. These students become frustrated when working in a group, and prefer to act independently. They often need a period of reflection before initiating an activity. They often excel at reading and writing. Student with an intrapersonal learning style will thrive in structured learning environments, and will prefer consistency to chaos. These students may become over-stimulated by contact with other people, and require frequent opportunities to recharge with solitude and contemplation. Intrapersonal learners tend to be reserved and thoughtful, but capable of developing strong relationships with a few select peers.

Practice Test

Reading Comprehension Questions

Questions 1 to 4 pertain to the following passage:

It is most likely that you have never had diphtheria. You probably don't even know anyone who has suffered from this disease. In fact, you may not even know what diphtheria is. Similarly, diseases like whooping cough, measles, mumps, and rubella may all be unfamiliar to you. In the nineteenth and early twentieth centuries, these illnesses struck hundreds of thousands of people in the United States each year, mostly children, and tens of thousands of people died. The names of these diseases were frightening household words. Today, they are all but forgotten. That change happened largely because of vaccines.

You probably have been vaccinated against diphtheria. You may even have been exposed to the bacterium that causes it, but the vaccine prepared your body to fight off the disease so quickly that you were unaware of the infection. Vaccines take advantage of your body's natural ability to learn how to combat many disease-causing germs, or microbes. What's more, your body remembers how to protect itself from the microbes it has encountered before. Collectively, the parts of your body that remember and repel microbes are called the immune system. Without the proper functioning of the immune system, the simplest illness—even the common cold—could quickly turn deadly.

On average, your immune system needs more than a week to learn how to fight off an unfamiliar microbe. Sometimes, that isn't enough time. Strong microbes can spread through your body faster than the immune system can fend them off. Your body often gains the upper hand after a few weeks, but in the meantime you are sick. Certain microbes are so virulent that they can overwhelm or escape your natural defenses. In those situations, vaccines can make all the difference.

Traditional vaccines contain either parts of microbes or whole microbes that have been altered so that they don't cause disease. When your immune system confronts these harmless versions of the germs, it quickly clears them from your body. In other words, vaccines trick your immune system in order to teach your body important lessons about how to defeat its opponents.

1. What is the main idea of the passage?
   A. The nineteenth and early twentieth centuries were a dark period for medicine.
   B. You have probably never had diphtheria.
   C. Traditional vaccines contain altered microbes.
   D. Vaccines help the immune system function properly.

2. Which statement is *not* a detail from the passage?
   A. Vaccines contain microbe parts or altered microbes.
   B. The immune system typically needs a week to learn how to fight a new disease.
   C. The symptoms of disease do not emerge until the body has learned how to fight the microbe.
   D. A hundred years ago, children were at the greatest risk of dying from now-treatable diseases.

3. What is the meaning of the word *virulent* as it is used in the third paragraph?
   A. tiny
   B. malicious
   C. contagious
   D. annoying

4. What is the author's primary purpose in writing the essay?
   A. to entertain
   B. to persuade
   C. to inform
   D. to analyze

Questions 5 to 8 pertain to the following passage :

Foodborne illnesses are contracted by eating food or drinking beverages contaminated with bacteria, parasites, or viruses. Harmful chemicals can also cause foodborne illnesses if they have contaminated food during harvesting or processing. Foodborne illnesses can cause symptoms ranging from upset stomach to diarrhea, fever, vomiting, abdominal cramps, and dehydration. Most foodborne infections are undiagnosed and unreported, though the Centers for Disease Control and Prevention estimates that every year about 76 million people in the United States become ill from pathogens in food. About 5,000 of these people die.

Harmful bacteria are the most common cause of foodborne illness. Some bacteria may be present at the point of purchase. Raw foods are the most common source of foodborne illnesses because they are not sterile; examples include raw meat and poultry contaminated during slaughter. Seafood may become contaminated during harvest or processing. One in 10,000 eggs may be contaminated with Salmonella inside the shell. Produce, such as spinach, lettuce, tomatoes, sprouts, and melons, can become contaminated with Salmonella, Shigella, or Escherichia coli (E. coli). Contamination can occur during growing, harvesting, processing, storing, shipping, or final preparation. Sources of produce contamination vary, as these foods are grown in soil and can become contaminated during growth, processing, or distribution. Contamination may also occur during food preparation in a restaurant or a home kitchen. The most common form of contamination from handled foods is the calicivirus, also called the Norwalk-like virus.

When food is cooked and left out for more than two hours at room temperature, bacteria can multiply quickly. Most bacteria don't produce an odor or change in color or texture, so they can be impossible to detect. Freezing food slows or stops bacteria's growth, but does not destroy the bacteria. The microbes can become reactivated when the food is thawed. Refrigeration also can slow the growth of some bacteria. Thorough cooking is required to destroy the bacteria.

5. What is the subject of the passage?
   A. foodborne illnesses
   B. the dangers of uncooked food
   C. bacteria
   D. proper food preparation

6. Which statement is *not* a detail from the passage?
   A. Every year, more than 70 million Americans contract some form of foodborne illness.
   B. Once food is cooked, it cannot cause illness.
   C. Refrigeration can slow the growth of some bacteria.
   D. The most common form of contamination in handled foods is calicivirus.

7. What is the meaning of the word *pathogens* as it is used in the first paragraph?
   A. diseases
   B. vaccines
   C. disease-causing substances
   D. foods

8. What is the meaning of the word *sterile* as it is used in the second paragraph?
   A. free of bacteria
   B. healthy
   C. delicious
   D. impotent

Questions 9 to 12 pertain to the following passage:

There are a number of health problems related to bleeding in the esophagus and stomach. Stomach acid can cause inflammation and bleeding at the lower end of the esophagus. This condition, usually associated with the symptom of heartburn, is called esophagitis, or inflammation of the esophagus. Sometimes a muscle between the esophagus and stomach fails to close properly and allows the return of food and stomach juices into the esophagus, which can lead to esophagitis. In another unrelated condition, enlarged veins (varices) at the lower end of the esophagus rupture and bleed massively. Cirrhosis of the liver is the most common cause of esophageal varices. Esophageal bleeding can be caused by a tear in the lining of the esophagus (Mallory-Weiss syndrome). Mallory-Weiss syndrome usually results from vomiting, but may also be caused by increased pressure in the abdomen from coughing, hiatal hernia, or childbirth. Esophageal cancer can cause bleeding.

The stomach is a frequent site of bleeding. Infections with Helicobacter pylori (H. pylori), alcohol, aspirin, aspirin-containing medicines, and various other medicines (such as nonsteroidal anti-inflammatory drugs [NSAIDs]—particularly those used for arthritis) can cause stomach ulcers or inflammation (gastritis). The stomach is often the site of ulcer disease. Acute or chronic ulcers may enlarge and erode through a blood vessel, causing bleeding. Also, patients suffering from burns, shock, head injuries, cancer, or those who have undergone extensive surgery may develop stress ulcers. Bleeding can also occur from benign tumors or cancer of the stomach, although these disorders usually do not cause massive bleeding.

9. What is the main idea of the passage?
   A. The digestive system is complex.
   B. Of all the digestive organs, the stomach is the most prone to bleeding.
   C. Both the esophagus and the stomach are subject to bleeding problems.
   D. Esophagitis afflicts the young and old alike.

10. Which statement is *not* a detail from the passage?
    A. Alcohol can cause stomach bleeding.
    B. Ulcer disease rarely occurs in the stomach.
    C. Benign tumors rarely result in massive bleeding.
    D. Childbirth is one cause of Mallory-Weiss syndrome.

11. What is the meaning of the word *rupture* as it is used in the first paragraph?
    A. tear
    B. collapse
    C. implode
    D. detach

12. What is the meaning of the word *erode* as it is used in the second paragraph?
    A. avoid
    B. divorce
    C. contain
    D. wear away

Questions 13 to 16 pertain to the following passage:

We met Kathy Blake while she was taking a stroll in the park . . . by herself. What's so striking about this is that Kathy is completely blind, and she has been for more than 30 years.

The diagnosis from her doctor was retinitis pigmentosa, or RP. It's an incurable genetic disease that leads to progressive visual loss. Photoreceptive cells in the retina slowly start to die, leaving the patient visually impaired.

"Life was great the year before I was diagnosed," Kathy said. "I had just started a new job; I just bought my first new car. I had just started dating my now-husband. Life was good. The doctor had told me that there was some good news and some bad news. 'The bad news is you are going to lose your vision; the good news is we don't think you are going to go totally blind.' Unfortunately, I did lose all my vision within about 15 years."

Two years ago, Kathy got a glimmer of hope. She heard about an artificial retina being developed in Los Angeles. It was experimental, but Kathy was the perfect candidate.

Dr. Mark Humayun is a retinal surgeon and biomedical engineer. "A good candidate for the artificial retina device is a person who is blind because of retinal blindness," he said. "They've lost the rods and cones, the light-sensing cells of the eye, but the rest of the circuitry is relatively intact. In the simplest rendition, this device basically takes a blind person and hooks them up to a camera."

It may sound like the stuff of science fiction . . . and just a few years ago it was. A camera is built into a pair of glasses, sending radio signals to a tiny chip in the back of the retina. The chip, small enough to fit on a fingertip, is implanted surgically and stimulates the nerves that lead to the vision center of the brain. Kathy is one of twenty patients who have undergone surgery and use the device.

It has been about two years since the surgery, and Kathy still comes in for weekly testing at the University of Southern California's medical campus. She scans back and forth with specially made, camera-equipped glasses until she senses objects on a screen and then touches the objects. The low-resolution image from the camera is still enough to make out the black stripes on the screen. Impulses are sent from the camera to the 60 receptors that are on the chip in her retina. So, what is Kathy seeing?

"I see flashes of light that indicate a contrast from light to dark—very similar to a camera flash, probably not quite as bright because it's not hurting my eye at all," she replied.

Humayun underscored what a breakthrough this is and how a patient adjusts. "If you've been blind for 30 or 50 years, (and) all of a sudden you get this device, there is a period of learning," he said. "Your brain needs to learn. And it's literally like seeing a baby crawl—to a child walk—to an adult run."

While hardly perfect, the device works best in bright light or where there is a lot of contrast. Kathy takes the device home. The software that runs the device can be upgraded. So, as the software is upgraded, her vision improves. Recently, she was outside with her husband on a moonlit night and saw something she hadn't seen for a long time.

"I scanned up in the sky (and) I got a big flash, right where the moon was, and pointed it out. I can't even remember how many years ago it's been that I would have ever been able to do that."

This technology has a bright future. The current chip has a resolution of 60 pixels. Humayun says that number could be increased to more than a thousand in the next version.

"I think it will be extremely exciting if they can recognize their loved ones' faces and be able to see what their wife or husband or their grandchildren look like, which they haven't seen," said Humayun.

Kathy dreams of a day when blindness like hers will be a distant memory. "My eye disease is hereditary," she said. "My three daughters happen to be fine, but I want to know that if my grandchildren ever have a problem, they will have something to give them some vision."

13. What is the primary subject of the passage?
    A. a new artificial retina
    B. Kathy Blake
    C. hereditary disease
    D. Dr. Mark Humayun

14. What is the meaning of the word *progressive* as it is used in the second paragraph?
    A. selective
    B. gradually increasing
    C. diminishing
    D. disabling

15. Which statement is *not* a detail from the passage?
    A. The use of an artificial retina requires a special pair of glasses.
    B. Retinal blindness is the inability to perceive light.
    C. Retinitis pigmentosa is curable.
    D. The artificial retina performs best in bright light.

16. What is the author's intention in writing the essay?
    A. to persuade
    B. to entertain
    C. to analyze
    D. to inform

Questions 17 to 21 pertain to the following passage:

Usher syndrome is the most common condition that affects both hearing and vision. The major symptoms of Usher syndrome are hearing loss and an eye disorder called retinitis pigmentosa, or RP. Retinitis pigmentosa causes night blindness and a loss of peripheral vision (side vision) through the progressive degeneration of the retina. The retina, which is crucial for vision, is a light-sensitive tissue at the back of the eye. As RP progresses, the field of vision narrows, until only central vision (the ability to see straight ahead) remains. Many people with Usher syndrome also have severe balance problems.

There are three clinical types of Usher syndrome. In the United States, types 1 and 2 are the most common. Together, they account for approximately 90 to 95 percent of all cases of juvenile Usher syndrome. Approximately three to six percent of all deaf and hearing-disabled children have Usher syndrome. In developed countries, such as the United States, about four in every 100,000 newborns have Usher syndrome.

Usher syndrome is inherited as an autosomal recessive trait. The term autosomal means that the mutated gene is not located on either of the chromosomes that determine sex; in other words, both males and females can have the disorder and can pass it along to a child. The word recessive means that in order to have Usher syndrome, an individual must receive a mutated form of the Usher syndrome gene from each parent. If a child has a mutation in one Usher syndrome gene but the other gene is normal, he or she should have normal vision and hearing. Individuals with a mutation in a gene that can cause an autosomal recessive disorder are called carriers, because they carry the mutated gene but show no symptoms of the disorder. If both parents are carriers of a mutated gene for Usher syndrome, they will have a one-in-four chance of producing a child with Usher syndrome.

Usually, parents who have normal hearing and vision do not know if they are carriers of an Usher syndrome gene mutation. Currently, it is not possible to determine whether an individual without a family history of Usher syndrome is a carrier. Scientists at the National Institute on Deafness and Other Communication Disorders (NIDCD) are hoping to change this, however, as they learn more about the genes responsible for Usher syndrome.

17. What is the main idea of the passage?
    A. Usher syndrome is an inherited condition that affects hearing and vision.
    B. Some people are carriers of Usher syndrome.
    C. Usher syndrome typically skips a generation.
    D. Scientists hope to develop a test for detecting the carriers of Usher syndrome.

18. What is the meaning of the word *symptoms* as it is used in the first paragraph?
    A. qualifications
    B. conditions
    C. disorders
    D. perceptible signs

19. Which statement is *not* a detail from the passage?
    A. Types 1 and 2 Usher syndrome are the most common in the United States.
    B. Usher syndrome affects both hearing and smell.
    C. Right now, there is no way to identify a carrier of Usher syndrome.
    D. Central vision is the ability to see straight ahead.

20. What is the meaning of the word *juvenile* as it is used in the second paragraph?
    A. bratty
    B. serious
    C. occurring in children
    D. improper

21. What is the meaning of the word *mutated* as it is used in the third paragraph?
    A. selected
    B. altered
    C. composed
    D. destroyed

Questions 22 to 27 pertain to the following passage:

The immune system is a network of cells, tissues, and organs that defends the body against attacks by foreign invaders. These invaders are primarily microbes—tiny organisms such as bacteria, parasites, and fungi—that can cause infections. Viruses also cause infections, but are too primitive to be classified as living organisms. The human body provides an ideal environment for many microbes. It is the immune system's job to keep the microbes out or destroy them.

The immune system is amazingly complex. It can recognize and remember millions of different enemies, and it can secrete fluids and cells to wipe out nearly all of them. The secret to its success is an elaborate and dynamic communications network. Millions of cells, organized into sets and subsets, gather and transfer information in response to an infection. Once immune cells receive the alarm, they produce powerful chemicals that help to regulate their own growth and behavior, enlist other immune cells, and direct the new recruits to trouble spots.

Although scientists have learned much about the immune system, they continue to puzzle over how the body destroys invading microbes, infected cells, and tumors without harming healthy tissues. New technologies for identifying individual immune cells are now allowing scientists to determine quickly which targets are triggering an immune response. Improvements in microscopy are permitting the first-ever observations of living B cells, T cells, and other cells as they interact within lymph nodes and other body tissues.

In addition, scientists are rapidly unraveling the genetic blueprints that direct the human immune response, as well as those that dictate the biology of bacteria, viruses, and parasites. The combination of new technology with expanded genetic information will no doubt reveal even more about how the body protects itself from disease.

22. What is the main idea of the passage?
    A. Scientists fully understand the immune system.
    B. The immune system triggers the production of fluids.
    C. The body is under constant invasion by malicious microbes.
    D. The immune system protects the body from infection.

23. Which statement is *not* a detail from the passage?
    A. Most invaders of the body are microbes.
    B. The immune system relies on excellent communication.
    C. Viruses are extremely sophisticated.
    D. The cells of the immune system are organized.

24. What is the meaning of the word *ideal* as it is used in the first paragraph?
    A. thoughtful
    B. confined
    C. hostile
    D. perfect

25. Which statement is *not* a detail from the passage?
    A. Scientists can now see T cells.
    B. The immune system ignores tumors.
    C. The ability of the immune system to fight disease without harming the body remains mysterious.
    D. The immune system remembers millions of different invaders.

26. What is the meaning of the word *enlist* as it is used in the second paragraph?
    A. call into service
    B. write down
    C. send away
    D. put across

27. What is the author's primary purpose in writing the essay?
    A. to persuade
    B. to analyze
    C. to inform
    D. to entertain

Questions 28 to 31 pertain to the following passage:

The federal government regulates dietary supplements through the United States Food and Drug Administration (FDA). The regulations for dietary supplements are not the same as those for prescription or over-the-counter drugs. In general, the regulations for dietary supplements are less strict.

To begin with, a manufacturer does not have to prove the safety and effectiveness of a dietary supplement before it is marketed. A manufacturer is permitted to say that a dietary supplement addresses a nutrient deficiency, supports health, or is linked to a particular body function (such as immunity), if there is research to support the claim. Such a claim must be followed by the words "This statement has not been evaluated by the Food and Drug Administration. This product is not intended to diagnose, treat, cure, or prevent any disease."

Also, manufacturers are expected to follow certain good manufacturing practices (GMPs) to ensure that dietary supplements are processed consistently and meet quality standards. Requirements for GMPs went into effect in 2008 for large manufacturers and are being phased in for small manufacturers through 2010.

Once a dietary supplement is on the market, the FDA monitors safety and product information, such as label claims and package inserts. If it finds a product to be unsafe, it can take action against the manufacturer and/or distributor and may issue a warning or require that the product be removed from the marketplace. The Federal Trade Commission (FTC) is responsible for regulating product advertising; it requires that all information be truthful and not misleading.

The federal government has taken legal action against a number of dietary supplement promoters or Web sites that promote or sell dietary supplements because they have made false or deceptive statements about their products or because marketed products have proven to be unsafe.

28. What is the main idea of the passage?
    A. Manufacturers of dietary supplements have to follow good manufacturing practices.
    B. The FDA has a special program for regulating dietary supplements.
    C. The federal government prosecutes those who mislead the general public.
    D. The FDA is part of the federal government.

29. Which statement is *not* a detail from the passage?
    A. Promoters of dietary supplements can make any claims that are supported by research.
    B. GMP requirements for large manufacturers went into effect in 2008.
    C. Product advertising is regulated by the FTC.
    D. The FDA does not monitor products after they enter the market.

30. What is the meaning of the phrase *phased in* as it is used in the third paragraph?
    A. stunned into silence
    B. confused
    C. implemented in stages
    D. legalized

31. What is the meaning of the word *deceptive* as it is used in the fifth paragraph?
    A. misleading
    B. malicious
    C. illegal
    D. irritating

Questions 32 to 35 pertain to the following passage:
Anemia is a condition in which there is an abnormally low number of red blood cells (RBCs). This condition also can occur if the RBCs don't contain enough hemoglobin, the iron-rich protein that makes the blood red. Hemoglobin helps RBCs carry oxygen from the lungs to the rest of the body.

Anemia can be accompanied by low numbers of RBCs, white blood cells (WBCs), and platelets. Red blood cells are disc-shaped and look like doughnuts without holes in the center. They carry oxygen and remove carbon dioxide (a waste product) from your body. These cells are made in the bone marrow and live for about 120 days in the bloodstream. Platelets and WBCs also are made in the bone marrow. White blood cells help fight infection. Platelets stick together to seal small cuts or breaks on the blood vessel walls and to stop bleeding.

If you are anemic, your body doesn't get enough oxygenated blood. As a result, you may feel tired or have other symptoms. Severe or long-lasting anemia can damage the heart, brain, and other organs of the body. Very severe anemia may even cause death.

Anemia has three main causes: blood loss, lack of RBC production, or high rates of RBC destruction. Many types of anemia are mild, brief, and easily treated. Some types can be prevented with a healthy diet or treated with dietary supplements. However, certain types of anemia may be severe, long lasting, and life threatening if not diagnosed and treated.

If you have the signs or symptoms of anemia, you should see your doctor to find out whether you have the condition. Treatment will depend on the cause and severity of the anemia.

32. What is the main idea of the passage?
    A. Anemia presents in a number of forms.
    B. Anemia is a potentially dangerous condition characterized by low numbers of RBCs.
    C. Anemia is a deficiency of WBCs and platelets.
    D. Anemia is a treatable condition.

33. Which statement is *not* a detail from the passage?
    A. There are different methods for treating anemia.
    B. Red blood cells remove carbon dioxide from the body.
    C. Platelets are made in the bone marrow.
    D. Anemia is rarely caused by blood loss.

34. What is the meaning of the word *oxygenated* as it is used in the third paragraph?
    A. containing low amounts of oxygen
    B. containing no oxygen
    C. consisting entirely of oxygen
    D. containing high amounts of oxygen

35. What is the meaning of the word *severity* as it is used in the fifth paragraph?
    A. seriousness
    B. disconnectedness
    C. truth
    D. swiftness

Questions 36 to 39 pertain to the following passage:

Contrary to previous reports, drinking four or more cups of coffee a day does not put women at risk of rheumatoid arthritis (RA), according to a new study partially funded by the National Institute of Arthritis and Musculoskeletal and Skin Diseases (NIAMS). The study concluded that there is little evidence to support a connection between consuming coffee or tea and the risk of RA among women.

Rheumatoid arthritis is an inflammatory autoimmune disease that affects the joints. It results in pain, stiffness, swelling, joint damage, and loss of function. Inflammation most often affects the hands and feet and tends to be symmetrical. About one percent of the U.S. population has rheumatoid arthritis.

Elizabeth W. Karlson, M.D., and her colleagues at Harvard Medical School and Brigham and Women's Hospital in Boston, Massachusetts, used the Nurses' Health Study, a long-term investigation of nurses' diseases, lifestyles, and health practices, to examine possible links between caffeinated beverages and RA risk. The researchers were able to follow up more than 90 percent of the original pool of 83,124 participants who answered a 1980 food frequency questionnaire, and no links were found. They also considered changes in diet and habits over a prolonged period of time, and when the results were adjusted for other factors, such as cigarette smoking, alcohol consumption, and oral contraceptive use, the outcome still showed no relationship between caffeine consumption and risk of RA.

Previous research had suggested an association between consuming coffee or tea and RA risk. According to Dr. Karlson, the data supporting that conclusion were inconsistent. Because the information in the older studies was collected at only one time, she says, consideration was not given to the other factors associated with RA, such as cigarette smoking and changes in diet and lifestyle over a follow-up period. The new study presents a more accurate picture of caffeine and RA risk.

36. What is the main idea of the passage?
    A. In the past, doctors have cautioned older women to avoid caffeinated beverages.
    B. Rheumatoid arthritis affects the joints of older women.
    C. A recent study found no link between caffeine consumption and RA among women.
    D. Cigarette smoking increases the incidence of RA.

37. Which statement is *not* a detail from the passage?
    A. Alcohol consumption is linked with RA.
    B. The original data for the study came from a 1980 questionnaire.
    C. Rheumatoid arthritis most often affects the hands and feet.
    D. This study included tens of thousands of participants.

38. What is the meaning of the word *symmetrical* as it is used in the second paragraph?
    A. affecting both sides of the body in corresponding fashion
    B. impossible to treat
    C. sensitive to the touch
    D. asymptomatic

39. What is the author's primary purpose in writing the essay?
    A. to entertain
    B. to inform
    C. to analyze
    D. to persuade

Questions 40 to 43 refer to the following passage:
　　Exercise is vital at every age for healthy bones. Not only does exercise improve bone health, but it also increases muscle strength, coordination, and balance, and it leads to better overall health. Exercise is especially important for preventing and treating osteoporosis.
　　Like muscle, bone is living tissue that responds to exercise by becoming stronger. Young women and men who exercise regularly generally achieve greater peak bone mass (maximum bone density and strength) than those who do not. For most people, bone mass peaks during the third decade of life. After that time, we can begin to lose bone. Women and men older than age 20 can help prevent bone loss with regular exercise. Exercise maintains muscle strength, coordination, and balance, which in turn prevent falls and related fractures. This is especially important for older adults and people with osteoporosis.
　　Weight-bearing exercise is the best kind of exercise for bones, which forces the muscle to work against gravity. Some examples of weight-bearing exercises are weight training, walking, hiking, jogging, climbing stairs, tennis, and dancing. Swimming and bicycling, on the other hand, are not weight-bearing exercises. Although these activities help build and maintain strong muscles and have excellent cardiovascular benefits, they are not the best exercise for bones.

40. What is the main idea of the passage?
    A. Weight-bearing exercise is the best for bones.
    B. Exercise increases balance.
    C. Exercise improves bone health.
    D. Women benefit from regular exercise more than men.

41. What is the meaning of the word *vital* as it is used in the first paragraph?
    A. deadly
    B. important
    C. rejected
    D. nourishing

42. Which statement is *not* a detail from the passage?
    A. Tennis is a form of weight-bearing exercise.
    B. Most people reach peak bone mass in their twenties.
    C. Swimming is not good for the bones.
    D. Bone is a living tissue.

43. What is the meaning of the word *fractures* as it is used in the second paragraph?
    A. breaks
    B. agreements
    C. tiffs
    D. fevers

Questions 44 to 47 pertain to the following passage :

Searching for medical information can be confusing, especially for first-timers. However, if you are patient and stick to it, you can find a wealth of information. Your community library is a good place to start your search for medical information. Before going to the library, you may find it helpful to make a list of topics you want information about and questions you have. Your list of topics and questions will make it easier for the librarian to direct you to the best resources.

Many community libraries have a collection of basic medical references. These references may include medical dictionaries or encyclopedias, drug information handbooks, basic medical and nursing textbooks, and directories of physicians and medical specialists (listings of doctors). You may also find magazine articles on a certain topic. Look in the Reader's Guide to Periodical Literature for articles on health and medicine from consumer magazines.

Infotrac, a CD-ROM computer database available at libraries or on the Web, indexes hundreds of popular magazines and newspapers, as well as medical journals such as the Journal of the American Medical Association and New England Journal of Medicine.

Your library may also carry searchable computer databases of medical journal articles, including MEDLINE/PubMed or the Cumulative Index to Nursing and Allied Health Literature. Many of the databases or indexes have abstracts that provide a summary of each journal article. Although most community libraries don't have a large collection of medical and nursing journals, your librarian may be able to get copies of the articles you want. Interlibrary loans allow your librarian to request a copy of an article from a library that carries that particular medical journal. Your library may charge a fee for this service. Articles published in medical journals can be technical, but they may be the most current source of information on medical topics.

44. What is the main idea of the passage?
    A. Infotrac is a useful source of information.
    B. The community library offers numerous resources for medical information.
    C. Searching for medical information can be confusing.
    D. There is no reason to prepare a list of topics before visiting the library.

45. What is the meaning of the word *popular* as it is used in the third paragraph?
    A. complicated
    B. old-fashioned
    C. beloved
    D. for the general public

46. Which statement is *not* a detail from the passage?
    A. Abstracts summarize the information in an article.
    B. Having a prepared list of questions enables the librarian to serve you better.
    C. Infotrac is a database on CD-ROM.
    D. The articles in popular magazines can be hard to understand.

47. What is the meaning of the word *technical* as it is used in the fourth paragraph?
    A. requiring expert knowledge
    B. incomplete
    C. foreign
    D. plagiarized

Vocabulary and General Knowledge Questions

1. What is the meaning of the word *prognosis*?
    A. forecast
    B. description
    C. outline
    D. schedule

2. What is the name for any substance that stimulates the production of antibodies?
    A. collagen
    B. hemoglobin
    C. lymph
    D. antigen

3. What is the best definition for the word *abstain*?
    A. offend
    B. retrain
    C. to refrain from
    D. defenestrate

4. Select the meaning of the underlined word in this sentence:
Jerry held out hope for recovery, in spite of the ominous results from the lab.
    A. threatening
    B. emboldening
    C. destructive
    D. insightful

5. What is the meaning of the word *incidence*?
    A. random events
    B. sterility
    C. autonomy
    D. rate of occurrence

6. Select the word that means "water loving."
    A. homologous
    B. hydrophilia
    C. dipsomaniac
    D. hydrated

7. Select the meaning of the underlined word in this sentence:
The occluded artery posed a significant threat to the long-term health of the patient.
    A. closed
    B. deformed
    C. enlarged
    D. engorged

8. What is the best description for the word *potent*?
    A. frantic
    B. determined
    C. feverish
    D. powerful

9. Select the meaning of the underlined word in this sentence:
The doctors were less concerned with Bill's respiration than with the <u>precipitous</u> rise in his blood pressure.
    A. detached
    B. sordid
    C. encompassed
    D. steep

10. Select the meaning of the underlined word in this sentence:
It is <u>vital</u> for the victim of a serious accident to receive medical attention immediately.
    A. recommended
    B. discouraged
    C. essential
    D. sufficient

11. What is the best description for the word *insidious*?
    A. stealthy
    B. deadly
    C. collapsed
    D. new

12. Select the word that means "take into the body."
    A. congest
    B. ingest
    C. collect
    D. suppress

13. What is the meaning of the word *proscribe*?
    A. anticipate
    B. prevent
    C. defeat
    D. forbid

14. Select the meaning of the underlined word in this sentence.
Wracked by abdominal pain, the victim of food poisoning moaned and rubbed his <u>distended</u> belly.
    A. concave
    B. sore
    C. swollen
    D. empty

15. Select the meaning of the underlined word in this sentence:
Despite the absence of <u>overt</u> signs, Dr. Harris suspected that Alicia might be suffering from the flu.
    A. concealed
    B. apparent
    C. expert
    D. delectable

16. Select the word that means "something added to resolve a deficiency or obtain completion."
    A. supplement
    B. complement
    C. detriment
    D. acumen

17. Select the word that means "a violent seizure."
    A. revelation
    B. nutrient
    C. contraption
    D. paroxysm

18. What is the meaning of *carnivore*?
    A. hungry
    B. meat eating
    C. infected
    D. demented

19. What is the meaning of *belligerent*?
    A. retired
    B. sardonic
    C. pugnacious
    D. acclimated

20. Select the word that means "on both sides."
    A. bilateral
    B. insufficient
    C. bicuspid
    D. congruent

21. Select the meaning of the underlined word in this sentence:
The medication should only be taken if the old symptoms <u>recur</u>.
    A. occur again
    B. survive
    C. collect
    D. desist

22. Select the word that means "likely to change."
    A. venereal
    B. motile
    C. labile
    D. entrail

23. What is the best description for the word *flaccid*?
    A. defended
    B. limp
    C. slender
    D. outdated

24. Select the word that means "both male and female."
    A. monozygotic
    B. heterogeneous
    C. homologous
    D. androgynous

25. What is the meaning of *terrestrial*?
    A. alien
    B. earthly
    C. foreign
    D. domestic

26. Select the word that means "improper or unfortunate."
    A. allocated
    B. untoward
    C. flaccid
    D. dilated

27. Select the meaning of the underlined word in this sentence:
At first, Gerald suspected that he had caught the disease at the office; later, though, he concluded that it was endogenous.
    A. contagious
    B. painful to the touch
    C. continuous
    D. growing from within

28. What is the meaning of *symptom*?
    A. result
    B. indication
    C. side effect
    D. precondition

29. Select the word that means "intrusive."
    A. convulsive
    B. destructive
    C. invasive
    D. connective

30. What is the meaning of *parameter*?
    A. guideline
    B. standard
    C. manual
    D. variable

31. Select the word that means "empty."
    A. holistic
    B. void
    C. concrete
    D. maladjusted

32. Select the meaning of the underlined word in this sentence:
Though chemotherapy had sent her cancer into remission, Glenda remained <u>lethargic</u> and depressed.
    A. nauseous
    B. sluggish
    C. contagious
    D. elated

33. Select the word that means "offsetting."
    A. compensatory
    B. defensive
    C. untoward
    D. confused

34. Select the word that means "degeneration or wasting away."
    A. dystrophy
    B. entropy
    C. atrophy
    D. apathy

35. What is the best description for the word *discrete*?
    A. calm
    B. subtle
    C. hidden
    D. separate

36. Select the meaning of the underlined word in this sentence:
In order to minimize scarring, the nurse reused the <u>site</u> of the previous injection.
    A. syringe
    B. location
    C. artery
    D. hole

37. Select the meaning of the underlined word in this sentence:
As a veteran of many flu seasons, the nurse knew how to minimize her <u>exposure</u> to the disease.
    A. laying open
    B. prohibition
    C. connection
    D. dislike

38. What is the meaning of *exacerbate*?
    A. implicate
    B. aggravate
    C. heal
    D. decondition

39. Select the word that means "nerve cell."
    A. neutron
    B. nucleus
    C. neuron
    D. neutral

40. Select the word that means "unfavorable."
    A. liberated
    B. adverse
    C. convenient
    D. occluded

41. Select the meaning of the underlined word in this sentence:
Dr. Grant ignored Mary's particular symptoms, instead administering a holistic treatment for her condition.
    A. insensitive
    B. ignorant
    C. specialized
    D. concerned with the whole rather than the parts

42. What is the best description for the word *suppress*?
    A. stop
    B. push up
    C. release
    D. strain

43. Select the word that means "about to happen."
    A. depending
    B. offending
    C. suspending
    D. impending

44. Select the meaning of the underlined word in this sentence:
The dermatologist was struck by the symmetric patterns of scarring on the patient's back.
    A. scabbed
    B. painful to the touch
    C. occurring in corresponding parts at the same time
    D. geometric

45. Select the word that means "open."
    A. inverted
    B. patent
    C. convent
    D. converted

46. Select the meaning of the underlined word in this sentence:
Despite an increase in the volume of his urine, the patient still reported bloating.
    A. quality
    B. length
    C. quantity
    D. loudness

47. What is the meaning of *repugnant*?
    A. destructive
    B. selective
    C. collective
    D. offensive

48. Select the word that means "enlarge."
    A. dilate
    B. protrude
    C. confuse
    D. occlude

49. What is the best description for the word *intact*?
    A. collapsed
    B. disconnected
    C. unbroken
    D. free

50. Select the word that means "the ability to enter, contact, or approach."
    A. ingress
    B. excess
    C. access
    D. success

Grammar Questions

1. Which word is *not* spelled correctly in the context of the following sentence?
Dr. Vargas was surprised that the prescription had effected Ron's fatigue so dramatically.
   A. surprised
   B. prescription
   C. effected
   D. fatigue

2. Select the word that makes this sentence grammatically correct:
Is the new student coming out to lunch with ____?
   A. we
   B. our
   C. us
   D. they

3. Select the word or phrase that makes this sentence grammatically correct:
____ picking up groceries one of the things you are supposed to do?
   A. Is
   B. Am
   C. Is it
   D. Are

4. Select the word that makes the following sentence grammatically correct.
These days, you can't ____ learning how to use a computer.
   A. not
   B. evading
   C. despite
   D. avoid

5. Which word is *not* spelled correctly in the context of the following sentence?
The climate hear is inappropriate for snow sports such as skiing.
   A. climate
   B. hear
   C. inappropriate
   D. skiing

6. Select the word or phrase that makes the following sentence grammatically correct.
____ screaming took the shopkeeper by surprise.
   A. We
   B. They
   C. Them
   D. Our

7. Select the word or phrase that makes the following sentence grammatically correct.
Why did we ____ try so hard?
   A. has to
   B. haven't
   C. had to
   D. have to

8. Select the word that makes the following sentence grammatically correct.
Tracey wore her hair in a French braid, ____ was the style at the time.
   A. among
   B. it
   C. that
   D. which

9. Select the phrase that makes the following sentence grammatically correct.
Working _____ the mission of the entire committee.
   A. to peace is
   B. toward peace was
   C. to peace was
   D. toward peace am

10. Select the phrase that makes the following sentence grammatically correct.
Janet called her _____ run after a squirrel.
   A. dog, who had
   B. dog that had
   C. dog, that had
   D. dog who had

11. Select the correct word for the blank in the following sentence.
After completing the intense surgery, Dr. Capra needed a long ____.
   A. brake
   B. break
   C. brink
   D. broke

12. Select the correct word for the blank in the following sentence.
The other day, Stan ____ reviewing his class notes in preparation for the final exam.
   A. begins
   B. begun
   C. begin
   D. began

13. Select the word or phrase that makes the following sentence grammatically correct.
It makes sense to maintain your current prescriptions, ____ they have worked so well in the past.
   A. although
   B. despite that
   C. since
   D. but

14. Select the word or phrase that makes the following sentence grammatically correct.
It seems like his blood pressure ___ every week.
   A. rises
   B. raises
   C. raise
   D. rise

15. Select the word or phrase that makes the following sentence correct.
___ their similar training, the two professionals drew radically different conclusions.
   A. Because of
   B. Among
   C. Despite
   D. Now that

16. Select the word or phrase that makes the following sentence grammatically correct.
Each of the two European capitals ___ named after a famous leader.
   A. are
   B. am
   C. as
   D. is

17. Which word is *not* used correctly in the context of the following sentence?
Before you walk any further, beware of the approaching traffic.
   A. before
   B. further
   C. beware
   D. approaching

18. What word is used incorrectly in the following sentence?
The little boy sat the red block atop the stack.
   A. little
   B. sat
   C. atop
   D. stack

19. Select the word or phrase that makes the following sentence grammatically correct.
Even though she was new, Lauren knew that ___ the patient's name would be an ethical violation.
   A. divulge
   B. to divulge
   C. to divulging
   D. divulged

20. Select the word or phrase that makes the following sentence grammatically correct.
The attendant looked ___ at everything related to the problem.
   A. close
   B. closet
   C. closely
   D. closedly

21. What word or phrase is used incorrectly in the following sentence?
Henry intuitively understood the doctor's illusion to his long-term depression.
    A. intuitively
    B. illusion
    C. long-term
    D. depression

22. Select the correct word for the blank in the following sentence.
If you want to join the club, you ___ contact the coach by Thursday.
    A. would
    B. should
    C. did
    D. have

23. Select the word that makes the following sentence grammatically correct.
Andy has ___ up a law practice of his own.
    A. seat
    B. set
    C. sit
    D. sat

24. Select the word or phrase that makes the following sentence grammatically correct.
He decided to buy a large coal furnace because he felt it would be _____ than a woodstove.
    A. more efficient
    B. efficienter
    C. more efficienter
    D. efficiency

25. What word is used incorrectly in the following sentence?
It is amazing how many soccer players has developed knee problems over the years.
    A. many
    B. players
    C. has
    D. developed

26. Select the word that makes the following sentence grammatically correct.
She asked ___ to take her around the corner to the drugstore.
    A. him
    B. his
    C. he
    D. his'

27. Select the word or phrase that makes the following sentence grammatically correct.
Felix was pleased ___ the progress he had made in his program.
    A. among
    B. with
    C. regards
    D. besides

28. Select the word or phrase that makes the following sentence grammatically correct.
After waking up, Dean eyed the cheesecake _____.
    A. hungry
    B. hungriest
    C. hungrily
    D. more hungry

29. Which word is *not* used correctly in the context of the following sentence?
After ringing up the nails, the cashier handed Nedra her recipe and change.
    A. ringing
    B. cashier
    C. recipe
    D. change

30. Select the correct word for the blank in the following sentence.
Sharon felt ____ about how her speech had gone.
    A. well
    B. good
    C. finely
    D. happily

31. What word is used incorrectly in the following sentence?
Brendan spent the day lying a brick foundation on the site.
    A. site
    B. on
    C. spent
    D. lying

32. Select the word or phrase that makes this sentence grammatically correct:
Children ____ obey their parents tend to do better in school.
    A. who
    B. which
    C. should
    D. to

33. Select the word or phrase that makes this sentence grammatically correct:
The development committee ____ a bargain with the city planners.
    A. striked
    B. stroke
    C. struck
    D. strike

34. Select the word or phrase that makes this sentence grammatically correct:
A child is not yet old enough to know what is healthy for _____.
    A. him or her
    B. them
    C. it
    D. she or he

35. Select the word or phrase that makes this sentence grammatically correct:
Theo was in great shape; he _____ all the way back to the pier.
   A. swam
   B. swimmed
   C. swum
   D. swim

36. Select the phrase that makes this sentence grammatically correct:
_____ went to the movies after having dinner at Lenny's.
   A. Her and I
   B. Her and me
   C. She and I
   D. She and me

37. Select the word or phrase that makes this sentence grammatically correct:
Before turning in, Brian made sure to ____ the alarm clock.
   A. sat
   B. sit
   C. set
   D. setted

38. What word is used incorrectly in the following sentence?
The dashboard shaked as he revved the engine.
   A. dashboard
   B. shaked
   C. as
   D. revved

39. Select the word or phrase that makes this sentence grammatically correct:
____ way he looked, Ted saw people milling about.
   A. Moreover
   B. Whichever
   C. Whomever
   D. Whether

40. Select the correct word for the blank in the following sentence.
The buried treasure had ____ there for centuries.
   A. laid
   B. layed
   C. lain
   D. laint

41. Select the word that makes this sentence grammatically correct:
In order to serve each patient better, the clinic decided to see ____ patients overall.
   A. less
   B. fewer
   C. lesser
   D. few

42. Select the word or phrase that makes this sentence grammatically correct:
It wasn't until ____ the interview that Kim realized she had forgotten her list of questions.
    A. despite
    B. after
    C. among
    D. between

43. Which word is used incorrectly in the following sentence?
The video store is on the way, so we should stop by and rent one.
    A. video
    B. way
    C. by
    D. one

44. Select the word that makes the following sentence grammatically correct.
____ are the best eye doctors in this county?
    A. Who
    B. Which
    C. Whom
    D. What

45. Select the word that makes this sentence grammatically correct:
While he was an apprentice, Steve ____ a great deal of time in the studio.
    A. spends
    B. spent
    C. spended
    D. spend

46. Select the word that correctly completes the following sentence.
The intern was surprised by the _____ of pain he was in after his first day of work.
    A. amount
    B. frequency
    C. number
    D. amplitude

47. What word is used incorrectly in the following sentence?
Whoever wrote the letter forgot to sign their name.
    A. Whoever
    B. wrote
    C. their
    D. name

48. Select the word or phrase that makes this sentence grammatically correct:
The child's fever was ____ high for him to lie comfortably in bed.
    A. to
    B. much
    C. too
    D. more

49. Select the word or phrase that makes the following sentence grammatically correct.
Sometimes, the condition _____ with an unusual symptom—vertigo.
   A. presence
   B. presents
   C. present
   D. prescience

50. Which word is *not* used correctly in the context of the following sentence?
There is no real distinction among the two treatment protocols recommended online.
   A. real
   B. among
   C. protocols
   D. online

Mathematics Questions

1. 474 + 2038 =
    A. 2512
    B. 2412
    C. 2521
    D. 2502

2. 32,788 + 1693 =
    A. 33,481
    B. 32,383
    C. 34,481
    D. 36,481

3. 3703 − 1849 =
    A. 1954
    B. 1854
    C. 1974
    D. 1794

4. 4790 − 2974 =
    A. 1816
    B. 1917
    C. 2109
    D. 1779

5. 229 × 738 =
    A. 161,622
    B. 167,670
    C. 169,002
    D. 171,451

6. 356 × 808 =
    A. 274,892
    B. 278,210
    C. 283,788
    D. 287,648

7. Round to the nearest whole number: 435 ÷ 7 =
    A. 16
    B. 62
    C. 74
    D. 86

8. Round to the nearest whole number: 4748 ÷ 12 =
    A. 372
    B. 384
    C. 396
    D. 412

9. Report all decimal places: 3.7 + 7.289 + 4 =
   A. 14.989
   B. 5.226
   C. 15.0
   D. 15.07

10. 4.934 + 7.1 + 9.08 =
    A. 21.114
    B. 21.042
    C. 20.214
    D. 59.13

11. 27 − 3.54 =
    A. 24.56
    B. 23.46
    C. 33.3
    D. 24.54

12. 28.19 − 9 =
    A. 28.1
    B. 18.19
    C. 27.29
    D. 19.19

13. Karen goes to the grocery store with $40. She buys a carton of milk for $1.85, a loaf of bread for $3.20, and a bunch of bananas for $3.05. How much money does she have left?
    A. $30.95
    B. $31.90
    C. $32.10
    D. $34.95

14. Round your answer to the tenths place: 0.088 × 277.9 =
    A. 21.90
    B. 2.5
    C. 24.5
    D. 24.46

15. Round your answer to the hundredths place: 28 ÷ 0.6 =
    A. 46.67
    B. 0.021
    C. 17.50
    D. 16.8

16. Roger's car gets an average of 25 miles per gallon. If his gas tank holds 16 gallons, about how far can he drive on a full tank?
    A. 41 miles
    B. 100 miles
    C. 320 miles
    D. 400 miles

17. Express the answer in simplest form: $\frac{3}{8} + \frac{2}{8} =$

   A. $\frac{1}{8}$

   B. $\frac{1}{2}$

   C. $\frac{5}{8}$

   D. $\frac{5}{16}$

18. Express the answer in simplest form: $\frac{2}{3} + \frac{2}{7} =$

   A. $\frac{20}{21}$

   B. $\frac{4}{10}$

   C. $\frac{4}{21}$

   D. $\frac{2}{5}$

19. Present the sum as a mixed number in simplest form: $1\frac{1}{2} + \frac{12}{9} =$

   A. $2\frac{3}{5}$

   B. $1\frac{3}{4}$

   C. $3\frac{1}{3}$

   D. $2\frac{5}{6}$

20. Aaron worked $2\frac{1}{2}$ hours on Monday, $3\frac{3}{4}$ hours on Tuesday, and $7\frac{2}{3}$ hours on Thursday. How many hours did he work in all?

   A. $10\frac{5}{6}$

   B. $12\frac{1}{2}$

   C. $13\frac{1}{4}$

   D. $13\frac{11}{12}$

21. Express the answer in simplest form: $\frac{23}{24} - \frac{11}{24} =$

   A. $\frac{11}{23}$

   B. $\frac{1}{2}$

   C. $\frac{2}{3}$

   D. $\frac{12}{24}$

22. Express the answer in simplest form: $3\frac{4}{7} - 2\frac{3}{14} =$

   A. $2\frac{3}{14}$

   B. $1\frac{1}{14}$

   C. $1\frac{5}{14}$

   D. $2\frac{3}{7}$

23. Express the answer in simplest form: Dean has brown, white, and black socks. One-third of his socks are white; one-sixth of his socks are black. How many of his socks are brown?

   A. $\frac{1}{3}$

   B. $\frac{2}{6}$

   C. $\frac{1}{2}$

   D. $\frac{3}{4}$

24. Express the answer in simplest form: A recipe calls for $1\frac{1}{2}$ cups sugar, $3\frac{2}{3}$ cups flour, and $\frac{2}{3}$ cup milk. If you want to double the recipe, what will be the total amount of cups of ingredients required?

   A. $11\frac{2}{3}$

   B. 8

   C. $12\frac{1}{6}$

   D. $6\frac{2}{3}$

25. Express your answer as a mixed number in simplest form: $4\frac{1}{3} \times \frac{2}{7} =$

   A. $6\frac{1}{3}$

   B. $3\frac{7}{10}$

   C. $\frac{8}{21}$

   D. $1\frac{5}{21}$

26. Express the answer as a mixed number or fraction in simplest form: $2\frac{3}{9} \times \frac{1}{3} =$

   A. $\frac{7}{8}$

   B. $2\frac{3}{7}$

   C. $\frac{12}{27}$

   D. $\frac{7}{9}$

27. Express the answer as a mixed number or fraction in simplest form: $\frac{5}{8} \div \frac{1}{5} =$
    A. $\frac{1}{8}$
    B. $2\frac{3}{4}$
    C. $3\frac{1}{3}$
    D. $3\frac{1}{8}$

28. Express the answer as a mixed number or fraction in simplest form: $\frac{2}{7} \div \frac{1}{6} =$
    A. $\frac{1}{21}$
    B. $2\frac{1}{12}$
    C. $1\frac{3}{4}$
    D. $1\frac{5}{7}$

29. Round to the nearest whole number: Bill got $\frac{7}{9}$ of the answers right on his chemistry test. On a scale of 1 to 100, what numerical grade would he receive?
    A. 77
    B. 78
    C. 79
    D. 80

30. Round to the hundredths place. Change the fraction to a decimal: $\frac{7}{8} =$
    A. 0.88
    B. 0.92
    C. 0.84
    D. 0.78

31. Round to the hundredths place. Change the fraction to a decimal: $4\frac{3}{7} =$
    A. 4.37
    B. 4.43
    C. 4.56
    D. 4.78

32. Change the decimal to the simplest equivalent proper fraction: 3.78 =
    A. $3\frac{3}{4}$
    B. $3\frac{7}{8}$
    C. $3\frac{39}{50}$
    D. $3\frac{78}{100}$

33. Change the decimal to the simplest equivalent proper fraction: 0.07 =
    A. $\frac{7}{10}$
    B. $\frac{0.07}{10}$
    C. $\frac{7}{100}$
    D. $\frac{70}{100}$

34. Change the decimal to the simplest equivalent proper fraction: 2.80 =
    A. $\frac{2.8}{10}$
    B. $2\frac{8}{10}$
    C. $\frac{0.28}{1}$
    D. $2\frac{4}{5}$

35. Change the fraction to the simplest possible ratio: $\frac{8}{14}$
    A. 2:3
    B. 4:7
    C. 4:6
    D. 3:5

36. Two-thirds of the students in Mr. Garcia's class are boys. If there are 27 students in the class, how many of them are girls?
    A. 1
    B. 9
    C. 12
    D. 20

37. Solve for x:
3:2 :: 24:x
    A. 16
    B. 12
    C. 2
    D. 22

38. Solve for x:
7:42 :: 4:x
    A. 12
    B. 48
    C. 24
    D. 16

39. Change the decimal to a percent: 0.64 =
    A. 0.64%
    B. 64%
    C. 6.4%
    D. 0.064%

40. Change the decimal to a percent: 0.000026 =
    A. 0.0026%
    B. 0.026%
    C. 2.6%
    D. 26%

41. Change the percent to a decimal: 38% =
    A. 3.8
    B. 0.038
    C. 38.0
    D. 0.38

42. Change the percent to a decimal: 17.6% =
    A. 17.6
    B. 1.76
    C. 0.176
    D. 0.0176

43. Change the percent to a decimal: 126% =
    A. 126.0
    B. 0.0126
    C. 0.126
    D. 1.26

44. Round to the nearest whole number. Change the fraction to a percent: $\frac{2}{9}=$
    A. 20%
    B. 21%
    C. 22%
    D. 23%

45. Round to the nearest whole number. Change the fraction to a percent: $\frac{9}{13}=$
    A. 33%
    B. 69%
    C. 72%
    D. 78%

46. Round to the nearest whole number: What is 17 out of 68, as a percent?
    A. 17%
    B. 25%
    C. 32%
    D. 68%

47. Round to the nearest percentage point: Gerald made 13 out of the 22 shots he took in the basketball game. What was his shooting percentage?
    A. 13%
    B. 22%
    C. 59%
    D. 67%

48. Round to the nearest whole number: What is 18% of 600?
    A. 108
    B. 76
    C. 254
    D. 176

49. Round to the tenths place: What is 6.4% of 32?
    A. 1.8
    B. 2.1
    C. 2.6
    D. 2.0

50. What is the numerical value of the Roman number XVII?
    A. 22
    B. 17
    C. 48
    D. 57

Biology Questions

1. If an organism is *AaBb*, which of the following combinations in the gametes is impossible?
    A. AB
    B. aa
    C. aB
    D. Ab

2. What is the typical result of mitosis in humans?
    A. two diploid cells
    B. two haploid cells
    C. four diploid cells
    D. four haploid cells

3. How does water affect the temperature of a living thing?
    A. Water increases temperature.
    B. Water keeps temperature stable.
    C. Water decreases temperature.
    D. Water does not affect temperature.

4. Which of the following is *not* a product of the Krebs cycle?
    A. carbon dioxide
    B. oxygen
    C. adenosine triphosphate (ATP)
    D. energy carriers

5. What kind of bond connects sugar and phosphate in DNA?
    A. hydrogen
    B. ionic
    C. covalent
    D. overt

6. What is the second part of an organism's scientific name?
    A. species
    B. phylum
    C. population
    D. kingdom

7. How are lipids different than other organic molecules?
    A. They are indivisible.
    B. They are not water soluble.
    C. They contain zinc.
    D. They form long proteins.

8. Which of the following is *not* a steroid?
    A. cholesterol
    B. estrogen
    C. testosterone
    D. hemoglobin

9. Which of the following properties is responsible for the passage of water through a plant?
    A. cohesion
    B. adhesion
    C. osmosis
    D. evaporation

10. Which hormone is produced by the pineal gland?
    A. insulin
    B. testosterone
    C. melatonin
    D. epinephrine

11. What is the name of the organelle that organizes protein synthesis?
    A. mitochondrion
    B. nucleus
    C. ribosome
    D. vacuole

12. During which phase is the chromosome number reduced from diploid to haploid?
    A. S phase
    B. interphase
    C. mitosis
    D. meiosis I

13. What is the name for a cell that does *not* contain a nucleus?
    A. eukaryote
    B. bacteria
    C. prokaryote
    D. cancer

14. What is the name for the physical presentation of an organism's genes?
    A. phenotype
    B. species
    C. phylum
    D. genotype

15. Which of the following forms of water is the densest?
    A. liquid
    B. steam
    C. ice
    D. All forms of water have the same density.

16. What is the longest phase in the life of a cell?
    A. prophase
    B. interphase
    C. anaphase
    D. metaphase

17. Which of the following is *not* found within a bacterial cell?
    A. mitochondria
    B. DNA
    C. vesicles
    D. ribosome

18. Which of the following is a protein?
    A. cellulose
    B. hemoglobin
    C. estrogen
    D. ATP

19. Which of the following structures is *not* involved in translation?
    A. tRNA
    B. mRNA
    C. ribosome
    D. DNA

20. Which of the following is necessary for cell diffusion?
    A. water
    B. membrane
    C. ATP
    D. gradient

21. How many different types of nucleotides are there in DNA?
    A. one
    B. two
    C. four
    D. eight

22. Which of the following cell types has no nucleus?
    A. platelet
    B. red blood cell
    C. white blood cell
    D. phagocyte

23. Which part of aerobic respiration uses oxygen?
    A. osmosis
    B. Krebs cycle
    C. glycolysis
    D. electron transport system

24. Which of the following is the most general taxonomic category?
    A. kingdom
    B. phylum
    C. genus
    D. order

25. What is the name of the process by which a bacterial cell splits into two new cells?
    A. mitosis
    B. meiosis
    C. replication
    D. fission

Chemistry Questions

1. Which of the following substances allows for the fastest diffusion?
    A. gas
    B. solid
    C. liquid
    D. plasma

2. What is the oxidation number of hydrogen in CaH_2?
    A. +1
    B. −1
    C. 0
    D. +2

3. Which of the following does *not* exist as a diatomic molecule?
    A. boron
    B. fluorine
    C. oxygen
    D. nitrogen

4. What is another name for aqueous HI?
    A. hydroiodate acid
    B. hydrogen monoiodide
    C. hydrogen iodide
    D. hydriodic acid

5. Which of the following could be an empirical formula?
    A. C_4H_8
    B. C_2H_6
    C. CH
    D. C_3H_6

6. What is the name for the reactant that is entirely consumed by the reaction?
    A. limiting reactant
    B. reducing agent
    C. reaction intermediate
    D. reagent

7. What is the name for the horizontal rows of the periodic table?
    A. groups
    B. periods
    C. families
    D. sets

8. What is the mass (in grams) of 7.35 mol water?
    A. 10.7 g
    B. 18 g
    C. 132 g
    D. 180.6 g

9. Which of the following orbitals is the last to fill?
    A. 1s
    B. 3s
    C. 4p
    D. 6s

10. What is the name of the binary molecular compound NO$_5$?
    A. nitro pentoxide
    B. ammonium pentoxide
    C. nitrogen pentoxide
    D. pentnitrogen oxide

11. What is the mass (in grams) of 1.0 mol oxygen gas?
    A. 12 g
    B. 16 g
    C. 28 g
    D. 32 g

12. Which kind of radiation has no charge?
    A. beta
    B. alpha
    C. delta
    D. gamma

13. What is the name of the state in which forward and reverse chemical reactions are occurring at the same rate?
    A. equilibrium
    B. constancy
    C. stability
    D. toxicity

14. What is 119°K in degrees Celsius?
    A. 32°C
    B. −154°C
    C. 154°C
    D. −32°C

15. What is the SI unit of energy?
    A. ohm
    B. joule
    C. henry
    D. newton

16. What is the name of the device that separates gaseous ions by their mass-to-charge ratio?
    A. mass spectrometer
    B. interferometer
    C. magnetometer
    D. capacitance meter

17. Which material has the smallest specific heat?
    A. water
    B. wood
    C. aluminum
    D. glass

18. What is the name for a reaction in which electrons are transferred from one atom to another?
    A. combustion reaction
    B. synthesis reaction
    C. redox reaction
    D. double-displacement reaction

19. What are van der Waals forces?
    A. the weak forces of attraction between two molecules
    B. the strong forces of attraction between two molecules
    C. hydrogen bonds
    D. conjugal bonds

20. Which of the following gases effuses the fastest?
    A. Cl_2
    B. O_2
    C. N_2
    D. H_2

21. Which of the following elements is *not* involved in many hydrogen bonds?
    A. fluorine
    B. carbon
    C. oxygen
    D. nitrogen

22. What is the mass (in grams) of 0.350 mol copper?
    A. 12.5 g
    B. 14.6 g
    C. 18.5 g
    D. 22.2 g

23. How many d orbitals are there in a d subshell?
    A. 5
    B. 7
    C. 9
    D. 11

24. What is the name for the number of protons in an atom?
    A. atomic identity
    B. atomic mass
    C. atomic weight
    D. atomic number

25. Which of the following elements is an alkali metal?
    A. magnesium
    B. rubidium
    C. hydrogen
    D. chlorine

Anatomy and Physiology Questions

1. What is the name of the structure that prevents food from entering the airway?
    A. trachea
    B. esophagus
    C. diaphragm
    D. epiglottis

2. Which substance makes up the pads that provide support between the vertebrae?
    A. bone
    B. cartilage
    C. tendon
    D. fat

3. How many different types of tissue are there in the human body?
    A. four
    B. six
    C. eight
    D. ten

4. What is the name of the outermost layer of skin?
    A. dermis
    B. epidermis
    C. subcutaneous tissue
    D. hypodermis

5. Which hormone stimulates milk production in the breasts during lactation?
    A. norepinephrine
    B. antidiuretic hormone
    C. prolactin
    D. oxytocin

6. Which of the following structures has the lowest blood pressure?
    A. arteries
    B. arteriole
    C. venule
    D. vein

7. Which of the heart chambers is the most muscular?
    A. left atrium
    B. right atrium
    C. left ventricle
    D. right ventricle

8. Which part of the brain interprets sensory information?
    A. cerebrum
    B. hindbrain
    C. cerebellum
    D. medulla oblongata

9. Which of the following proteins is produced by cartilage?
   A. actin
   B. estrogen
   C. collagen
   D. myosin

10. Which component of the nervous system is responsible for lowering the heart rate?
    A. central nervous system
    B. sympathetic nervous system
    C. parasympathetic nervous system
    D. distal nervous system

11. Which type of substance breaks down to form urea?
    A. lipid
    B. protein
    C. carbohydrate
    D. iron

12. What is the name for a joint that can only move in two directions?
    A. hinge
    B. insertion
    C. ball and socket
    D. flange

13. In which of the following muscle types are the filaments arranged in a disorderly manner?
    A. cardiac
    B. smooth
    C. skeletal
    D. rough

14. How much air does an adult inhale in an average breath?
    A. 500 mL
    B. 750 mL
    C. 1000 mL
    D. 1250 mL

15. Which type of cell secretes antibodies?
    A. bacterial cell
    B. viral cell
    C. lymph cell
    D. plasma cells

16. Which force motivates filtration in the kidneys?
    A. osmosis
    B. smooth muscle contraction
    C. peristalsis
    D. blood pressure

17. Which of the following hormones decreases the concentration of blood glucose?
    A. insulin
    B. glucagon
    C. growth hormone
    D. glucocorticoids

18. Which structure controls the hormones secreted by the pituitary gland?
    A. hypothalamus
    B. adrenal gland
    C. testes
    D. pancreas

19. How much of a female's blood volume is composed of red blood cells?
    A. 10%
    B. 25%
    C. 40%
    D. 70%

20. Which type of cholesterol is considered to be the best for health?
    A. LDL
    B. HDL
    C. VLDL
    D. VHDL

21. Where are the vocal cords located?
    A. bronchi
    B. trachea
    C. larynx
    D. epiglottis

22. Where does gas exchange occur in the human body?
    A. alveoli
    B. bronchi
    C. larynx
    D. pharynx

23. Which structure of the nervous system carries action potential in the direction of a synapse?
    A. cell body
    B. axon
    C. neuron
    D. myelin

24. Where is the parathyroid gland located?
    A. neck
    B. back
    C. side
    D. brain

25. What is the name of the process in the lungs by which oxygen is transported from the air to the blood?
   A. osmosis
   B. diffusion
   C. dissipation
   D. reverse osmosis

Answer Key and Explanations

Reading Comprehension Answer Key and Explanations

1. D: The main idea of this passage is that vaccines help the immune system function properly. Identifying main ideas is one of the key skills tested by the HESI exam. One of the common traps that many test-takers fall into is assuming that the first sentence of the passage will express the main idea. Although this will be true for some passages, often the author will use the first sentence to attract interest or to make an introductory, but not central, point. On this question, if you assume that the first sentence contains the main idea, you will mistakenly choose answer B. Finding the main idea of a passage requires patience and thoroughness; you cannot expect to know the main idea until you have read the entire passage. In this case, a diligent reading will show you that answer choices A, B, and C express details from the passage, but only answer choice D is a comprehensive summary of the author's message.

2. C: This passage does not state that the symptoms of disease will not emerge until the body has learned to fight the disease. The reading comprehension section of the HESI exam will include several questions that require you to identify details from a passage. The typical structure of these questions is to ask you to identify the answer choice that contains a detail not included in the passage. This question structure makes your work a little more difficult, because it requires you to confirm that the other three details are in the passage. In this question, the details expressed in answer choices A, B, and D are all explicit in the passage. The passage never states, however, that the symptoms of disease do not emerge until the body has learned how to fight the disease-causing microbe. On the contrary, the passage implies that a person may become quite sick and even die before the body learns to effectively fight the disease.

3. B: In the third paragraph, the word *virulent* means "malicious." The reading comprehension section of the HESI exam will include several questions that require you to define a word as it is used in the passage. Sometimes the word will be one of those used in the vocabulary section of the exam; other times, the word in question will be a slightly difficult word used regularly in academic and professional circles. In some cases, you may already know the basic definition of the word. Nevertheless, you should always go back and look at the way the word is used in the passage. The HESI exam will often include answer choices that are legitimate definitions for the given word, but which do not express how the word is used in the passage. For instance, the word *virulent* could in some circumstances mean contagious or annoying. However, since the passage is not talking about transfer of the disease and is referring to a serious illness, malicious is the more appropriate answer.

4. C: The author's primary purpose in writing this essay is to inform. The reading comprehension section of the HESI exam will include a few questions that ask you to determine the purpose of the author. The answer choices are always the same: The author's purpose is to entertain, to persuade, to inform, or to analyze. When an author is *writing to entertain*, he or she is not including a great deal of factual information; instead, the focus is on vivid language and interesting stories. *Writing to persuade* means "trying to convince the reader of something." When a writer is just trying to provide the reader with information, without any particular bias, he or she is *writing to inform*. Finally, *writing to analyze* means to consider a subject already well known to the reader. For instance, if the above passage took an objective look at the pros and cons of various approaches to fighting disease, we would say that the passage was a piece of analysis. Because the purpose of this

passage is to present new information to the reader in an objective manner, however, it is clear that the author's intention is to inform.

5. A: The subject of this passage is foodborne illnesses. Identifying the subject of a passage is similar to identifying the main idea. Do not assume that the first sentence of the passage will declare the subject. Oftentimes, an author will approach his or her subject by first describing some related, familiar subject. In this passage, the author does introduce the subject of the passage in the first sentence. However, it is only by reading the rest of the passage that you can determine the subject. One way to figure out the subject of a passage is to identify the main idea of each paragraph, and then identify the common thread in each.

6. B: This passage never states that cooked food cannot cause illness. Indeed, the first sentence of the third paragraph states that harmful bacteria can be present on cooked food that is left out for two or more hours. This is a direct contradiction of answer choice B. If you can identify an answer choice that is clearly contradicted by the text, you can be sure that it is not one of the ideas advanced by the passage. Sometimes the correct answer to this type of question will be something that is contradicted in the text; on other occasions, the correct answer will be a detail that is not included in the passage at all.

7. C: In the first paragraph, the word *pathogens* means "disease-causing substances." The vocabulary you are asked to identify in the reading comprehension section of the HESI exam will tend to be health related. The exam administrators are especially interested in your knowledge of the terminology used by doctors and nurses. Some of these words, however, are rarely used in normal conversation, so they may be unfamiliar to you. The best way to determine the meaning of an unfamiliar word is to examine how it is used in context. In the last sentence of the first paragraph, it is clear that pathogens are some substances that cause disease. Note that the pathogens are not diseases themselves; we would not say that an uncooked piece of meat "has a disease," but rather that consuming it "can cause a disease." For this reason, answer choice C is better than answer choice A.

8. A: In the second paragraph, the word *sterile* means "free of bacteria." This question provides a good example of why you should always refer to the word as it is used in the text. The word *sterile* is often used to describe "a person who cannot reproduce." If this definition immediately came to mind when you read the question, you might have mistakenly chosen answer D. However, in this passage the author describes raw foods as *not sterile*, meaning that they contain bacteria. For this reason, answer choice A is the correct response.

9. C: The main idea of the passage is that both the esophagus and the stomach are subject to bleeding problems. The structure of this passage is simple: The first paragraph discusses bleeding disorders of the esophagus, and the second paragraph discusses bleeding disorders of the stomach. Remember that statements can be true, and can even be explicitly stated in the passage, and can yet not be the main idea of the passage. The main idea given in answer choice A is perhaps true, but is too general to be classified as the main idea of the passage.

10. B: The passage never states that ulcer disease rarely occurs in the stomach. On the contrary, in the second paragraph the author states that ulcer disease *can* affect the blood vessels in the stomach. The three other answer choices can be found within the passage. The surest way to answer a question like this is to comb through the passage, looking for each detail in turn. This is a time-consuming process, however, so you may want to follow any initial intuition you have. In other words, if you are suspicious of one of the answer choices, see if you can find it in the passage.

Often you will find that the detail is expressly contradicted by the author, in which case you can be sure that this is the right answer.

11. A: In the first paragraph, the word *rupture* means "tear." All of the answer choices are action verbs that suggest destruction. In order to determine the precise meaning of rupture, then, you must examine its usage in the passage. The author is describing a condition in which damage to a vein causes internal bleeding. Therefore, it does not make sense to say that the vein has *collapsed* or *imploded*, as neither of these verbs suggests a ripping or opening in the side of the vein. Similarly, the word *detach* suggests an action that seems inappropriate for a vein. It seems quite possible, however, for a vein to *tear*: Answer choice A is correct.

12. D: In the second paragraph, the word *erode* means "wear away." Your approach to this question should be the same as for question 11. Take a look at how the word is used in the passage. The author is describing a condition in which ulcers degrade a vein to the point of bleeding. Obviously, it is not appropriate to say that the ulcer has *avoided*, *divorced*, or *contained* the vein. It *is* sensible, however, to say that the ulcer has *worn away* the vein.

13. A: The primary subject of the passage is a new artificial retina. This question is a little tricky, because the author spends so much time talking about the experience of Kathy Blake. As a reader, however, you have to ask yourself whether Mrs. Blake or the new artificial retina is more essential to the story. Would the author still be interested in the story if a different person had the artificial retina? Probably. Would the author have written about Mrs. Blake if she hadn't gotten the artificial retina? Almost certainly not. Really, the story of Kathy Blake is just a way for the author to make the artificial retina more interesting to the reader. Therefore, the artificial retina is the primary subject of the passage.

14. B: In the second paragraph, the word *progressive* means "gradually increasing." The root of the word is *progress*, which you may know means "advancement toward a goal." With this in mind, you may be reasonably certain that answer choice B is correct. It is never a bad idea to examine the context, however. The author is describing *progressive visual loss*, so you might be tempted to select answer choice C or D, since they both suggest loss or diminution. Remember, however, that the adjective *progressive* is modifying the noun *loss*. Since the *loss* is increasing, the correct answer is B.

15. C: The passage never states that retinitis pigmentosa (RP) is curable. This question may be somewhat confusing, since the passage discusses a new treatment for RP. However, the passage never declares that researchers have come up with a cure for the condition; rather, they have developed a new technology that allows people who suffer from RP to regain some of their vision. This is not the same thing as curing RP. Kathy Blake and others like her still have RP, though they have been assisted by this exciting new technology.

16. D: The author's intention in writing this essay is to inform. You may be tempted to answer that the author's intention is to entertain. Indeed, the author expresses his message through the story of Kathy Blake. This story, however, is not important by itself. It is clearly included as a way of explaining the new camera glasses. If the only thing the reader learned from the passage was the story of Kathy Blake, the author would probably be disappointed. At the same time, the author is not really trying to persuade the reader of anything. There is nothing controversial about these new glasses: Everyone is in favor of them. The mission of the author, then, is simply to inform the reader.

17. A: The main idea of the passage is that Usher syndrome is an inherited condition that affects hearing and vision. Always be aware that some answers may be included in the passage but not the

main idea. In this question, answer choices B and D are both true details from the passage, but neither of them would be a good summary of the article. One way to approach this kind of question is to consider what you would be likely to say if someone asked you to describe the article in a single sentence. Often, the sentence you come up with will closely mimic one of the answer choices. If so, you can be sure that answer choice is correct.

18. D: In the first paragraph, the word *symptoms* means "perceptible signs." The word *symptoms* is used frequently in medical contexts, though many people do not entirely understand its meaning. Symptoms are only those signs of illness that can be observed by someone besides the person with the illness. A stomachache, for instance, is not technically considered a symptom, since it cannot be observed by anyone other than the person who has it. A rash, however, is considered a symptom because other people can see it. The best definition for *symptoms*, then, is perceptible signs; that is, signs that can be perceived.

19. B: The passage does not state that Usher syndrome affects both hearing and smell. On the contrary, the passage only states that Usher syndrome affects hearing and vision. You should not be content merely to note that sentence in the passage and select answer choice B. In order to be sure, you need to quickly scan the passage to determine whether there is any mention of problems with the sense of smell. This is because the mention of impaired hearing and vision does not make it impossible for smell to be damaged as well. It is a good idea to practice scanning short articles for specific words. In this case, you would want to scan the article looking for words like *smell* and *nose*.

20. C: In the second paragraph, the word *juvenile* means "occurring in children." Examine the context in which the word is used. Remember that the context extends beyond just the immediate sentence in which the word is found. It can also include adjacent sentences and paragraphs. In this case, the word juvenile is immediately followed by a further explanation of Usher syndrome as it appears in children. You can be reasonably certain, then, that juvenile Usher syndrome is the condition as it presents in children. Although the word *juvenile* is occasionally used in English to describe immature or annoying behavior, it is clear that the author is not here referring to a *bratty* form of Usher syndrome.

21. B: In the third paragraph, the word *mutated* means "altered." This word comes from the same root as mutant; a *mutant* is an organism in which the chromosomes have been changed somehow. The context in which the word is used makes it clear that the author is referring to a scenario in which one of the parent's chromosomes has been altered. One way to approach this kind of problem is to substitute the answer choice into the passage to see if it still makes sense. Clearly, it would not make sense for a chromosome to be *selected*, since chromosomes are passed on and inherited without conscious choice. Neither does it make sense for a chromosome to be destroyed, because a basic fact of biology is that all living organisms have chromosomes.

22. D: The main idea of the passage is that the immune system protects the body from infection. The author repeatedly alludes to the complexity and mystery of the immune system, so it cannot be true that scientists fully understand this part of the body. It is true that the immune system triggers the production of fluids, but this description misses the point. Similarly, it is true that the body is under constant invasion by malicious microbes; however, the author is much more interested in the body's response to these microbes. For this reason, the best answer choice is D.

23. C: The passage never states that viruses are extremely sophisticated. In fact, the passage explicitly states the opposite. However, in order to know this you need to understand the word *primitive*. The passage says that viruses are too primitive, or early in their development, to be

classified as living organisms. A primitive organism is simple and undeveloped—exactly the opposite of sophisticated. If you do not know the word *primitive*, you can still answer the question by finding all three of the answer choices in the passage.

24. D: In the first paragraph, the word *ideal* means "perfect." Do not be confused by the similarity of the word *ideal* to *idea* and mistakenly select answer choice A. Take a look at the context in which the word is used. The author is describing how many millions of microbes can live inside the human body. It would not make sense, then, for the author to be describing the body as a *hostile* environment for microbes. Moreover, whether or not the body is a confined environment would not seem to have much bearing on whether it is good for microbes. Rather, the paragraph suggests that the human body is a perfect environment for microbes.

25. B: The passage never states that the immune system ignores tumors. Indeed, at the beginning of the third paragraph, the author states that scientists remain puzzled by the body's ability to fight tumors. This question is a little tricky, because it is common knowledge that many tumors prove fatal to the human body. However, you should not take this to mean that the body does not at least try to fight tumors. In general, it is best to seek out direct evidence in the text rather than to rely on what you already know. You will have enough time on the HESI exam to fully examine and research each question.

26. A: In the second paragraph, the word *enlist* means "call into service." The use of this word is an example of figurative language, the use of a known image or idea to elucidate an idea that is perhaps unfamiliar to the reader. In this case, the author is describing the efforts of the immune system as if they were a military campaign. The immune system *enlists* other cells, and then directs these *recruits* to areas where they are needed. You are probably familiar with *enlistment* and *recruitment* as they relate to describe military service. The author is trying to draw a parallel between the enlistment of young men and women and the enlistment of immune cells. For this reason, "call into service" is the best definition for *enlist*.

27. C: The author's primary purpose in writing this essay is to inform. As you may have noticed, the essays included in the reading comprehension section of the HESI exam were most often written to inform. This should not be too surprising; after all, the most common intention of any writing on general medical subjects is to provide information rather than to persuade, entertain, or analyze. This does not mean that you can automatically assume that "to inform" will be the answer for every question of this type. However, if you are in doubt, it is probably best to select this answer. In this case, the passage is written in a clear, declarative style with no obvious prejudice on the part of the author. The primary intention of the passage seems to be providing information about the immune system to a general audience.

28. B: The main idea of the passage is that the Food and Drug Administration (FDA) has a special program for regulating dietary supplements. This passage has a straightforward structure: The author introduces his subject in the first paragraph and uses the four succeeding paragraphs to elaborate. All of the other possible answers are true statements from the passage but cannot be considered the main idea. One way to approach questions about the main idea is to take sentences at random from the passage and see which answer choice they could potentially support. The main idea should be strengthened or supported by most of the details from the passage.

29. D: The passage never states that the Food and Drug Administration (FDA) ignores products after they enter the market. In fact, the entire fourth paragraph describes the steps taken by the FDA to regulate products once they are available for purchase. In some cases, questions of this type

will contain answer choices that are directly contradictory. Here, for instance, answer choices A and B cannot be true if answer choice D is true. If there are at least two answer choices that contradict another answer choice, it is a safe bet that the contradicted answer choice cannot be correct. If you are at all uncertain about your logic, however, you should refer to the passage.

30. C: In the third paragraph, the phrase *phased in* means "implemented in stages." Do not be tempted by the similarity of this phrase to the word *fazed*, which can mean "confused or stunned." The author is referring to manufacturing standards that have already been implemented for large manufacturers and are in the process of being implemented for small manufacturers. It would make sense, then, for these standards to be implemented in *phases*: that is, to be *phased in*.

31. A: In the fifth paragraph, the word *deceptive* means "misleading." The root of the word *deceptive* is the same as for the words *deceive* and *deception*. Take a look at the context in which the word is used. The author states that the FDA prevents certain kinds of advertising. It would be somewhat redundant for the author to mean that the FDA prevents *illegal* advertising; this goes without saying. At the same time, it is unlikely that the FDA spends its time trying to prevent merely *irritating* advertising; the persistent presence of such advertising makes this answer choice inappropriate. Left with a choice between *malicious* and *misleading* advertising, it makes better sense to choose the latter, since being mean and nasty would be a bad technique for selling a product. It is common, however, for an advertiser to deliberately mislead the consumer.

32. B: The main idea of the passage is that anemia is a potentially dangerous condition characterized by low numbers of RBCs (red blood cells). All of the other answer choices are true (although answer C leaves out RBCs), but only answer choice C expresses an idea that is supported by the others. When you are considering a question of this type, try to imagine the answer choices as they would appear on an outline. If the passage above were placed into outline form, which answer choice would be the most appropriate title? Which answer choices would be more appropriate as supporting details? Try to get in the habit of imagining a loose outline as you are reading the passages on the HESI exam.

33. D: The passage never states that anemia is rarely caused by blood loss. On the contrary, in the first sentence of the fourth paragraph the author lists three causes of anemia, and blood loss is listed first. Sometimes, answer choices for this type of question will refer to details not explicitly mentioned in the passage. For instance, answer choice A is true without ever being stated in precisely those terms. Since the passage mentions several different treatments for anemia, however, you should consider the detail in answer choice A to be in the passage. In other words, it is not enough to scan the passage looking for an exact version of the detail. Sometimes, you will have to use your best judgment.

34. D: In the third paragraph, the word *oxygenated* means "containing high amounts of oxygen." This word is not in common usage, so it is absolutely essential for you to refer to its context in the passage. The author states in the second paragraph that anemia is in part a deficiency of the red blood cells that carry oxygen throughout the body. Then in the first sentence of the third paragraph, the author states that anemic individuals do not get enough oxygenated blood. Given this information, it is clear that *oxygenated* must mean carrying high amounts of oxygen, because it has already been stated that anemia consists of a lack of oxygen-rich blood.

35. A: In the fifth paragraph, the word *severity* means "seriousness." This word shares a root with the word *severe*, but not with the word *sever*. As always, take a look at the word as it is used in the passage. In the final sentence of the passage, the author states that the treatment for anemia will

depend on the *cause and severity* of the condition. In the previous paragraph, the author outlined a treatment for anemia and indicated that the proper response to the condition varies. The author even refers to the worst cases of anemia as being *severe*. With this in mind, it makes the most sense to define *severity* as seriousness.

36. C: The main idea of the passage is that a recent study found no link between caffeine consumption and rheumatoid arthritis (RA) among women. As is often the case, the first sentence of the passage contains the main idea. However, do not assume that this will always be the case. Furthermore, do not assume that the first sentence of the passage will only contain the main idea. In this passage, for instance, the author makes an immediate reference to the previous belief in the correlation between caffeine and RA. It would be incorrect, however, to think that this means answer choice A is correct. Regardless of whether or not the main idea is contained in the first sentence of the passage, you will need to read the entire text before you can be sure.

37. A: The passage never states that alcohol consumption is linked with RA. The passage does state that the new study took into account alcohol consumption when evaluating the long-term data. This is a good example of a question that requires you to spend a little bit of time rereading the passage. A quick glance might lead you to believe that the new study had found a link between alcohol and RA. Tricky questions like this make it even more crucial for you to go back and verify each answer choice in the text. Working through this question by using the process of elimination is the best way to ensure the correct response.

38. A: In the second paragraph, the word *symmetrical* means "affecting both sides of the body in corresponding fashion." This is an example of a question that is hard to answer even after reviewing its context in the passage. If you have no idea what *symmetrical* means, it will be hard for you to select an answer: All of them sound plausible. In such a case, the best thing you can do is make an educated guess. One clue is that the author has been describing a condition that affects the hands and the feet. Since people have both right and left hands and feet, it makes sense that inflammation would be described as *symmetrical* if it affects both the right and left hand or foot.

39. B: The author's primary purpose in writing this essay is to inform. You may be tempted to select answer choice D on the grounds that the author is presenting a particular point of view. However, there is no indication that the author is trying to persuade the reader of anything. One clear sign that an essay is written to persuade is a reference to what the reader already thinks. A persuasive essay assumes a particular viewpoint held by the reader and then argues against that viewpoint. In this passage, the author has no allegiance to any idea; he or she is only reporting the results of the newest research.

40. C: The main idea of the passage is that exercise improves bone health. This short passage has a simple structure: The author presents the thesis (main idea) and then spends the rest of the essay supporting it. When a passage is as clearly organized as this one, there should be little mystery about the main idea. If you look at the first sentences of paragraphs two and three, you will see that both contain the words *exercise* and *bones*. This is a good sign that either answer choice A or C is correct. Once you note that weight-bearing exercise is not discussed until the final paragraph, it seems clear that the correct answer must be C.

41. B: In the first paragraph, the word *vital* means "important." On first looking at this word, you might note its similarity to other words having to do with life and liveliness: *vitality*, *revive*, and *vivacious*, to name just a few. This knowledge can help guide your response, though you shouldn't make any assumptions based on it. Otherwise, you might mistakenly select answer choice D. The

author states that exercise is *vital* for healthy bones. It would not make sense to say that exercise is *nourishing* for healthy bones, because it would also be so for unhealthy bones. The author is not describing the condition of healthy bones, but rather how bones can be made healthy. For this reason, it makes the most sense to select answer choice B.

42. C: The passage never states that swimming is not good for the bones. This question is a little bit tricky, because the author does state that non-weight-bearing forms of exercise, including swimming, are not *as* good for the bones as weight-bearing exercises. However, just because swimming is not as good for the bones as running does not mean that it is bad for the bones. In fact, swimming works every major muscle system of the body and contributes to overall health, which includes bone health. Be on guard for questions like this that try to fool you into putting words in the author's mouth.

43. A: In the second paragraph, the word *fractures* means "breaks." In the second paragraph, the author declares that exercise reduces the risk of falls and fractures. To begin with, it makes sense to assume that broken bones would be one of the possible results of a fall. We are all aware that older people are more likely to break their bones by falling in the shower or on the stairs. On occasion, authors will use the word *fracture* to describe a damaged relationship, which may tempt you to select *tiffs*. In this case, however, the context makes clear that the author is describing broken bones.

44. B: The main idea of the passage is that the community library offers numerous resources for medical information. While most of the articles used in the reading comprehension section of the HESI exam will be about scientific or health-related concepts directly, some will touch on health and medicine in a more indirect manner. In this article, the author outlines some of the useful sources of medical information that can be obtained at the local library. Answer choices A and C are true, but do not express the general, overarching message of the article. Answer choice D is not true and is directly contradicted by the article itself.

45. D: In the third paragraph, the word *popular* means "for the general public." This word is more often used to describe someone or something that is well known or liked, so you might be tempted to select answer choice C. Take a look at the word as it is used in the context of the third paragraph, however. The author states that the library contains popular magazines and newspapers and then adds that the library also contains medical journals. Popular magazines and newspapers, then, are not the same thing as professional trade journals. Because the latter are known to be complicated and technical (that is, requiring professional expertise), you can guess that *popular* magazines are for a general reading audience.

46. D: The passage does not state that the articles in popular magazines can be hard to understand. If you are working in order, you can use your knowledge of the word *popular* to figure out the answer to this question. Specifically, you will know that the word describes publications that are written for a general, nonexpert audience. With this in mind, it seems unlikely that the articles would also be hard to understand. The other three details are explicit in the passage, so the answer must be D.

47. A: In the fourth paragraph, the word *technical* means "requiring expert knowledge." Again, some of the details gleaned from your work in the preceding questions can help you. The word *technical* is used to describe medical journals. As has already been shown, the author states that medical journals are written for an expert audience and can be difficult for a nonprofessional to understand.

If this is the case, you can infer that the word *technical* must mean requiring expert knowledge, answer choice A.

Vocabulary and General Knowledge Answer Key and Explanations

1. A: The best definition for the word *prognosis* is "forecast." A prognosis is a probable result or course of a disease. The prognosis usually includes the likelihood of recovery for the patient. A prognosis is distinct from a *diagnosis*, which is just the description of the patient's condition. Likewise, a *description* is not the same thing as a prognosis, because it does not include a suggestion of what will happen in the future. An *outline* is an organized description of a subject, and therefore is not similar to a prognosis. Finally, a *schedule* is a plan for the future, rather than a prediction.

2. D: The name for a substance that stimulates the production of antibodies is an *antigen*. An antigen is any substance perceived by the immune system as dangerous. When the body senses an antigen, it produces an antibody. *Collagen* is one of the components of bone, tendon, and cartilage. It is a spongy protein that can be turned into gelatin by boiling. *Hemoglobin* is the part of red blood cells that carries oxygen. In order for the blood to carry enough oxygen to the cells of the body, there has to be a sufficient amount of hemoglobin. *Lymph* is a near-transparent fluid that performs a number of functions in the body: It removes bacteria from tissues, replaces lymphocytes in the blood, and moves fat away from the small intestine. Lymph contains white blood cells. As you can see, some of the questions in the vocabulary section will require technical knowledge.

3. C: The best definition for the word *abstain* is "to refrain from." Doctors often ask their patients to abstain from certain behaviors that have a negative impact on health. For example, a patient recovering from a viral infection might be asked to abstain from alcohol, so as to prevent weakening of the immune system. To *offend* is "to annoy or irritate." A health-care worker should take care to avoid offending a patient. *Retrain* means "to teach someone how to do a job again." For instance, a nurse might have to be retrained after a long period of not performing a particular task. To *defenestrate* means "to throw out the window." This word is unlikely to be used in a health context.

4. A: The best synonym for *ominous* as it is used in this sentence is "threatening." An ominous symptom, for instance, is one that suggests the presence of serious disease. The word *emboldening* means "making bold." A patient who is regaining strength might be emboldened to try new and more difficult activities. The word *destructive* means "causing damage, chaos, or loss." A destructive condition or behavior has a negative effect on the patient's health. The word *insightful* means "thoughtful or provocative." As a health practitioner, you should try to be insightful so that you can come up with creative solutions to your patients' problems.

5. D: The word *incidence* means "rate of occurrence." A doctor will often refer to the incidence of a particular disease or condition as a measure of its severity or longevity. *Random events* are referred to as "incidents." *Sterility* means "free of living bacteria and microorganisms." It is absolutely necessary for a medical environment to be sterile so that patients will not get infections. *Autonomy* means "self-control and self-determination." A health-care worker should try to promote the autonomy of the patient whenever possible, although autonomy should never be more important than health and well-being.

6. B: *Hydrophilia* means "water loving." One could say that humans have a hydrophilic body, because our bodies crave constant infusions of water. The word *homologous* means "corresponding

or having the same relative position or structure." A *dipsomaniac* is a person who cannot resist alcoholic drinks. Dipsomania is a compulsion that must be treated with behavioral therapy or medications such as Antabuse, which causes a violent physical reaction to alcohol. The word *hydrated* means "full of water or sufficiently full of water." Patients need to be hydrated, and medical workers need to be hydrated while they are performing their duties.

7. A: The closest meaning for the word *occluded* as it is used in this sentence is "closed." Occluded means "blocked or obstructed." The word is commonly used to describe arteries that no longer allow the passage of blood. The word *deformed* means "misshapen or out of the normal shape." Any deformed body part is a cause for concern. The word *engorged* means "overfull, especially of blood or food." The organs of the body may become engorged when they are infected or diseased. *Enlarged* means "made larger."

8. D: The best definition for the word *potent* is "powerful." A strong drug may be referred to as potent. The ability of a man to reproduce is sometimes referred to as his potency. The word *frantic* means "frenzied or anxious." A medical worker should never be frantic when dealing with patients and should do his or her best to keep patients from becoming frantic. The word *determined* means "set on a particular path." Whenever possible, a health-care worker should try to ensure that patients are determined to take the necessary steps toward recovery and good health. The word *feverish* can mean either "having a high temperature" or "being worried and anxious." A feverish patient should be comforted and given plenty of fluids.

9. D: The word *precipitous* as it is used this sentence means "steep." Doctors will often refer to a precipitous change in blood pressure. In general, precipitous changes are dangerous to the health. The word *detached* means "unconnected or aloof." A common example is a detached retina, a condition in which part of the eye becomes disconnected, and vision is damaged. The word *sordid* means "dirty" or "vile." The word *encompassed* means "surrounded or entirely contained within." For instance, a doctor might describe a treatment protocol as encompassing all aspects of the patient's life.

10. C: The word *vital* as it is used this sentence means "essential." Medical workers will often refer to a patient's vital signs, meaning blood pressure, heart rate, and temperature. The word *recommended* means "preferred by some authority." The recommended course of treatment is the one outlined and prescribed by a doctor. The word *discouraged* means "disappointed and doubtful of success." Health-care workers should try to prevent patients from becoming discouraged, since this can further diminish quality of life and chances of recovery. The word *sufficient* means "having enough to accomplish the necessary task." As an example, a doctor might inquire to make sure that a patient is receiving sufficient fluids or food.

11. A: The best definition of the word *insidious* is "stealthy." An insidious disease takes root and develops in the body slowly, so that by the time the patient is aware of it, the damage can be severe and even fatal. Cancer is the classic example of insidious disease, because it may take root in the body and develop for a long period without any perceptible signs or symptoms. An insidious disease may be *deadly*, but it is not necessarily so. The words *collapsed* and *new* have no innate relationship to the word *insidious*.

12. B: The word *ingest* means "take into the body." The rate at which a patient ingests food and fluids is important when establishing a treatment protocol. To *congest* is "to fill to excess or to overcrowd." Chest congestion is a common complaint, which may be rooted in serious or minor causes. To *collect* is "to gather together." A health-care worker needs to collect information on

patients so as to serve them effectively. To *suppress* means "to hold down or hold back." Patients should be encouraged not to suppress any information during a medical examination; keeping important facts from the doctor or nurse can prevent effective treatment.

13. D: The word *proscribe* means "forbid." A doctor often will proscribe certain foods or behaviors if they would negatively impact patient health. To *anticipate* is "to expect ahead of time." A doctor tries to anticipate how a disease will progress or how a patient will respond to treatment, though it is impossible to do this all the time. To *prevent* is "to keep from happening." Health-care workers try to prevent accidents and mistakes from happening on the job. To *defeat* is "to achieve victory over." The primary goal of treatment is to defeat whatever conditions are adversely affecting the patient's health.

14. C: The word *distended* as it is used in this sentence means "swollen." Doctors will often refer to a distended abdomen, which accompanies gassiness or bloating. The word *concave* means "shaped like the inside of a bowl." Many structures of the human body, for instance the inside of the ear and the arch of the foot, are described as concave. A distended body part may be *sore*, but it is not necessarily so. A distended artery, for instance, may have no accompanying pain. Also, though a distended body part may be *empty*, this is not always the case. In cases of starvation, the stomach may become distended; however, other body parts may become distended from being full to excess.

15. B: The word *overt* as it is used in this sentence means "apparent." Overt signs are those that can be seen by someone other than the person who is experiencing them. A rash is an overt sign; a stomachache is not. The word *concealed* means "hidden." Concealed signs cannot be perceived with the senses; a rise in blood pressure, for instance, is a concealed sign of illness. The word *expert*, used as an adjective, means "knowledgeable about a particular subject." When dealing with an unfamiliar situation, for instance, a doctor might call in an expert practitioner. The word *delectable* means "tasty or delicious."

16. A: The word *supplement* means "something added to resolve a deficiency or obtain completion." A doctor might recommend a particular nutritional supplement to address a patient's needs. A *complement* completes something or makes it perfect. Doctors try to put together complementary treatments that will reinforce and support one another. The word *detriment* means "loss, damage, or injury." A patient should be dissuaded from behaviors that will work to their detriment. The word *acumen* means "expertise" or "special knowledge in some area." A health-care worker will develop acumen based on his or her professional experience.

17. D: The word *paroxysm* means "a violent seizure." A patient who is suffering from paroxysms needs to be stabilized and treated immediately. A *revelation* is "a sudden realization or flash of knowledge." Sometimes, a doctor will puzzle over a case until he or she has a revelation and realizes what needs to be done. A *nutrient* is "something that provides nutrition, or sustenance, to the body." Tests may indicate that a patient needs more of a particular nutrient in order to improve his or her health. A *contraption* is "a mechanical device." Health-care workers must learn how to use all sorts of contraptions in order to perform their duties.

18. B: The word *carnivore* means "meat eating." A patient who is not a carnivore might be in danger of anemia (iron deficiency) or other malnutrition. On the other hand, excessive consumption of red meat can lead to heart disease and obesity. *Hungry* means "feeling hunger." The word *infected* means "contaminated by germs." An infected body part needs to be sterilized and treated immediately. The word *demented* means "crazy or insane," especially when this behavior is the

result of the condition known as dementia. A demented individual may not be able to make health-related decisions.

19. C: The word *belligerent* means "pugnacious." *Pugnacious* means "ready to fight." Belligerent patients may be resistant to treatment and disdainful of the doctor's or nurse's authority. The word *retired* means "withdrawn from business." The word *sardonic* means "mocking or sneering." This word is unlikely to come up in a medical context, though a health-care worker should avoid being sardonic. The word *acclimated* means "used to or accustomed to." Often, it takes a while for patients to become acclimated to a course of treatment or to a new lifestyle imposed upon them by diminishing health.

20. A: The word *bilateral* means "on both sides." This word is typically used to describe conditions that afflict both sides of the body. For instance, a patient suffering from bilateral partial paralysis might have numbness in both his right and left arms. The word *insufficient* means "lacking in necessary qualities." A patient might have insufficient blood flow to a certain area, or an insufficient amount of a certain nutrient. A *bicuspid* is anything that ends in two points. Many teeth are referred to as bicuspids because of their shape. The word *congruent* means "agreeing or in complete accord."

21. A: The word *recur* as it is used in this sentence means "occur again." Doctors often refer to the recurrence of a disease or symptom. In some cases, the recurrence of a disease indicates that the treatment used in the past was ineffective. *Recur* has the same root as *occur*, with the prefix *re-*, meaning "back or again." To *survive* means "to remain alive." To *collect* means "to bring together into one place." To *desist* means "to cease or stop doing something." A doctor might advise a patient to desist from a certain behavior in order to improve his or her health.

22. C: The word *labile* means "likely to change." This word is often used as a synonym for unstable. Blood pressure that fluctuates rapidly may be described as labile. The word *venereal* is used to describe conditions that relate to sexual intercourse. Venereal disease, for instance, is acquired during sexual contact. Chlamydia, gonorrhea, and syphilis are all examples of venereal disease. The word *motile* means "moving or capable of moving." A doctor will often refer to a part of the body as motile when its movements have been compromised in the past. An *entrail* is one of the internal parts of an animal or human body. It most often refers to the intestines.

23. B: The best description for the word *flaccid* is "limp." A flaccid part of the body is lacking in muscle tone. The word *defended* means "driven danger away from." The word *slender* means "thin or skinny, but not to the extent of being unhealthy." In general, patients who are slender recover better from injury and illness than patients who are overweight or obese. The word *outdated* describes "something that has become irrelevant with age." As medical technology becomes increasingly sophisticated, much of the equipment that used to be essential has now become outdated.

24. D: The word *androgynous* means "both male and female." Some children are born with androgynous characteristics, and their sexuality may remain ambiguous (hard to determine) for their entire life. *Monozygotic* means "derived from one fertilized egg." Identical twins are often referred to as monozygotic because they emerge from an individual zygote (fertilized egg). The word *exogenous* is used to describe "conditions that originate outside of the body." It is not to be confused with *heterogeneous*, which means "having different parts." *Homologous* means "corresponding or having the same relative position." A dog's body is said to be homologous to a cat's because their legs are in the same place.

25. B: The word *terrestrial* means "earthly." It can also be used to refer to things that are from the land rather than from the water. The word *alien*, when used as an adjective, describes "things that are unfamiliar or from an outside source." *Alien* does not only refer to creatures from outer space. A patient who has come down with a mystery ailment might try to identify some contact with alien substances. The word *foreign* is used to describe "people or things that are from some other area or country." In an area where medical procedures are being performed, foreign objects are usually forbidden. The word *domestic* is used to describe "things that are of the home or household."

26. B: The word *untoward* means "improper or unfortunate." Health-care workers should avoid untoward actions when dealing with their patients. This means acting according to the professional code of ethics. *Allocated* means "reserved for a particular purpose." For example, a patient may be put on a specific exercise regimen. The patient then needs to allocate a certain part of the day for this activity, so that it is sure to be done. *Flaccid* means "limp or lacking in muscle tone." If a patient is experiencing any degree of paralysis, the affected part of the body may be flaccid. *Dilated* means "expanded or made larger." The pupils of the eyes become dilated in the dark so that more light can enter the lens.

27. D: The word *endogenous* as it is used in this sentence means "growing from within." Doctors occasionally refer to endogenous cholesterol, which comes from inside the body rather than from the diet. *Contagious* means "capable of spreading from person to person." A person with a contagious disease needs to be kept away from other people. Often, diseases are only contagious for a limited time. *Continuous* means "proceeding on without stopping." If a patient is suffering from continuous back pain, for instance, he or she is experiencing the pain at all times.

28. B: The word *symptom* means "indication." A symptom is any subjective indication of disease. A symptom can be perceived only by the patient. Lower back pain, for instance, is a symptom, because it cannot be perceived by anyone else. Symptoms are distinct from signs, which are apparent to the patient and other people. Bleeding and high blood pressure are both signs. In medicine, an *indication* is "a sign or symptom that suggests a particular treatment." For example, some rashes are an indication for topical ointment. A *side effect*, on the other hand, is "any effect in addition to the intended effect." The term is often used to describe the unpleasant additional effects of treatment or medication. As an example: Side effects of chemotherapy are nausea and fatigue. A *precondition* is "something that must happen or be true before something else can happen." For example, when a patient has the flu, keeping liquids down is a precondition for trying to eat solid foods.

29. C: The word *invasive* means "intrusive." An invasive disease seeks to penetrate the body and cause damage. Strep throat, a bacterial infection, is an example of an invasive disease. The word *convulsive* means "afflicted by spasms or seizures." A patient who suffers from epilepsy or extreme fever may become convulsive. Convulsive patients need to be stabilized so that they don't hurt themselves. The word *destructive* is used to describe "things that cause damage, injury, or loss." Health-care workers try to steer patients away from destructive behaviors. The word *connective* is used to describe "structures that bring other things into contact." The connective tissues of the body include cartilage, ligaments, and tendons.

30. A: The word *parameter* means "guideline." A doctor will often lay out certain parameters at the beginning of treatment. These are not specific rules, but rather they are the general ideas that will inform the entire course of treatment. Parameters are the boundaries of treatment. A *standard*, on the other hand, is "an established basis of comparison." A *manual* is "a book that explains how to

perform a particular task." A *variable* is "something that changes." The amount of food a patient is given might be considered to be a variable, for example.

31. B: The word *void* means "empty." Doctors may refer to a patient's bowels as void when they do not contain any digested food matter. *Holistic* means "concerned with the whole of something rather than with the particular parts." Doctors try to put together a holistic treatment plan so that the patient's general level of health will be improved. *Concrete* is a building material, but the word is also used as an adjective to describe "things that are real, sturdy, and well established." Doctors try to establish concrete standards for measuring a patient's condition, rather than relying on general impressions. *Maladjusted* means "poorly accustomed or acclimated." Although it often takes time for a patient to adjust to a new treatment protocol, some patients will remain maladjusted and require a change in treatment.

32. B: The word *lethargic* as it is used in this sentence means "sluggish." Lethargy is a symptom of many forms of illness. It is also a side effect of chemotherapy. *Nauseous* means "sickened, or suffering from an upset stomach." Nausea is a common side effect of chemotherapy as well; it is just not the one described in this sentence. *Contagious* means "capable of spreading from person to person." Many viral and bacterial infections are contagious. *Elated* means "ecstatic," or "wildly happy." It is usually a good thing when a patient is elated, although manic-depressive patients may alternate between excessive elation and near-suicidal sadness.

33. A: The word *compensatory* means "offsetting." A patient may develop compensatory behaviors to make up for a developing health condition. *Defensive* means "protective" or "intending to repel an attack." Sometimes, patients will feel defensive in the presence of a health professional. *Untoward* means "unfavorable, improper, or unfortunate." Untoward events will inevitably occur during the course of treatment; it is the job of the staff to continue their work regardless. *Confused* means "perplexed or bewildered." Some patients, especially the very young or very old, may become confused during treatment. When confusion is identified, health-care workers should slow down and help the patient feel more comfortable.

34. C: The word *atrophy* means "degeneration or wasting away." Doctors often refer to muscle atrophy, which occurs when a patient is immobile for a long period. Physical therapy and massage are two common ways to prevent muscle atrophy when a patient cannot move because of injury or illness. *Dystrophy* is "weakening, degeneration, or abnormal growth of muscle." You may have heard of muscular dystrophy, a hereditary disease in which the muscles gradually lose their strength. *Entropy* is "the tendency toward chaos and disorder." This term is occasionally used in a medical context to describe a patient's tendency toward decline and decrease in function. It is the job of the health-care worker to fight against entropy. *Apathy* is "a lack of caring." Patients who are suffering from serious injury or illness, especially those who have a poor long-term prognosis, may descend into apathy. A health-care worker should try to use his or her influence to improve mood and combat apathy.

35. D: The best description for the word *discrete* is "separate." Discrete symptoms, for example, are those that do not have any connection to one another, though they spring from the same source. The word *subtle* is used to describe things that are "delicate or mysterious in their meaning or intent." Sometimes, the signs of disease will be subtle. Although today's health-care system has amazing technology for spotting the signs of disease, health-care workers still must be on the lookout for the subtle signs of disease.

36. B: The word *site* as it is used in this sentence means "location." Doctors will often refer to the site of an injection or a planned surgery. A *syringe* is "the device used to inject or withdraw fluid from the body." Medical personnel who specialize in withdrawing blood from patients are called phlebotomists. An *artery* is "a blood vessel that carries blood away from the heart to nourish the rest of the body." Although the site to which the author is referring in this sentence is a *hole*, it will not always be so. For this reason, "hole" cannot be the best definition for *site*.

37. A: The word *exposure* as it is used in this sentence means "laying open." The most common usage of this term is in reference to the sun, although exposure to toxic chemicals is also a major health concern. A doctor will often ask a patient to limit his or her exposure to some environmental element. *Prohibition* is "the act of forbidding." Often, a doctor will place a prohibition on certain behaviors or foods if they are believed to adversely affect health. The words *connection* and *dislike* have no relation to exposure.

38. B: The word *exacerbate* means "aggravate." The first commandment of medical care is "do no harm," which essentially means do nothing to exacerbate the patient's illness or injury. Behaviors or foods that exacerbate the symptoms of illness or injury should be stopped immediately. To *implicate* is "to demonstrate involvement or assign blame." Often, during the examination period, a doctor or nurse will implicate seemingly unrelated behaviors in a patient's condition. Once a behavior has been implicated, the doctor and patient will work together to eliminate its negative effects on health. To *decondition* is "to weaken or diminish the conditioned response to a certain stimulus." Part of working in health care is helping people make positive choices. In part, this is accomplished by deconditioning them to stimuli that provoke a negative response.

39. C: The word *neuron* means "nerve cell." The human body has millions of neurons, with billions of connections between them. A *neutron* is "the part of an atom that has neither positive nor negative charge." Neutrons are located in the nucleus of the atom. The *nucleus* is "the central part of a cell or atom, around which the other parts cluster." The HESI exam requires you to know the names and functions of all the cell parts. *Neutral* means "not taking part in or not taking sides in a dispute." A neutral behavior or medication is one that has neither a positive nor a negative effect on health.

40. B: The word *adverse* means "unfavorable." Unhealthy behaviors have an adverse effect on well-being. *Liberated* means "freed." The general goal of health care is to liberate patients from the negative effects of illness or injury. *Convenient* means "easily accessible and available." When health care is convenient, patients are more likely to acquire it. Health-care workers should strive to make their services convenient for patients whenever possible. *Occluded* means "blocked or closed." Patients with a high level of cholesterol are at risk of developing occluded arteries. Another instance in which the term is used is when a patient is choking: In this case, the patient's airway is said to be occluded.

41. D: The word *holistic* as it is used in this sentence means "concerned with the whole rather than the parts." Doctors try to consider the patient's health from a holistic perspective; that is, they try to improve health in its entirety rather than to eliminate specific symptoms. The word *insensitive* means "not responsive." The word *ignorant* means "lacking knowledge." Health-care workers cannot be ignorant of the latest findings and information in their field. The word *specialized* means "adapted to or trained in a specific discipline or task." Because of the technological complexity of modern medical practice, most careers in health care are specialized.

42. A: The best description for the word *suppress* is "stop." Sometimes, a patient will suppress their symptoms if they are not psychologically ready to face illness. However, the suppression of illness tends to create other problems. Ultimately, it is better not to suppress illness, but to face it directly. To *strain* is "to work hard or overextend." This word is used in a couple of different ways in health care. A patient may be suffering from a specific muscle strain after excessive exercise or hyperextension. Also, a doctor may prohibit a patient from straining in his or her professional life if it is causing fatigue and making the patient vulnerable to disease.

43. D: The word *impending* means "about to happen." A doctor might refer to impending symptoms, which are the symptoms the patient is likely to start experiencing in the near future. *Depending* means "relying on or placing trust in." Because most patients have no medical expertise, they are depending on doctors and nurses to choose the appropriate course of action. *Offending* means "annoying or irritating." *Suspending* means "stopping for an undetermined period." If a treatment is not working, for instance, or if it is causing unforeseen negative side effects, then a doctor may suspend it until more information can be gathered.

44. C: The word *symmetric* as it is used in this sentence means "occurring in corresponding parts at the same time." Some illnesses will cause symmetric rashes, meaning that both the right and left sides of the body are afflicted with similarly shaped inflammation. The word *scabbed* means "covered with wounds." The word *geometric* is used to describe "things that resemble the classic geometric shapes, such as the circle, square, or triangle." On occasion, a doctor may use this word to describe the pattern of a wound or rash.

45. B: The word *patent* means "open." Doctors will describe an artery as patent when it allows a free flow of blood. Similarly, a patent airway allows for unrestricted breathing. *Inverted* means turned upside down or backwards. Sometimes, a patient will be inverted in order to stimulate blood flow to certain parts of the body. A *convent* is "a home for nuns or monks." This word has no relevance to health care, but it is included because the HESI exam will sometimes try to tempt you with answer choices that sound like the right answer. The word *converted* means "changed or altered." A patient may have his or her diet converted in order to meet the needs of a treatment protocol.

46. C: The word *volume* as it is used in this sentence means "quantity." Doctors will refer to an increase in the volume of urine or some other body product as an indication of health. Volume is calculated as length × width × height (or depth); it is a three-dimensional measure. *Length*, on the other hand, is "a two-dimensional measure of distance." *Quality* means "degree of excellence." Quantity can be measured in any kind of units. *Loudness* might be the right answer if *volume* were being used in a different way, as "the relative power of a sound." In this sentence, however, the word is not being used to describe a sound.

47. D: The word *repugnant* means "offensive, especially to the senses or the morals." For instance, a patient may find a certain kind of medicine repugnant, in which case the doctor must either figure out a way to disguise the taste or consider a different form of treatment. The word *destructive* means "causing damage, injury, or loss." Patients should be steered away from destructive behaviors. *Selective* means "choosy or capable of making a thoughtful choice." In general, it is good to be selective, although a patient who is too selective about his or her diet may develop a nutritional deficiency. *Collective* means "combined or grouped together to form a whole." Health care seeks to treat the collective symptoms of the patient, rather than to focus on specific problems.

48. A: The word *dilate* means "enlarge." Dilation is often expressed as measurement, typically in units of centimeters. For instance, when the body becomes hot, the arteries dilate and blood rushes to the extremities. To *protrude* means "to stick out." Sometimes when a patient breaks a bone severely, part of the bone will protrude from the skin. To *occlude* means "to close up or block." Airways and arteries are the most common parts of the body to become occluded. Either of these occlusions needs to be dealt with immediately before other treatment can be administered.

49. C: The best description for the word *intact* is "unbroken." The word can be used in a number of different contexts. For instance, if a patient presents with severe pain in his or her side, the doctor might worry about the possibility of a ruptured appendix. After an X-ray reveals no damage to the appendix, however, the doctor might say that the organ is intact.

50. C: The word *access* means the ability "to enter, contact, or approach." It is important for patients to have easy access to health-care services. If patients do not have convenient access to services, they will be less likely to take actions to improve health. *Ingress* is "entering or going in." In some cases, a doctor will have to perform tests to determine a disease's path of ingress to the body. *Excess* is "too much or an overabundance of something." In general, excess of any kind is bad for the health. Even excessive exercise can be detrimental to health. During an initial examination, the doctor will try to identify areas in which the patient needs attention. *Success* is "the attainment of goals, whether personal, emotional, professional, physical, or financial." Obviously, the success of the patient is the top priority for all health-care workers.

Grammar Answer Key and Explanations

1. C: The word *effected* is not spelled correctly in the context of this sentence. In order to answer this question, you need to know the difference between *affect* and *effect*. The former is a verb and the latter is a noun. In other words, *affect* is something that you do and *effect* is something that is. In this sentence, the speaker is describing something that the prescription medication *did*. Therefore, the appropriate word is a verb. *Effect*, however, is a noun. For this reason, instead of *effected* the author should have used the word *affected*.

2. C: The word *us* makes the sentence grammatically correct. *Us* is the objective case of *we*. In this case, *us* is being used as an indirect object. An indirect object is the noun to which the action of the verb refers. In the sentence *He gave her a sandwich*, the indirect object is *her* (and the direct object is *sandwich*). All of the answer choices for this question are in the first-person plural, with the exception of answer choice D, which is in the third-person plural. The appropriate third-person plural form to complete this sentence is *them*.

3. A: The word *is* makes the sentence grammatically correct. In order to answer this question, you need to determine what the object of the verb will be. One way to do this is to rearrange the question as if it were a declarative sentence: *Picking up the groceries ____ one of the things you are supposed to do*. Expressed like this, it is easy to see that the subject of the sentence is "picking up the groceries." This is a third-person singular subject (that is, it is an "it"), so it receives the third-person present indicative verb form, *is*.

4. D: The word *avoid* makes the sentence grammatically correct. To *avoid* is to keep from doing something. The sentence states that it is impossible to function in the modern world without learning how to use a computer. The word *evade* has a similar meaning to *avoid*, but the verb form used here does not fit into the sentence correctly. The best way to approach this kind of question on

the HESI exam is to read the sentence aloud softly, substituting in the various answer choices. If you used this strategy on question 4, you would immediately notice that answer choice B does not correctly complete the sentence.

5. B: The word *hear* is not spelled correctly in the context of this sentence. The speaker has mixed up the homophones *hear* and *here*. *Homophones* are words that sound the same but are spelled differently and have a different meaning. Homophones are not to be confused with *homonyms*, which are spelled the same but have a different meaning. In question 5, the author is trying to describe the place where the climate is; that is, he or she is describing the climate *here*. Unfortunately, the author uses the word *hear*, which is a verb meaning "to listen."

6. D: The word *our* makes the sentence grammatically correct. *Our* is the possessive case of *we*, In this case, our is being used as an attributive adjective. An adjective is a word that modifies (or describes) a noun. *Our* is called an attributive adjective because it is attributing (assigning) ownership of the screaming to a particular party, *us*. Answer choices A and D are in the first-person plural; answer choices B and C are in the third-person plural. Neither B nor C, however, is in the possessive case. The sentence could be effectively completed with *their*, but this choice is not available.

7. D: The phrase *have to* makes the sentence grammatically correct. The speaker is trying to express that his group was forced to try hard. For this reason, it is essential for the verb *have* to be used. *Have* is an auxiliary verb indicating obligation. It agrees with the first-person plural pronoun *we*. An auxiliary verb accompanies another verb and makes some alterations in mood or tense. In this case, the addition of the verb have indicates that the speaker and others were obliged to try hard. *Can*, *will*, and *have* are all common examples of auxiliary verbs.

8. D: The word *which* makes the sentence grammatically correct. In this sentence, *which* is used as a relative pronoun. A relative pronoun introduces a relative clause, which is so called because it "relates" to the antecedent. The antecedent is the word that the relative pronoun refers to. In this sentence, the antecedent is "French braid," and the subsequent relative clause gives the reader more information about the French braid. Answer choice C is also a relative pronoun, but it is rarely used after a comma.

9. B: The phrase *toward peace was* makes this sentence grammatically correct. The word *toward* is a preposition that can mean "in the direction of" or "with a view to obtaining." It is in this last sense that the word is being used in this sentence. Peace is an abstract concept, not a physical destination that one could actually reach. For this reason, it does not make sense to select answer choices A or C. Answer choice D has an incorrect verb form; since the subject of the sentence is "working toward peace," the third-person singular verb form is correct.

10. A: The phrase *dog, who had* makes the sentence grammatically correct. To begin with, it is necessary for there to be a comma separating these two clauses, because the second clause is nonrestrictive. A clause is considered nonrestrictive if it could not stand by itself and if the rest of the sentence would still make sense were it removed. If the portion of this sentence after the comma were removed, the sentence would be *Janet called her dog*. Obviously, this is still a coherent sentence. Also, *who* is used here instead of *which* because the antecedent, *dog*, has an identity and personality.

11. B: The word *break* correctly completes this sentence. This question hinges on the different meanings that can be assigned to the word *break*. A *break* can be a brief period of rest from work or

some tiring activity, or it can be the act of destroying or disconnecting something. The first usage is as a noun, and the second usage is as a verb. In this sentence, the author is expressing that Dr. Capra needed something, which means you should use the noun form. Also, remember that a *brake* is the mechanism for stopping a vehicle.

12. D: The word *began* properly completes the sentence. The sentence begins with the phrase "the other day," which indicates that the action described took place sometime in the recent past. A past tense verb form is appropriate, then. The verb *begun* is the past participle of *begin*. A past participle describes action that took place before but is now complete. This sentence does not indicate, however, that the action is now complete. For all we know, Stan could still be reviewing his class notes. For this reason, the past tense *began* is the correct answer.

13. C: The word *since* makes the sentence grammatically correct. In this sentence, *since* is being used as a conjunction meaning "because." The word can also be used as an adverb or a preposition indicating an interval from some past time to the present. In this sentence, however, the right answer is indicated by the context. The first part of the sentence states that the current prescription is to be maintained; this suggests that the speaker has a positive attitude toward it. It makes sense, then, that the prescription would have worked well in the past, and that this would be the reason for continuing it.

14. A: The word *rises* makes the sentence grammatically correct. At the heart of this question is the distinction between *rise* and *raise*, which can be summed up in one sentence: To *raise* is to cause to *rise*. This probably requires a little explanation. *Raise* is generally a transitive verb, meaning that it has to be done to something. In other words, it needs an object. One *raises* a window or *raises* a question, but a window or question does not *raise* itself. *Rise*, on the other hand, is typically used as an intransitive verb. This means that it does not take an object. I *rise* from sleep; I do not *rise myself* from sleep. In the sentence for question 14, the blood pressure is doing the action described by the verb, and there is no object. For this reason, *rises* is correct.

15. C: The word *despite* completes the sentence correctly. *Despite* is a preposition meaning "notwithstanding" or "in spite of." A preposition is a word that indicates relationship. *At*, *by*, *with*, and *before* are all prepositions. All of the answer choices for question 15 include prepositions. So in order to answer the question, you need to determine which relationship the author is most likely trying to express. The first clause indicates that the two professionals had similar training, and the second clause that indicates they drew different conclusions. It would not make sense for them to draw different conclusions *because of* their similar training; one would expect both professionals to approach a question in the same way. Answer choices B and D create an incoherent statement when they are substituted into the sentence. The answer must therefore be C.

16. D: The word *is* makes the sentence grammatically correct. In order to answer this question correctly, you need to be able to identify the subject. Although it may seem as if the subject is *the two European capitals*, this is actually a clause related to the subject *each*. *Each* is a singular pronoun, in which two or more things are being considered individually. In this case, each of these things is an "it," so the appropriate verb form will be the third-person singular present indicative *is*.

17. B: The word *further* is not used correctly in the context of this sentence. Here, the word *farther* would be more appropriate. The distinction between *further* and *farther* is likely to appear in at least one question on the HESI exam. For the purposes of the examination, you just need to know that *farther* can be used to describe physical distance, while *further* cannot. In this sentence, the

speaker is describing a distance to be walked, which is a physical distance. For this reason, the word *further* is incorrect.

18. B: The word *sat* is used incorrectly in this sentence. The word *set* would be a good substitution for *sat*. The distinction between *sit* and *set* is likely to appear at least once during the HESI exam. *Sit* is an intransitive verb that does not need an object. One does not *sit* something else, one just *sits*. *Set*, meanwhile, is a transitive verb that requires an object. One *sets* an alarm clock or a table, one does not just *set*. In the sentence on question 18, the little boy is placing something, namely the red block. A transitive verb is required, therefore. For this reason, the past tense of *set* (also *set*) is correct, while the past tense of *sit* (*sat*) is not.

19. B: The phrase *to divulge* makes the sentence grammatically correct. *To divulge* is the infinitive form of a verb meaning to "reveal or disclose information." The verb can stay in the present tense because the speaker is describing what Laura knew at a particular time in the past. In other words, the author has already established the past tense with the word *knew*. It would also be appropriate to fill this blank with the word *divulging*. However, this is not one of the answer choices.

20. C: The word *closely* makes the sentence grammatically correct. Remember that an adjective is a word that describes a noun, while an adverb describes an adjective, a verb, or another adverb. In this sentence, you are looking for the right word to describe how the attendant *looked*. This means that you are looking for an adverb. Most of the time, adverbs end in *-ly*. On question 20, answer choices C and D both have this ending. Answer choice D, however, does not really make sense when substituted into the sentence.

21. B: The word *illusion* is used incorrectly in this sentence. Instead, the author should have used the word *allusion*. An illusion is a false or deceptive image. For example, a magician pulling a rabbit out a hat is a famous illusion. The magician does not actually produce the rabbit out of thin air, but is able to create the image of having done so. An *allusion*, on the other hand, is an indirect reference. If the doctor had said something like, "in light of your past issues," and Henry knew that the doctor meant his depression, then the doctor would have made an allusion.

22. B: The word *should* correctly completes the sentence. All of the answer choices are auxiliary verbs, which are verbs that accompany other verbs and add some element of tone or mood. In order to determine the appropriate auxiliary verb for this sentence, you need to take a close look at the context. The *if* that initiates the sentence suggests that the author is making a conditional statement. In other words, in order to join the club, a condition must be met: Namely, the coach must be contacted by Thursday. For this reason, *should* is the appropriate auxiliary verb. When should is placed before a verb, it adds a note of obligation or recommendation. For instance, saying "you should brush your teeth" is like saying "brushing your teeth is a healthful act that you ought to do."

23. B: The word *set* makes the sentence grammatically correct. This questions centers on the distinction between *set* and *sit*. *Set* is transitive and needs to have an object. This means that it has to be done to something (there are a few exceptions, like *the sun sets*). The past tense and past participle of *set* are both *set*. *Sit*, meanwhile, is intransitive and takes no object. You don't sit something; you just sit. The past tense and past participle of *sit* is *sat*. In this case, the blank must be filled by a transitive verb, because the verb is acting on something else: the law practice. For this reason, *set* is the correct answer.

24. A: The phrase *more efficient* makes the sentence grammatically correct. Here, the author is attempting to describe a comparison between two things: the coal furnace and the woodstove. The comparative form of an adjective usually ends with *-er*: *taller*, *wiser*, *cleaner*, for example. In some cases, however, the word *more* is placed in front of the unchanged adjective. As a general rule, multisyllabic words are more likely to use the *more* construction than the *-er* construction. That is the case with *efficient*. Unfortunately, there is no easy rule for memorizing the comparative forms of common English adjectives. Reading is one way to develop a good eye for proper usage.

25. C: The word *has* is used incorrectly in this sentence. The auxiliary verb *have* would be a correct substitution for *has*. *Have* and *has* are auxiliary verbs that, along with *developed*, form a past participle. A past participle is used for action that took place in the past and is now complete. The subject of the sentence is soccer players, which means the verb has to be in the third-person plural. *Has*, however, is the third-person singular. *Have* is in the third-person plural and would therefore be a better choice.

26. A: The word *him* makes the sentence grammatically correct. In this sentence, the blank needs to be filled by a direct object, because you are looking for the person, place, or thing to which the action of the verb is being done. Here, we are looking to identify the person who was asked. For that reason, we need the objective case of *he*, which is *him*. The objective case of *she* is *her*. There will probably be several questions in the grammar section of the HESI exam that require you to differentiate between a pronoun used as a subject and a pronoun used as an object.

27. B: The word *with* makes the sentence grammatically correct. *With* is a preposition that can mean a number of different things. Perhaps the most common meaning of *with* is "in the company of." In this sentence, however, a more accurate meaning is "in regard to." The word *among* is not appropriate here, because progress is not something one could physically be in the middle of. That is, *progress* is not a group of individual things. The word *regards* is not grammatically appropriate for this sentence, although the sentence could be correctly completed with the phrase *with regard to*. Finally, the word *besides* is incorrect because it would not make sense for Felix to not be pleased with his own progress.

28. C: The word *hungrily* makes the sentence grammatically correct. In order to answer this question, you must know the difference between an adjective and an adverb. An adjective modifies a noun. For instance, in the phrase *the delicious meatball*, *delicious* is an adjective. An adverb, on the other hand, modifies an adjective, a verb, or another adverb. In the phrase *walking quickly away*, *quickly* is an adverb. In the sentence for this question, it seems clear that the answer must modify the verb *eyed*. After all, it would not make much sense for the cheesecake to be hungry. This means that an adverb is required. The adverbial form of *hungry* is *hungrily*.

29. C: The word *recipe* is not used correctly in the context of this sentence. The author of this sentence has apparently confused the word *recipe* and *receipt*. A *recipe* is a list of instructions for making something, usually a food or beverage. You might have a recipe for chocolate chip cookies, for instance. A *receipt*, on the other hand, is a printed acknowledgement of having received a certain amount of money and goods. The slip of paper you are handed after paying for something in a store is a receipt. The HESI exam will most likely contain a few questions that require you to identify mixed-up word choices.

30. B: The word *good* properly completes this sentence. This question centers on the distinction between good and well, and, more generally, between adjectives and adverbs. An adjective is used to describe a noun or a pronoun. In the phrase *the red bicycle*, for example, *red* is an adjective

describing *bicycle*. An adverb, on the other hand, describes a verb, an adjective, or another adverb. Words that end in *-ly* are usually adverbs, describing the way something is done. As an example, in the phrase *running steadily*, *steadily* is an adverb. To succeed on the HESI exam, you need to know that g*ood* is an adjective and *well* is an adverb. In question 30, you are looking for a word that describes how Sharon felt, not one that describes her act of feeling. For this reason, you should select the adjective *good*.

31. D: The word *lying* is used incorrectly in this sentence. It would be correct to use the verb *laying* instead. The distinction between *laying* and *lying* is tricky. *Laying* is typically used as a transitive verb, meaning that it is done to something. One lays bricks or lays carpet, for instance. Lie, on the other hand, is an intransitive verb: It is not done to something; it is just done. You *lie* on the floor, for instance. The definition of *lay* is to place; to *lie* is to take a horizontal position. In this sentence, the subject (Brendan) is laying something (bricks), so it is incorrect to use the verb *lying*.

32. A: The word *who* makes the sentence grammatically correct. In this sentence, *who* is being used as a relative pronoun: that is, a pronoun introducing a clause that describes a noun already mentioned. The noun being referred to, known as the antecedent, is *children*. Because children are people with a personality and identity, the pronoun *who* is used rather than *which*. *Which* is used as a relative pronoun when the antecedent is an inanimate object, such as a box or a house.

33. C: The word *struck* makes the sentence grammatically correct. *Struck* is the past tense and past participle of *strike*, meaning "to hit" or "to beat." *Striked* is not a word. In this case, however, the author is using the common expression "struck a bargain." This expression is frequently used to describe deal making or the end of negotiations. These kinds of conversational phrases may be especially difficult for students whose native language is not English. If you are unfamiliar with expressions in English, you may want to pick up a glossary of slang or colloquial expressions.

34. A: The phrase *him or her* makes the sentence grammatically correct. In this case, we are looking for a word or words that can serve as the object of the preposition *for*. *She* and *he* are nominative forms, meaning that they can only be used as the subject of a sentence or a clause. *Them* can be the object of a preposition, but it is plural and, therefore, cannot correctly refer to the singular subject *a child*. (Incidentally, the use of *they* and *them* to refer to a singular subject is one of the most common grammatical errors, and will almost certainly appear in one or more questions on the HESI exam.) For a similar reason, you cannot use *it* to refer to *a child*. The correct answer, then, is *him or her*.

35. A: The word *swam* makes the sentence grammatically correct. *Swam* is the past tense of the verb *swim*. The context of this sentence makes clear that the action took place in the past; the author uses the past tense verb *was* and describes an action that has already been completed. *Swimmed* is an incorrect verb form. *Swum* is the past participle of *swim*; it would be appropriate if the sentence read *he had swum* or *he has swum*. The absence of these auxiliary verbs means that the simple past tense is appropriate here.

36. C: The phrase *she and I* makes the sentence grammatically correct. The blank needs to be filled by the subject of the sentence. The subject of a sentence or clause is the person, place, or thing that performs the verb. There are a couple of ways to determine that this sentence needs a subject. To begin with, the blank is at the beginning of the sentence, where the subject most often is found. Also, when you read the sentence, you will notice that it is unclear who went to the movies. Because you are looking for the subject, you need the nominative pronouns *she and I*.

37. C: The word *set* makes the sentence grammatically correct. This question requires knowledge of the distinction between *set* and *sit*. *Set* is a transitive verb meaning "to place in a particular position." Transitive verbs have to be done *to* something. *Sit*, meanwhile, is an intransitive verb meaning "to assume a seated posture." In this case, Brian is performing the action of the verb on something in particular: the alarm clock. For this reason, the verb *set* is appropriate.

38. B: The word *shaked* is incorrect in this sentence. In fact, *shaked* is not a word at all. The past tense of *shake* is *shook*. This is similar to the word *take*, which has as its past tense *took* rather than *taked*. There is no real reason for this, making it yet another usage pattern in English that does not conform to any strict rules. After all, the past tense of *wake* is *waked* rather than *wook*. There is no easy way to know all of these rules and exceptions, but a good way to acquire a sense of standard English usage is to become widely read and use a dictionary.

39. B: The word *whichever* makes the sentence grammatically correct. In this sentence, *whichever* is being used as an adjective modifying *way*. The presence of this adjective indicates that Ted was looking in any number of different ways. *Moreover* is an adverb meaning "in addition" or "besides." *Whomever* is the form of whoever used as a direct object, indirect object, or object of a preposition. *Whether* is a conjunction that suggests alternatives or sets of two choices.

40. C: The word *lain* properly completes the sentence. On this question, the presence of the word *had* is the biggest clue to the right answer. *Had* indicates that the verb phrase is being used as a past participle. A past participle is the verb form used to describe action that took place in the past and has been completed. In other words, the treasure started lying there a long time ago, and its position was fully established in the past. Remember that *lain* is the past participle of *lie*, and *laid* is the past participle of *lay*. The verb here is clearly intransitive (that is, it does not act on something else, it just does something), so the correct form is *lain*.

41. B: The word *fewer* makes the sentence grammatically correct. The distinction between fewer and less will most likely appear on your HESI exam. In general, *fewer* is used for things that can be counted and *less* is used for things that cannot be counted. So, for instance, one would say "fewer attendees at this year's conference" and "less confidence in the economy." In this sentence, the adjective is modifying *patients*, who of course can be counted quite easily. So, the correct answer is *fewer*.

42. B: The word *after* makes the sentence grammatically correct. *After* is a conjunction meaning "behind in place or position." A conjunction is a part of speech that connects different words, phrase, and ideas. *And*, *but*, and *because* are all conjunctions. In order to find the appropriate word to complete the sentence in question 42, you need to take a close look at the context. The sentence indicates that Kim realized she had forgotten her list of questions at some time relating to the interview. In other words, it seems clear that the blank must be completed with some word relating to time. Kim either made this realization before, during, or after the interview. Since *after* is one of the answer choices, it must be the correct answer.

43. D: The word *one* is used incorrectly in this sentence. Here, *one* is being used as a pronoun: a stand-in for some other noun. The problem is that it is unclear to what it is referring. The only possible reference for *one* is video store, and it does not make sense to say that "we should rent a video store." Most of the time, we would read this sentence and just assume that the author meant that we should rent a video. However, on the HESI exam, you must be alert for unclear wording.

44. A: The word *who* makes this sentence correct. *Who* is an interrogative pronoun that can be either singular or plural. A pronoun is a word that stands in for another noun. In this case, the pronoun is used so that the author can inquire about the noun to which the pronoun is referring. Once the question is answered, the names of the best eye doctors could be substituted for *who* to make a complete sentence. In any case, *who* is appropriate because the pronoun is referring to people who have both personality and identity; if they were objects, it would be appropriate to use *which* or *what*. *Whom* is a pronoun in the objective cases and is therefore not appropriate for this sentence.

45. B: The word *spent* makes this sentence grammatically correct. The sentence is clearly describing action that took place in the past, because the introductory clause begins with the word *while*. It cannot be determined whether this action is ongoing or has been completed. The past tense of the verb *spend* is *spent*. Unfortunately, there is no rule to guide this past tense; as a matter of fact, the past tense of the verb *mend* is *mended*, which might lead you to believe that *spended* is correct. Reading a variety of materials is the best way to develop an ear for proper usage.

46. A: The word *amount* correctly completes this sentence. This question centers on the distinction between *amount* and *number*. An *amount* is a quantity that cannot be counted, while a *number* is a quantity that can be counted. There is no way to count pain, so *amount* is a better word choice than *number*. *Frequency* is rate of occurrence, or how often something happens. If a doctor asks how often a patient gets a migraine, for instance, she is asking about the *frequency* of the headaches. *Amplitude* is the specific breadth or width. Amplitude is mainly used to describe waves; the difference in height between the top of a wave (crest) and the bottom (trough) is the amplitude.

47. C: The word *their* is used incorrectly in this sentence. The problem is that *whoever* as it is used here is a singular subject, while *their* is a plural possessive pronoun. *Whoever* can be either singular or plural, depending on how it is used. In this case, however, because the author is describing a letter writer who forgot to sign the letter, it seems clear that *whoever* is meant as a singular. For this reason, the author should use *his or her* instead of *their*.

48. C: The word *too* makes the sentence grammatically correct. Clearly, the author is trying to express that the child's fever was excessively high. Of the four answer choices, three convey this idea. Only answer choice A (the preposition *to*) can be immediately eliminated. The best way to find the final answer is to substitute each of the answer choices into the sentence and read the result. Answer choice B requires the addition of the word *too* to make any sense. Answer choice C, then, must be the correct answer.

49. B: The word *presents* makes the sentence grammatically correct. The author is referring to the symptoms that will be displayed when a patient has a particular condition: that is, the presentation of the condition. Because the subject of the sentence (*condition*) is singular, it is proper to use the verb form ending in an *s*. For this reason, you should select answer choice B rather than answer choice C. *Presence* is the quality of being there. When a teacher is calling roll and a student responds to his name by saying "present," he is using a form of this word to indicate that he is there. Of course, *present* can also mean a gift. *Prescience*, on the other hand, is foreknowledge, or knowledge ahead of time. You can exercise prescience by learning the content of the HESI exam and practicing with this study guide.

50. B: The preposition *among* is not used correctly in the context of the sentence. In this case, the word *between* would be more appropriate. *Among* and *between* both mean "in the midst of some other things." However, *between* is used when there are only two other things, and *among* is used

when there are more than two. For example, it would be correct to say "between first and second base" or "among several friends." In this sentence, the preposition *among* is inappropriate for describing placement amid "two treatment protocols."

Mathematics Answer Key and Explanations

1. A: The answer is 2512. To solve this problem, you must know how to add numbers with multiple digits. It may be easier for you to complete this problem if you align the numbers vertically. The crucial thing when setting up the vertical problem is to make sure that the place values are lined up correctly. In this problem, the larger number (2038) should be placed on top, such that the 8 is over the 4, the 3 is over the 7, and so on. Then add the place value farthest to the right. In this case, the 4 and the 8 that we find in the ones place have a sum of 12; the 2 is placed in the final sum, and the 1 is carried over to the next place value to the left, the tens. The tens place is the next to be added: 3 plus 7 equal 10, with the addition of the carried 1 making 11. Again, the first 1 is carried over to the next place value. The problem proceeds on in this vein.

2. C: The answer is 34,481. This problem requires you to understand addition of multiple-digit numbers. As in the first problem, the most important step is properly aligning the two addends in vertical formation, such that the final 8 in 32,788 is above the final 3 in 1693. Again, as in the first problem, you will be required to carry numbers over. It is a good idea to practice these addition problems and pay special attention to carrying over, since errors in this area can produce answers that look correct. The administrators of the HESI exam will sometimes try to take advantage of these common errors by making a couple of the wrong answers the results one would get by failing to carry over a digit.

3. B: The answer is 1854. To solve this problem, you must know how to subtract one multiple-digit number from another. As with the above addition problems, the most important step in this kind of problem is to set up the proper vertical alignment. In subtraction problems, the larger number must always be on top, and there can be only two terms in all (an addition problem can have an infinite number of terms). In this problem, the ones places should be aligned such that the 3 in 3703 is above the 9 in 1849. This problem also requires you to understand what to do when you have a larger value on the bottom of a subtraction problem. In this case, the 3 on the top of the ones place is smaller than the 9 beneath it, so it must borrow 1 from the number to its left. Unfortunately, there is a 0 to the left of the three, so we must extract a 1 from the next place over again. The 7 in 3703 becomes a 6, the 0 becomes a 10 only to have 1 taken away, leaving it as a 9. The 3 in the ones place becomes 13, from which we can now subtract the 9.

4. A: The answer is 1816. This problem requires you to understand subtraction with multiple-digit numbers. As in problem 3, the most important step is to align the problem vertically such that the 0 in 4790 is above the 4 in 2974. Again as in problem 3, you will have to borrow from the place value to the left when the number on the bottom is bigger than the number on top. Be sure to practice this kind of problem with special attention to borrowing from adjacent place values. The HESI exam will often include a few wrong answers that you could mistakenly derive by simply forgetting how to borrow.

5. C: The answer is 169,002. To solve this problem, you must know how to multiply numbers with several digits. These problems often intimidate students because they produce such large numbers, but they are actually quite simple. As with the above addition and subtraction problems, the crucial first step is to align the terms vertically such that the 8 in 738 is above the 9 in 229. In

multiplication, it is a good idea to put the larger number on top, although it is only essential to do so when one of the terms has more place values than the other. In a multiple-digit multiplication problem, every digit gets multiplied by every other digit: First the 9 in 229 is multiplied by the three digits in 738, moving from right to left. Only the digit in the ones place is brought down; the digit in the tens place is placed above the digit to the immediate left and added to the product of the next multiplication. In this problem, then, the 9 and 8 produce 72: The 2 is placed below, and the 7 is placed above the 3 in 738. Then the 9 and the 3 are multiplied and produce 27, to which the 7 is added, making 24. The 4 comes down, the 2 goes above the first 2 in 229, and the process continues. The product of 9 multiplied by 738 is placed below and is added to the products of 2 and 738 and 2 and 738, respectively. For each successive product, the first digit goes one place value to the left. So, in other words, 0 is placed under the 2. These three products are added together to calculate the final product of 738 and 229.

6. D: The answer is 287,648. This problem requires you to understand multiplication of numbers with several digits. The difficulties you may face with this problem are identical to those of problem 5. Be sure set up your vertical alignment properly, such that the 8 in 808 is above the 6 in 356. Multiply the 6 in 356 by 8, 0, and 8, proceeding from right to left. Then multiply the 5 in 356 by 8, 0, and 8; finally, multiply the 3 in 356 by 8. For each successive product, add one zero at the extreme right of the product. Add the three products together to find your final answer.

7. B: The answer is 62. To solve this problem, you must know how to divide a multiple-digit number by a single-digit number. To begin with, set up the problem as $7\overline{)435}$. Then determine the number of times that 7 will go into 43 (one way to do this is to multiply 7 by various numbers until you find a product that is either 43 exactly or no more than 6 fewer than 43). In this case, you will find that 7 goes into 43 six times. Place the 6 above the 3 in 435 and multiply the 6 by 7. The product, 42, should be subtracted from 43, leaving a difference of 1. Since 7 cannot go into 1, bring down the 5 to create 15. The 7 will go into 15 twice, so place a 2 to the right of the 6 on top of the problem. At this point, you should recognize that only answer choice B can be correct. If you proceed further, however, you will find that 435 must become 435.0 so that the 0 can be brought down to make a large enough number to be divided by 7. Once a decimal point is introduced to the dividend, a decimal point must be placed directly above it in the quotient. If you continue working this problem, you will end up with an answer of 62.14 ... Note that the instructions tell you only to round to the nearest whole number. Once you have solved to the tenths place, there is no need to continue.

8. C: The answer is 396. To solve this problem, you must understand division involving multiple-digit numbers. To begin with, set up the problem as $12\overline{)4,748}$. Then solve the problem according to the procedure you followed in problem 7. Since you are asked to round to the nearest whole number, you must solve this problem to the tenths place. If your calculations are correct, you will have a 6 in the tenths place, meaning that the answer should be rounded up from 395 to 396.

9. A: The answer is 14.989. To solve this problem, you must know how to add a series of numbers when some of the numbers include decimals. As with addition problems 1 and 2, the most important first step is to set up the proper vertical alignment. This step is even more important when working with decimals. Be sure that all of the decimal points are in alignment; in other words, the 7 in 3.7 should be above the 2 in 7.289. Since the final term, 4, is a whole number, we assume a 0 in the tenths place. Similarly, you may assume zeros in the hundredths and thousandths places, if you prefer to have a digit in every relevant place. Then beginning at the rightmost place value (in

this case, the thousandths), add the terms together as you would with whole numbers. The decimal point of the sum should be aligned with the decimal points of the terms.

10. A: The answer is 21.114. This problem requires you to understand addition involving a series of numbers, some of which include decimals. This problem is solved in the same manner as problem 9. Be sure to align the terms correctly, such that the 9 in 4.934 is above the 1 in 7.1 and the 0 in 9.08. Assume zeros for the hundredths and thousandths place of 7.1 and for the thousandths place of 9.08. The usual rules for carrying in addition still apply when working with decimals.

11. B: The answer is 23.46. To solve this problem, you must know how to subtract a number with a decimal from a whole number. At first glance, this problem seems complex, but it is actually quite simple once you set it up in a vertical form. Remember that the decimal point must remain aligned and that a decimal point can be assumed after the 7 in 27. In order to solve this problem, you should assume zeros for the tenths and hundredths places of 27. The problem is solved as 27.00 – 3.54. Obviously, in order to solve this problem you will have to borrow from the 7 in 27.00. The normal rules for borrowing in subtraction still apply when working with decimals. Be sure to keep the decimal point of the difference aligned with the decimal points of the terms.

12. D: The answer is 19.19. This problem requires you to understand subtraction of a whole number from a number with a decimal. This problem is somewhat similar to problem 11, although here the decimal is on the top in your vertical alignment. Assume zeros for the tenths and hundredths place of the bottom term, creating the problem 28.19 – 9.00. Be sure to keep your decimal point in the same position in the difference as in the terms. HESI exam administrators often try to fool test-takers by including some possible answers that have the correct digits, but in which the decimal point is misplaced.

13. B: The answer is $31.90. To solve this problem, you must know how to solve word problems involving decimal subtraction. In this scenario, Karen starts out with a certain amount of money and spends some of it on groceries. To calculate how much money she has left, simply subtract the money spent from the original figure: 40 – 1.85 – 3.20 – 3.05. There is no reason to include the dollar sign in your calculations, so long as you remember that it exists. You cannot subtract the costs of these items at the same time, so you must either subtract them one by one or add them up and subtract the sum from 40. Either way will generate the right answer.

14. C: The answer is 24.5. This problem requires you to understand multiplication including numbers with decimals. In some ways, multiplying decimals is easier than adding or subtracting them. This is because the decimal points can be ignored until the very end of the process. Simply set this problem up such that the longer term, 277.9, is on top (this term is considered longer because the initial 0 in 0.088 performs no function). Then multiply according to the usual system: Multiply the rightmost 8 by 9, 7, 7, and 2, and then do the same for the next 8. Add the two products together. Finally, count up the number of decimal places to the right of the decimal point in both terms. In this problem, there are four: 0.088 and 277.9. This means that there should be four places to the right of the decimal point in the product. Once the product is found, you must round it to the tenths place. This is done by assessing the digit in the place to the right of the tenths place (that is, the hundredths place). If that digit is lower than 5, round down; if it is 5 or greater, round up. In this case, there is a 5 in the hundredths place, so the 4 in the tenths place becomes a 5.

15. A: The answer is 46.67. To solve this problem, you must know how to divide a whole number by a decimal. To begin with, set the problem up in the form $0.6\overline{)28}$. You cannot perform division when

the divisor is less than one, however, so shift the decimal point one place to the right. For every action in the divisor, an identical action must be taken in the dividend: Shift the decimal point (which can be assumed after the 8 in 28) in the dividend as well. The problem is now $6 \overline{)280}$. This problem can now be solved just like problems 7 and 8. Remember to round your answer to the hundredths place for this problem (this means you will need to solve to the thousandths place). With a knowledge of place value, you can immediately eliminate answer choices B and D, since they are solved to the nearest thousandth and tenth place, respectively.

16. D: The answer is 400 miles. This problem requires you to understand word problems involving mileage rates and multiplication. The problem states that the car gets an average 25 miles per gallon; in other words, every gallon of fuel powers the car for approximately 25 miles. If the car holds 16 gallons of gas, then, and each of these gallons provides 25 miles of travel, you can set up the following equation: 25 miles/gallon × 16 gallons = 400 miles. Since the first term has gallons in the denominator and the second term has gallons in what would be the numerator (if it were expressed as 16 gallons/1), these units cancel each other out and leave only miles.

17. C: The answer is $\frac{5}{8}$. To solve this problem, you must know how to add fractions with like denominators. This kind of operation is actually quite simple. The denominator of the sum remains the same; the calculation is performed by adding the numerators. On problems like this, HESI exam administrators will probably try to fool you by including one possible answer in which the denominators have been added; in this problem, for instance, you would end up with answer choice D if you added both numerator and denominator. Do not assume that you have answered the question correctly because your calculations match one of the answer choices. Always check your work.

18. A: The answer is $\frac{20}{21}$. This problem requires you to understand addition of fractions with unlike denominators. The denominator is the bottom term in a fraction; the top term is called the numerator. In order to perform addition with a fraction, all of the terms must have the same denominator. In order to derive the lowest common denominator in this problem, you must list the multiples for 3 and 7 until you find one that both have in common. In increasing order, multiples of 3 are 3, 6, 9, 12, 15, 18, and 21; multiples of 7 are 7, 14, and 21. The lowest common multiple is 21. This is also the lowest common denominator for the two fractions. To convert each term into a fraction with this common denominator, you must multiply both numerator and denominator by the same number. To make the denominator of $\frac{2}{3}$ into 21, you must multiply by 7; therefore, you must also multiply the numerator, 2, by 7. The new fraction is $\frac{14}{21}$. For the second term, you must multiply numerator and denominator by 3: $\frac{2}{7} \times \frac{3}{3} = \frac{6}{21}$. The new addition problem is $\frac{14}{21} + \frac{6}{21}$. Remember that when adding fractions, only the numerators are combined.

19. D: The answer is $2\frac{5}{6}$. To solve this problem, you must know how to add mixed numbers and improper fractions. To begin with, convert the mixed number (a mixed number includes a whole number and a fraction) into an improper fraction (a fraction in which the numerator is larger than

the denominator). This is done by multiplying the whole number by the denominator and adding the product to the numerator: 1 × 2 + 1 = 3. The problem is now $\frac{3}{2}+\frac{12}{9}$. Then find the lowest common denominator by listing some multiples of 2 and 9. The lowest common multiple is 18, so you must convert both terms: $\frac{3}{2}\times\frac{9}{9}=\frac{27}{18}$, and $\frac{12}{9}\times\frac{2}{2}=\frac{24}{18}$. The problem is now $\frac{27}{18}+\frac{24}{18}=\frac{51}{18}$. This fraction is converted into a mixed number by dividing the numerator by the denominator: $\frac{51}{18}=2\frac{15}{18}$, which can be simplified to $2\frac{5}{6}$ by dividing both numerator and denominator by 3.

20. D: The answer is $13\frac{11}{12}$. This problem requires you to understand addition involving mixed numbers. The calculation required by this problem is straightforward: In order to derive the number of hours worked by Aaron, add up the three mixed numbers. To make this possible, you will need to find the lowest common multiple of 2, 4, and 3, so that you can establish a common denominator. The lowest common denominator for this problem is 12. You can either add up the whole numbers separately from the fractions or convert the mixed numbers into improper fractions and add them in that form. Either way will yield the correct answer.

21. B: The answer is $\frac{1}{2}$. To solve this problem, you must understand subtraction involving fractions with like denominators. As with addition involving fractions with like denominators, you should only subtract the numerators. So, this problem is solved $\frac{23}{24}-\frac{11}{24}=\frac{12}{24}$. This answer can be simplified by dividing by the greatest common factor (a factor is any number that can be divided into the given number equally). The factors of 12 are 1, 2, 3, 4, 6, and 12. The factors of 24 are 1, 2, 3, 4, 6, 8, 12, and 24. The greatest common factor of 12 and 24, then, is 12. Divide both numerator and denominator by 12 to derive the answer in simplest form: $(\frac{12}{12})/(\frac{24}{12})=\frac{1}{2}$.

22. C: The answer is $1\frac{5}{14}$. This problem requires you to understand subtraction with mixed numbers. In order to perform this problem, you must convert these mixed numbers into improper fractions with the same denominator. Remember that mixed numbers are converted into improper fractions by multiplying the denominator by the whole number and adding the product to the numerator: $3\frac{4}{7}$ becomes $\frac{25}{7}$, and $2\frac{3}{14}$ becomes $\frac{31}{14}$. Next, find the lowest common denominator by listing multiples of 7 and 14. Since 14 is a multiple of 7, you only have to alter the first term. Multiply both numerator and denominator by 2: $\frac{25}{7}\times\frac{2}{2}=\frac{50}{14}$. The problem is now $\frac{50}{14}-\frac{31}{14}=\frac{19}{14}$. Convert this improper fraction into a mixed number by dividing the numerator by the denominator: $\frac{19}{14}=1\frac{5}{14}$. The mixed number cannot be simplified further.

23. C: The answer is $\frac{1}{2}$. To solve this problem, you must know how to solve word problems requiring fraction addition and subtraction. You are given the proportions of Dean's socks that are white and black. The best approach to this problem is adding together the two known quantities and subtracting the sum from 1. First you need to find a common denominator for $\frac{1}{3}$ and $\frac{1}{6}$. The lowest common multiple of these two numbers is 6, so convert $\frac{1}{3}$ by multiplying the numerator and denominator by 2. The new equation will be $\frac{2}{6} + \frac{1}{6} = \frac{3}{6}$. This sum is equivalent to $\frac{1}{2}$, meaning that half of Dean's socks are either white or black. The other half, then, are brown. If you need to perform the calculation, however, it will look like this: $\frac{2}{2} - \frac{1}{2} = \frac{1}{2}$.

24. A: The answer is $11\frac{2}{3}$. This problem requires you to understand word problems involving the addition and multiplication of mixed numbers and improper fractions. To begin with, convert the three mixed numbers to improper fractions by multiplying the whole number by the denominator and adding the product to the numerator. The resulting fractions will be $\frac{3}{2}$ (sugar), $\frac{11}{3}$ (flour), and $\frac{2}{3}$ (milk). Then find the lowest common multiple of 2 and 3 which is 6 and convert the three fractions so that they have this denominator: $\frac{9}{6}$ (sugar), $\frac{22}{6}$ (flour), and $\frac{4}{6}$ (milk). Add these fractions together and multiply the sum by two to double the recipe: $\frac{9}{6} + \frac{22}{6} + \frac{4}{6} = \frac{35}{6} \times 2 = \frac{70}{6}$. Finally, convert this improper fraction to a simple mixed number by dividing numerator by denominator and simplifying the leftover fraction: $\frac{70}{6} = 11\frac{4}{6} = 11\frac{2}{3}$.

25. D: The answer is $1\frac{5}{21}$. To solve this problem, you must know how to multiply mixed numbers and fractions. Unlike fraction addition and subtraction, fraction multiplication does not require a common denominator. However, it is necessary to convert mixed numbers into improper fractions. This is done by multiplying the whole number by the denominator and adding the product to the numerator: in this case, 4 × 3 + 1 = 13. So the problem is now $\frac{13}{3} \times \frac{2}{7}$. Fraction multiplication is performed by multiplying numerator by numerator and denominator by denominator: (13 × 2)/(3 × 7) = $\frac{26}{21}$. This improper fraction can be converted into a mixed number by dividing numerator by denominator, which gives $1\frac{5}{21}$. Note that since 26 and 21 have no common factors other than 1, the improper fraction cannot be simplified.

26. D: The answer is $\frac{7}{9}$. This problem requires you to understand multiplication of mixed numbers and fractions. The process is the same as for the previous problem: Convert $2\frac{3}{9}$ into the mixed number $\frac{21}{9}$ (if you like, you can simplify this fraction by dividing top and bottom by 3). Then multiply numerator by numerator and denominator by denominator. If you did not simplify the first fraction, you will have a product of $\frac{21}{27}$. This fraction can be simplified by dividing the numerator and denominator by 3: (21/3)/(27/3) = 7/9.

27. D: The answer is $3\frac{1}{8}$. To solve this problem, you must know how to divide fractions. The process of dividing fractions is similar to that of multiplying fractions, except that the second term must be inverted. Once this is done, the numerator is multiplied by the numerator, and the denominator is multiplied by the denominator. The inversion of a number is also known as the reciprocal. So, in this problem, solve by multiplying $\frac{5}{8}$ by the reciprocal of $\frac{1}{5}$, which is $\frac{5}{1}$ (finding the reciprocal of a fraction simply means switching the numerator with the denominator). The problem is solved as (5 × 5)/(8 × 1) = $\frac{25}{8}$. Convert this improper fraction into a mixed number according to the usual procedure.

28. D: The answer is $1\frac{5}{7}$. This problem requires you to understand how to divide fractions. The procedure is the same as for the previous problem: Invert the second term and change the problem to one of multiplication: 2/7 × 6/1 = $\frac{12}{7}$. Convert this improper fraction into a mixed number according to the usual procedure. The fraction cannot be simplified because 12 and 7 do not share any factors other than 1.

29. B: The answer is 78. To solve this problem, you must know how to convert a fraction into a ratio. In this problem, you are being asked to convert the fraction into a value on a scale from 1 to 100, which is basically like being asked to convert it into a percentage. To do so, divide the numerator by the denominator. The answer will be a repeating seven: $0.7\overline{777}$. Calculate to the thousandth place in order to determine the value. Because the digit in the thousandths place is a 7, you will round up the digit to the left to establish the final answer, 78.

30. A: The answer is 0.88. This problem requires you to understand the conversion of fractions to decimals. The process is fairly simple: Divide the numerator by the denominator. In order to make this possible, you will have to write 7 as 7.0. The resulting quotient will be 0.875. Remember that the instructions require you to round to the nearest hundredths place. The digit in the thousandths place will be 5, meaning that you need to round up. The final answer is 0.88.

31. B: The answer is 4.43. To solve this problem, you must know how to convert mixed numbers into decimals. Perhaps the easiest way to perform this operation is to convert the mixed number into an improper fraction and then divide the numerator by the denominator. Convert the mixed number into an improper fraction by multiplying the whole number by the denominator and adding the product to the numerator: 4 × 7 + 3 = 31, so the improper fraction is $\frac{31}{7}$. Next divide 31 by 7, according to the same procedure used in problems 7 and 8. Remember that when you have to add 0 to 31 in order to continue your calculations, you must put a decimal point directly above in the quotient. Also, since the problem asks you to round to the hundredths place, you must solve the problem to the nearest thousandth.

32. C: The answer is $3\frac{39}{50}$. This problem requires you to understand the conversion of decimals into mixed numbers. 3.78 has value into the hundredths place, so your fraction will have a denominator of 100. There are three whole units and seventy-eight hundredths, a mixed number that can be written as $3\frac{78}{100}$. Next, you must simplify this fraction. The only common factor of 78 and 100 is 2; divide both numerator and denominator by 2 to derive the answer, $3\frac{39}{50}$. This fraction cannot be simplified any further.

33. C: The answer is $\frac{7}{100}$. To solve this problem, you must know how to convert decimals into fractions. Remember that all of the numbers to the right of a decimal point represent values less than one. So, a decimal number such as this will not include any whole numbers when it is converted into a fraction. The 7 is in the hundredths place, so the number is properly expressed as $\frac{7}{100}$. The fraction cannot be simplified because 7 and 100 do not share any factors besides one.

34. D: The answer is $2\frac{4}{5}$. This problem requires you to understand how to convert a decimal into a fraction or, in this case, a mixed number. Because there are values to the left of the decimal point, you can tell that this number will be equivalent to a mixed number. Indeed, the number 2.80 is equivalent to $2\frac{80}{100}$. Next, list the factors of 80 (1, 2, 4, 5, 8, 10, 16, 20, 40, 80) and 100 (1, 2, 4, 5, 10, 20, 25, 50, 100). The greatest common factor is 20, so divide both numerator and denominator by 20 to derive the simplest form of the fraction, $2\frac{4}{5}$.

35. D: The answer is 4:7. To solve this problem, you must know how to convert fractions into ratios. A ratio expresses the relationship between two numbers. For instance, the ratio 2:3 suggests that for every 2 of one thing, there will be 3 of the other. If we applied this ratio to the length and width of a rectangle, for instance, we would be saying that for every 2 units of length, the rectangle must have 3 units of width. A fraction is just one way to express a ratio: The fraction $\frac{8}{14}$ is equivalent to

the ratio 8:14. To simplify the ratio, divide both sides by the greatest common factor, 2. The simplest form of this ratio is 4:7.

36. B: The answer is 9. This problem requires you to understand how to approach word problems involving fractions and ratios. You are given the total number of students in the class and the fraction of students who are boys: With this information, you can determine the number of boys by multiplying $\frac{2}{3}$ by 27. You will find that there are 18 boys in the class. You can then find the number of girls by subtracting the number of boys from the total number of students: 27 − 18 = 9. There are nine girls in the class.

37. A: The answer is 16. To solve this problem, you must understand proportions. A proportion is a comparison between two or more equivalent ratios. A simple proportion is 1:2 :: 2:4, which can be expressed in words as "1 is to 2 as 2 is to 4." Just as 2 is twice 1, 4 is twice 2. Problem 37 asks you to identify a missing term in a proportion. One way to do this is to set up the problem as a set of equivalent fractions and solve for the variable: $\frac{3}{2} = \frac{24}{x}$. To solve this equation, cross-multiply. You will end up with 3x = 48. To find the value of x, divide both sides by 3.

38. C: The answer is 24. This problem requires you to understand proportions. You can use the same procedure to solve this problem as you used to solve problem 37. Set up the proportion in the same way as a pair of equivalent fractions: $\frac{7}{42} = \frac{4}{x}$. Then solve for x. To do this, you must cross-multiply (producing 7x = 168), and then divide both sides by 7. Your calculations should determine that x = 24.

39. B: The answer is 64%. To solve this problem, you must know how to convert a decimal into a percent. A percentage is a number expressed in terms of hundredths. When we say, for instance, that a candidate received 55% of the vote, we mean that she received 55 out of every 100 votes cast. When we say that the sales tax is 6%, we mean that for every 100 cents in the price another 6 cents are added to the final cost. To convert a decimal into a percentage, multiply it by 100 or just shift the decimal point two places to the right. In this case, by moving the decimal point two places to the right you can derive the correct answer, 64%.

40. A: The answer is 0.0026%. This problem requires you to understand the conversion of decimals into percentages. Remember that percent is equivalent to quantity out of a hundred; 75%, for instance, is 75 out of 100. To convert a decimal into a percentage, then, multiply the given decimal by 100. A simple way to perform this calculation is to shift the decimal point two places to the right. So for this problem, 0.000026 is equivalent to 0.0026%.

41. D: The answer is 0.38. To solve this problem, you must know how to convert percentages into decimals. This is done by shifting the decimal point two places to the right. This operation is the same as dividing the percentage by 100. In this problem, assume that the decimal is after the eight in 38%. The equivalent decimal, then, is 0.38.

42. C: The answer is 0.176. This problem requires you to understand the conversion of percentages into decimals. A percentage is an amount out of 100; 17.6%, then, is equivalent to 17.6 out of 100,

or $\frac{17.6}{100}$. A percentage can be converted into decimal form by dividing it by 100, or, more simply, by shifting the decimal point two places to the left. Therefore, 17.6% is equivalent to 0.176.

43. D: The answer is 1.26. To solve this problem, you must know how to convert percentages into decimals. Remember that a percentage is really just an expression of a value in terms of hundredths. That is, 25% is the same as 25 out of 100. To convert a percentage into a decimal, shift the decimal point two places to the left. In this case, the decimal point is assumed to be after the six in 126%. By shifting the decimal point two places to the left, you find that the equivalent decimal is 1.26.

44. C: The answer is 22%. This problem requires you to understand how to convert fractions into percentages. To do so, divide the numerator by the denominator. This requires placing a decimal point and 0 after the 2. Remember that the instructions ask you to round your quotient to the nearest whole number. The quotient will be an endlessly repeating 0.2, which means that you will round down to 22%. You only need to solve this equation to the thousandths place in order to obtain sufficient information to answer the question.

45. B: The answer is 69%. To solve this problem, you must know how to convert fractions into percentages. This is done by dividing the numerator by the denominator. In this case, the problem is set up as $13\overline{)9.0}$, because a decimal point and 0 are required to make the calculation possible.

Although the decimal point is there, you should still treat 9.0 as if it were 90 when performing your division. Since 13 will go into 90 six times, you can place a 6 above the 0 in 9.0. Remember that your quotient will have a decimal point in the identical place; that is, directly to the left of the 6. If you continue your calculations, you will derive an answer of 0.692... However, once you derive that first 6, you should be able to select the correct answer choice. Remember that percentage is the same as hundredths; in other words, 69% is the same as sixty-nine hundredths.

46. B: The answer is 25%. This problem requires you to understand how to convert fractions into percentages. One way to make this conversion is to divide 17 by 68, which will create a decimal quotient, and then convert this decimal into a percentage. The procedure for division is the same as was used in problem 45; simply divide the numerator (17) by the denominator (68). In order to do so, you will have to express 17 as 17.0. Take the resulting quotient, 0.25, and convert it into a percentage by multiplying it by a hundred or simply shifting the decimal point two places to the right. Of course, you may skip this last step if your quotient makes the right answer apparent. In this problem, for instance, a quotient of 0.25 suggests that only answer choice B can be correct.

47. C: The answer is 59%. To solve this problem, you must know how to convert a fraction into a percentage. Gerald made 13 out of 22 shots, a performance that can also be expressed by the fraction 13/22. To convert this fraction into a percentage, divide the numerator by the denominator: $22\overline{)13}$. Once you derive the initial 5 in the quotient, you can be fairly certain that answer choice C is correct. Whenever possible, try to take these kinds of shortcuts to save yourself some time. Although the HESI exam gives you plenty of time to complete all of the questions, by saving a little time here and there you can give yourself more opportunities to work through the harder problems.

48. A: The answer is 108. This problem requires you to understand how to find equivalencies involving percentages. One way to solve this problem is to set up the equation $\frac{18}{100} = \frac{x}{600}$. In words, this equation states that 18 out of 100 is equal to some unknown amount out of 600. The first step in solving such an equation is to cross-multiply; in other words, 18 × 600 = 100x. This produces 10,800 = 100x, a problem that can be solved for x by dividing both sides by 100. This calculation shows that x = 108, meaning that 108 is 18% of 600.

49. D: The answer is 2.0. To solve this problem, you must know how to find equivalencies involving percentages. This problem can be solved with the same strategy used in problem 48. To begin with, set up the following equation: $\frac{6.4}{100} = \frac{x}{32}$. Next cross-multiply: 6.4 × 32 = 100x. This produces 204.8 = 100x, which is solved for x by dividing both sides of the equation by 100. The value of x is 2.048, which is rounded to 2.0.

50. B: The answer is 17. This problem requires you to know about Roman numerals. This system of numeration is still used in a number of professional contexts. The Roman numerals are as follows: I (1), V (5), X (10), L (50), C (100), D (500), and M (1000). You may also see the lowercase versions of these letters used. The order of the numerals is typically largest to smallest. However, when a smaller number is placed in front of a larger one, the smaller number is to be subtracted from the larger one that follows. For instance, the Roman numeral XIV is 14, as the 1 (I) is to be subtracted from the 5 (V). If the number had been written XVI, it would represent 16, as the 1 (I) is to be added to the 5 (V).

Biology Answer Key and Explanations

1. B: It is impossible for an *AaBb* organism to have the *aa* combination in the gametes. It is impossible for each letter to be used more than one time, so it would be impossible for the lowercase *a* to appear twice in the gametes. It would be possible, however, for *Aa* to appear in the gametes, since there is one uppercase *A* and one lowercase *a*. Gametes are the cells involved in sexual reproduction. They are germ cells.

2. A: The typical result of mitosis in humans is two diploid cells. *Mitosis* is the division of a body cell into two daughter cells. Each of the two produced cells has the same set of chromosomes as the parent. A diploid cell contains both sets of homologous chromosomes. A haploid cell contains only one set of chromosomes, which means that it only has a single set of genes. For the HESI exam, you will need to know about all the different stages of cell division for both human and plant cells.

3. B: Water stabilizes the temperature of living things. The ability of warm-blooded animals, including human beings, to maintain a constant internal temperature is known as *homeostasis*. Homeostasis depends on the presence of water in the body. Water tends to minimize changes in temperature because it takes a while to heat up or cool down. When the human body gets warm, the blood vessels dilate and blood moves away from the torso and toward the extremities. When the body gets cold, blood concentrates in the torso. This is the reason why hands and feet tend to get especially cold in cold weather. The HESI exam will require you to understand the basic processes of the human body.

4. B: Oxygen is not one of the products of the Krebs cycle. The *Krebs cycle* is the second stage of cellular respiration. In this stage, a sequence of reactions converts pyruvic acid into carbon dioxide.

This stage of cellular respiration produces the phosphate compounds that provide most of the energy for the cell. The Krebs cycle is also known as the citric acid cycle or the tricarboxylic acid cycle. The HESI exam may require you to know all stages of cellular respiration: the process in which a plant cell converts carbon dioxide into oxygen.

5. C: The sugar and phosphate in DNA are connected by covalent bonds. A *covalent bond* is formed when atoms share electrons. It is very common for atoms to share pairs of electrons. An *ionic bond* is created when one or more electrons are transferred between atoms. *Ionic bonds*, also known as *electrovalent bonds*, are formed between ions with opposite charges. There is no such thing as an *overt bond* in chemistry. The HESI exam will require you to understand and have some examples of these different types of bonds.

6. A: The second part of an organism's scientific name is its species. The system of naming species is called binomial nomenclature. The first name is the *genus*, and the second name is the *species*. In binomial nomenclature, species is the most specific designation. This system enables the same name to be used all around the world, so that scientists can communicate with one another. Genus and species are just two of the categories in biological classification, otherwise known as taxonomy. The levels of classification, from most general to most specific, are kingdom, phylum, class, order, family, genus, and species. As you can see, binomial nomenclature only includes the two most specific categories.

7. B: Unlike other organic molecules, lipids are not water soluble. Lipids are typically composed of carbon and hydrogen. Three common types of lipid are fats, waxes, and oils. Indeed, lipids usually feel oily when you touch them. All living cells are primarily composed of lipids, carbohydrates, and proteins. Some examples of fats are lard, corn oil, and butter. Some examples of waxes are beeswax and carnauba wax. Some examples of steroids are cholesterol and ergosterol.

8. D: *Hemoglobin* is not a steroid. It is a protein that helps to move oxygen from the lungs to the various body tissues. Steroids can be either synthetic chemicals used to reduce swelling and inflammation or sex hormones produced by the body. *Cholesterol* is the most abundant steroid in the human body. It is necessary for the creation of bile, though it can be dangerous if the levels in the body become too high. *Estrogen* is a female steroid produced by the ovaries (in females), testes (in males), placenta, and adrenal cortex. It contributes to adolescent sexual development, menstruation, mood, lactation, and aging. *Testosterone* is the main hormone produced by the testes; it is responsible for the development of adult male sex characteristics.

9. A: The property of cohesion is responsible for the passage of water through a plant. *Cohesion* is the attractive force between two molecules of the same substance. The water in the roots of the plant is drawn upward into the stem, leaves, and flowers by the presence of other water molecules. *Adhesion* is the attractive force between molecules of different substances. *Osmosis* is a process in which water diffuses through a selectively permeable membrane. *Evaporation* is the conversion of water from a liquid to a gas.

10. C: *Melatonin* is produced by the pineal gland. One of the primary functions of melatonin is regulation of the circadian cycle, which is the rhythm of sleep and wakefulness. *Insulin* helps regulate the amount of glucose in the blood. Without insulin, the body is unable to convert blood sugar into energy. *Testosterone* is the main hormone produced by the testes; it is responsible for the development of adult male sex characteristics. *Epinephrine*, also known as adrenaline, performs a number of functions: It quickens and strengthens the heartbeat and dilates the bronchioles. Epinephrine is one of the hormones secreted when the body senses danger.

11. C: *Ribosomes* are the organelles that organize protein synthesis. A ribosome, composed of RNA and protein, is a tiny structure responsible for putting proteins together. The *mitochondrion* converts chemical energy into a form that is more useful for the functions of the cell. The *nucleus* is the central structure of the cell. It contains the DNA and administrates the functions of the cell. The *vacuole* is a cell organelle in which useful materials (for example, carbohydrates, salts, water, and proteins) are stored.

12. D: During *meiosis I,* the chromosome number is reduced from diploid to haploid. *Interphase* is the period of the cell cycle that occurs in between divisions of the cell. In *meiosis*, the homologous chromosomes in a diploid cell separate, reducing the number of chromosomes in each cell by half. *Mitosis* is the phase of cell division in which the cell nucleus divides. *S phase* is the part of the mitotic cycle in which DNA is synthesized.

13. C: Prokaryotic cells do not contain a nucleus. A *prokaryote* is simply a single-celled organism without a nucleus. It is difficult to identify the structures of a prokaryotic cell, even with a microscope. These cells are usually shaped like a rod, a sphere, or a spiral. A *eukaryote* is an organism containing cells with nuclei. Bacterial cells are prokaryotes, but since there are other kinds of prokaryotes, *bacteria* cannot be the correct answer to this question. *Cancer* cells are malignant, atypical cells that reproduce to the detriment of the organism in which they are located.

14. A: *Phenotype* is the physical presentation of an organism's genes. In other words, the phenotype is the physical characteristics of the organism. Phenotype is often contrasted with *genotype*, the genetic makeup of an organism. The genotype of the organism is not visible in its presentation, although some of the characteristics encoded in the genes have to do with physical presentation. A *phylum* is a group of classes that are closely related. A *species* is a group of like organisms that are capable of breeding together and producing similar offspring.

15. A: Liquid is the densest form of water. Water can exist in three states, depending on temperature. Ranging from coldest to hottest, these states are solid, liquid, and gaseous—or ice, water, and steam. Water freezes at zero degrees Celsius. Although the solidity of ice might lead one to believe that it is the densest form of water, water actually expands about nine percent when it is frozen. This is the reason why ice will float in water. Steam is the least dense form of water.

16. B: *Interphase* is the longest phase in the life of a cell. Interphase occurs between cell divisions. *Prophase* is the initial stage of mitosis. It is also the longest stage. During prophase, the chromosomes become visible, and the centrioles divide and position themselves on either side of the nucleus. *Anaphase* is the third phase of mitosis, in which chromosome pairs divide and take up positions on opposing poles. *Metaphase* is the second stage of mitosis. In it, the chromosomes align themselves across the center of the cell.

17. A: Bacterial cells do not contain *mitochondria*. Bacteria are prokaryotes composed of single cells; their cell walls contain peptidoglycans. The functions normally performed in the mitochondria are performed in the cell membrane of the bacterial cell. *DNA* is the nucleic acid that contains the genetic information of the organism. It is in the shape of a double helix. DNA can reproduce itself and can synthesize RNA. A *vesicle* is a small cavity containing fluid. A *ribosome* is a tiny particle composed of RNA and protein, in which polypeptides are constructed.

18. B: *Hemoglobin* is a protein. Proteins contain carbon, nitrogen, oxygen, and hydrogen. These substances are required for the growth and repair of tissue and the formation of enzymes.

Hemoglobin is found in red blood cells and contains iron. It is responsible for carrying oxygen from the lungs to the various body tissues. *Adenosine triphosphate* (ATP) is a compound used by living organisms to store and use energy. *Estrogen* is a steroid hormone that stimulates the development of female sex characteristics. *Cellulose* is a complex carbohydrate that composes the better part of the cell wall.

19. D: Deoxyribonucleic acid (*DNA*) is not involved in translation. *Translation* is the process by which messenger RNA (*mRNA*) messages are decoded into polypeptide chains. Transfer RNA (*tRNA*) is a molecule that moves amino acids into the ribosomes during the synthesis of protein. Messenger RNA carries sets of instructions for the conversion of amino acids into proteins from the RNA to the other parts of the cell. *Ribosomes* are the tiny particles in the cell where proteins are put together. Ribosomes are composed of ribonucleic acid (RNA) and protein.

20. A: Water is required for cell diffusion. Diffusion is the movement of molecules from an area of high concentration to an area of lower concentration. This process takes place in the body in a number of different areas. For instance, nutrients diffuse from partially digested food through the walls of the intestine into the bloodstream. Similarly, oxygen that enters the lungs diffuses into the bloodstream through membranes at the end of the alveoli. In all these cases, the body has evolved special membranes that only allow certain materials through.

21. C: There are four different nucleotides in DNA. *Nucleotides* are monomers of nucleic acids, composed of five-carbon sugars, a phosphate group, and a nitrogenous base. Nucleotides make up both DNA and RNA. They are essential for the recording of an organism's genetic information, which guides the actions of the various cells of the body. Nucleotides are also a crucial component of adenosine triphosphate (ATP), one of the parts of DNA and a chemical that enables metabolism and muscle contractions.

22. B: *Red blood cells* do not have a nucleus. These cells are shaped a little like a doughnut, although the hole in the center is not quite open. The other three types of cell have a nucleus. *Platelets*, which are fragments of cells and are released by the bone marrow, contribute to blood clotting. *White blood cells*, otherwise known as leukocytes, help the body fight disease. A *phagocyte* is a cell that can entirely surround bacteria and other microorganisms. The two most common phagocytes are neutrophils and monocytes, both of which are white blood cells.

23. D: The *electron transport system* enacted during aerobic respiration requires oxygen. This is the last component of biological oxidation. *Osmosis* is the movement of fluid from an area of high concentration through a partially permeable membrane to an area of lower concentration. This process usually stops when the concentration is the same on either side of the membrane. *Glycolysis* is the initial step in the release of glucose energy. The *Krebs cycle* is the last phase of the process in which cells convert food into energy. It is during this stage that carbon dioxide is produced and hydrogen is extracted from molecules of carbon.

24. A: *Kingdom* is the largest, most expansive taxonomic category. A *genus* is a group of related species, which are capable of breeding and producing similar offspring. In binomial nomenclature, genus is the first name. An *order* is any group of similar families. A *phylum* is any group of closely related classes. The HESI exam requires you to know the name and relative specificity of each taxonomic category. They are listed here in order from most general to most specific: kingdom, phylum, class, order, family, genus, and species.

25. D: *Fission* is the process of a bacterial cell splitting into two new cells. Fission is a form of asexual reproduction in which an organism divides into two components; each of these two parts will develop into a distinct organism. The two cells, known as daughter cells, are identical. *Mitosis*, on the other hand, is the part of eukaryotic cell division in which the cell nucleus divides. In *meiosis*, the homologous chromosomes in a diploid cell separate, reducing the number of chromosomes in each cell by half. In *replication*, a cell creates duplicate copies of DNA.

Chemistry Answer Key and Explanations

1. A: Diffusion is fastest through gases. The next fastest medium for diffusion is liquid, followed by plasma, and then solids. In chemistry, diffusion is defined as the movement of matter by the random motions of molecules. In a gas or a liquid, the molecules are in perpetual motion. For instance, in a quantity of seemingly immobile air, molecules of nitrogen and oxygen are constantly bouncing off each other. There is even some miniscule degree of diffusion in solids, which rises in proportion to the temperature of the substance.

2. B: The oxidation number of the hydrogen in CaH_2 is –1. The oxidation number is the positive or negative charge of a monoatomic ion. In other words, the oxidation number is the numerical charge on an ion. An ion is a charged version of an element. Oxidation number is often referred to as oxidation state. Oxidation number is sometimes used to describe the number of electrons that must be added or removed from an atom in order to convert the atom to its elemental form.

3. A: Boron does not exist as a diatomic molecule. The other possible answer choices, fluorine, oxygen, and nitrogen, all exist as diatomic molecules. A diatomic molecule always appears in nature as a pair: The word *diatomic* means "having two atoms." With the exception of astatine, all of the halogens are diatomic. Chemistry students often use the mnemonic BrINClHOF (pronounced "brinkelhoff") to remember all of the diatomic elements: bromine, iodine, nitrogen, chlorine, hydrogen, oxygen, and fluorine. Note that not all of these diatomic elements are halogens.

4. D: Hydriodic acid is another name for aqueous HI. In an aqueous solution, the solvent is water. Hydriodic acid is a polyatomic ion, meaning that it is composed of two or more elements. When this solution has an increased amount of oxygen, the *-ate* suffix on the first word is converted to *-ic*. The HESI exam will require you to know the fundamentals of naming chemicals. This process can be quite complex, so you should carefully review this material before your exam.

5. C: CH could be an empirical formula. An empirical formula is the smallest expression of a chemical formula. To be empirical, a formula must be incapable of being reduced. For this reason, answer choices A, B, and D are incorrect, as they could all be reduced to a simpler form. Note that empirical formulas are not the same as compounds, which do not have to be irreducible. Two compounds can have the same empirical formula but different molecular formulas. The molecular formula is the actual number of atoms in the molecule.

6. A: A limiting reactant is entirely used up by the chemical reaction. Limiting reactants control the extent of the reaction and determine the quantity of the product. A reducing agent is a substance that reduces the amount of another substance by losing electrons. A reagent is any substance used in a chemical reaction. Some of the most common reagents in the laboratory are sodium hydroxide and hydrochloric acid. The behavior and properties of these substances are known, so they can be effectively used to produce predictable reactions in an experiment.

7. B: The horizontal rows of the periodic table are called periods. The vertical columns of the periodic table are known as groups or families. All of the elements in a group have similar properties. The relationships between the elements in each period are similar as you move from left to right. The periodic table was developed by Dmitri Mendeleev to organize the known elements according to their similarities. New elements can be added to the periodic table without necessitating a redesign.

8. C: The mass of 7.35 mol water is 132 grams. You should be able to find the mass of various chemical compounds when you are given the number of mols. The information required to perform this function is included on the periodic table. To solve this problem, find the molecular mass of water by finding the respective weights of hydrogen and oxygen. Remember that water contains two hydrogen molecules and one oxygen molecule. The molecular mass of hydrogen is roughly 1, and the molecular mass of oxygen is roughly 16. A molecule of water, then, has approximately 18 grams of mass. Multiply this by 7.35 mol, and you will obtain the answer 132.3, which is closest to answer choice C.

9. D: Of these orbitals, the last to fill is 6s. Orbitals fill in the following order: 1s, 2s, 2p, 3s, 3p, 4s, 3d, 4p, 5s, 4d, 5p, 6s, 4f, 5d, 6p, 7s, 5f, 6d, and 7p. The number is the orbital number, and the letter is the sublevel identification. Sublevel s has one orbital and can hold a maximum of two electrons. Sublevel p has three orbitals and can hold a maximum of six electrons. Sublevel d has five orbitals and can hold a maximum of 10 electrons. Sublevel f has seven orbitals and can hold a maximum of 14 electrons.

10. C: Nitrogen pentoxide is the name of the binary molecular compound NO_5. The format given in answer choice C is appropriate when dealing with two nonmetals. A prefix is used to denote the number of atoms of each element. Note that when there are seven atoms of a given element, the prefix *hepta-* is used instead of the usual *septa-*. Also, when the first atom in this kind of binary molecular compound is single, it does not need to be given the prefix *mono-*.

11. D: The mass of 1.0 mol oxygen gas is 32 grams. The molar mass of oxygen can be obtained from the periodic table. In most versions of the table, the molar mass of the element is directly beneath the full name of the element. There is a little trick to this question. Oxygen is a diatomic molecule, which means that it always appears in pairs. In order to determine the mass in grams of 1.0 mol of oxygen gas, then, you must double the molar mass. The listed mass is 16, so the correct answer to the problem is 32.

12. D: Gamma radiation has no charge. This form of electromagnetic radiation can travel a long distance and can penetrate the human body. Sunlight and radio waves are both examples of gamma radiation. Alpha radiation has a 2+ charge. It only travels short distances and cannot penetrate clothing or skin. Radium and uranium both emit alpha radiation. Beta radiation has a 1– charge. It can travel several feet through the air and is capable of penetrating the skin. This kind of radiation can be damaging to health over a long period of exposure. There is no such thing as delta radiation.

13. A: When forward and reverse chemical reactions are taking place at the same rate, a chemical reaction has achieved equilibrium. This means that the respective concentrations of reactants and products do not change over time. In theory, a chemical reaction will remain in equilibrium indefinitely. One of the common tasks in the chemistry lab is to find the equilibrium constant (or set of relative concentrations that result in equilibrium) for a given reaction. In thermal equilibrium, there is no net heat exchange between a body and its surroundings. In dynamic equilibrium, any motion in one direction is offset by an equal motion in the other direction.

14. B: 119°K is equivalent to −154 degrees Celsius. It is likely that you will have to perform at least one temperature conversion on the HESI exam. To convert degrees Kelvin to degrees Celsius, simply subtract 273. To convert degrees Celsius to degrees Kelvin, simply add 273. To convert degrees Kelvin into degrees Fahrenheit, multiply by 9/5 and subtract 460. To convert degrees Fahrenheit to degrees Kelvin, add 460 and then multiply by 5/9. To convert degrees Celsius to degrees Fahrenheit, multiply by 9/5 and then add 32. To convert degrees Fahrenheit to degrees Celsius, subtract 32 and then multiply by 5/9.

15. B: The *joule* is the SI unit of energy. Energy is the ability to do work or generate heat. In regard to electrical energy, a joule is the amount of electrical energy required to pass a current of one ampere through a resistance of one ohm for one second. In physical or mechanical terms, the joule is the amount of energy required for a force of one newton to act over a distance of one meter. The *ohm* is a unit of electrical resistance. The *henry* is a unit of inductance. The *newton* is a unit of force.

16. A: A *mass spectrometer* separates gaseous ions according to their mass-to-charge ratio. This machine is used to distinguish the various elements in a piece of matter. An *interferometer* measures the wavelength of light by comparing the interference phenomena of two waves: an experimental wave and a reference wave. A *magnetometer* measures the direction and magnitude of a magnetic field. Finally, a *capacitance meter* measures the capacitance of a capacitor. Some sophisticated capacitance meters may also measure inductance, leakage, and equivalent series resistance.

17. C: Of the given materials, aluminum has the smallest specific heat. The specific heat of a substance is the amount of heat required to raise the temperature of one gram of the substance by one degree Celsius. In some cases, specific heat is expressed as a ratio of the heat required to raise the temperature of one gram of a substance by one degree Celsius to the heat required to raise the temperature of one gram of water by one degree Celsius.

18. C: In a *redox* reaction, also known as an oxidation-reduction reaction, electrons are transferred from one atom to another. A redox reaction changes the oxidation numbers of the atoms. In a *combustion* reaction, one material combines with an oxidizer to form a product and generate heat. In a *synthesis* reaction, multiple chemicals are combined to create a more complex product. In a *double-displacement* reaction, two chemical compounds trade bonds or ions and create two different compounds. Other common chemical reactions you may need to know for the HESI exam are the acid-base reaction, analysis reaction, single-displacement reaction, isomerization reaction, and hydrolysis reaction.

19. A: van der Waals forces are the weak forces of attraction between two molecules. The van der Waals force is considered to be any of the attractive or repulsive forces between electrons that are not related to electrostatic interaction or covalent bonds. Compared to other chemical bonds, the strength of van der Waals forces is small. However, these forces have a great effect on a substance's solubility and other characteristics. The HESI exam may require you to demonstrate knowledge of all the major chemical forces.

20. D: Of the given gases, H_2 effuses the fastest. It has the smallest molecular weight, and it is therefore capable of moving faster than the molecules represented by the other answer choices. In chemistry, effusion is defined as the flow of a gas through a small opening. The rate of effusion of a substance is inversely proportional to the square root of the density of the substance. This means

that the less dense a substance is, the faster it will effuse. This agrees with the common observation that thick smoke tends to linger in the same form for a longer period than thin smoke or steam.

21. B: Carbon is not involved in many hydrogen bonds. A hydrogen bond occurs when an atom of hydrogen that has a covalent bond with an electronegative atom forms a bond with a third atom. The original covalent bond involving hydrogen gives away protons, and the third element receives them. One of the reasons that fluorine, oxygen, and nitrogen are frequently part of a hydrogen bond is that they have a strong electronegativity and are therefore able to form more durable bonds. Chlorine is another element frequently involved in hydrogen bonds.

22. D: The mass of 0.350 mol copper is 22.2 grams. This problem requires the use of the periodic table. There you will see that the molecular mass of copper is approximately 63.5. Take this figure and multiply it by the amount of copper given by the question: 0.350 mol. The resulting figure is 22.225, which, rounded to the nearest tenth, is 22.2 grams. In order to succeed on the HESI exam, you will need to be able to perform these simple calculations of mass.

23. A: There are five d orbitals in a d subshell (or sublevel). Each of these orbitals can hold two electrons, so sublevel d is capable of holding 10 electrons. The s subshell has one orbital, the p subshell has three orbitals, the d subshell has five orbitals, and the f subshell has seven orbitals. In chemistry, the electron configuration of an atom is expressed in the following form, using helium as an example: $1s^2$. In this notation, the 1 indicates that the electrons are found in the first energy level of the atom, the s indicates that the electrons are in a spherical orbit, and the superscript 2 indicates that there are 2 total electrons in the first energy level subshell.

24. D: The number of protons in an atom is the atomic number. Protons are the fundamental positive unit of an atom. They are located in the nucleus. In a neutral atom (an atom with neither positive nor negative charge), the number of protons in the nucleus is equal to the number of electrons orbiting the nucleus. When it needs to be expressed, atomic number is written as a subscript in front of the element's symbol, for example in $_{13}Al$. Atomic mass, meanwhile, is the average mass of the various isotopes of a given element. Atomic identity and atomic weight are not concepts in chemistry.

25. B: Rubidium is an alkali metal. The alkali metals are located in group 1 of the periodic table. These soft substances melt at a low temperature and are typically white in color. The alkali metals are lithium, sodium, potassium, rubidium, cesium, and francium. Rubidium, cesium, and francium are not commonly encountered in the natural world. The alkali metals are highly reactive, meaning that they easily engage in chemical reactions when combined with other elements. These metals have a low density and tend to react violently with water.

Anatomy and Physiology Answer Key and Explanations

1. D: The epiglottis covers the trachea during swallowing, thus preventing food from entering the airway. The trachea, also known as the windpipe, is a cylindrical portion of the respiratory tract that joins the larynx with the lungs. The esophagus connects the throat and the stomach. When a person swallows, the esophagus contracts to force the food down into the stomach. Like other structures in the respiratory system, the esophagus secretes mucus for lubrication.

2. B: The pads that support the vertebrae are made up of cartilage. Cartilage, a strong form of connective tissue, cushions and supports the joints. Cartilage also makes up the larynx and the

outer ear. Bone is a form of connective tissue that comprises the better part of the skeleton. It includes both organic and inorganic substances. Tendons connect the muscles to other structures of the body, typically bones. Tendons can increase and decrease in length as the bones move. Fat is a combination of lipids; in humans, fat forms a layer beneath the skin and on the outside of the internal organs.

3. A: There are four different types of tissue in the human body: epithelial, connective, muscle, and nerve. *Epithelial* tissue lines the internal and external surfaces of the body. It is like a sheet, consisting of squamous, cuboidal, and columnar cells. They can expand and contract, like on the inner lining of the bladder. *Connective* tissue provides the structure of the body, as well as the links between various body parts. Tendons, ligaments, cartilage, and bone are all examples of connective tissue. *Muscle* tissue is composed of tiny fibers, which contract to move the skeleton. There are three types of muscle tissue: smooth, cardiac, and skeletal. *Nerve* tissue makes up the nervous system; it is composed of nerve cells, nerve fibers, neuroglia, and dendrites.

4. B: The epidermis is the outermost layer of skin. The thickness of this layer of skin varies over different parts of the body. For instance, the epidermis on the eyelids is very thin, while the epidermis over the soles of the feet is much thicker. The dermis lies directly beneath the epidermis. It is composed of collagen, elastic tissue, and reticular fibers. Beneath the dermis lies the subcutaneous tissue, which consists of fat, blood vessels, and nerves. The subcutaneous tissue contributes to the regulation of body temperature. The hypodermis is the layer of cells underneath the dermis; it is generally considered to be a part of the subcutaneous tissue.

5. C: *Prolactin* stimulates the production of breast milk during lactation. *Norepinephrine* is a hormone and neurotransmitter secreted by the adrenal gland that regulates heart rate, blood pressure, and blood sugar. *Antidiuretic hormone* is produced by the hypothalamus and secreted by the pituitary gland. It regulates the concentration of urine and triggers the contractions of the arteries and capillaries. *Oxytocin* is a hormone secreted by the pituitary gland that makes it easier to eject milk from the breast and manages the contractions of the uterus during labor.

6. D: Of the given structures, veins have the lowest blood pressure. *Veins* carry oxygen-poor blood from the outlying parts of the body to the heart. An *artery* carries oxygen-rich blood from the heart to the peripheral parts of the body. An *arteriole* extends from an artery to a capillary. A *venule* is a tiny vein that extends from a capillary to a larger vein.

7. C: Of the four heart chambers, the left ventricle is the most muscular. When it contracts, it pushes blood out to the organs and extremities of the body. The right ventricle pushes blood into the lungs. The atria, on the other hand, receive blood from the outlying parts of the body and transport it into the ventricles. The basic process works as follows: Oxygen-poor blood fills the right atrium and is pumped into the right ventricle, from which it is pumped into the pulmonary artery and on to the lungs. In the lungs, this blood is oxygenated. The blood then reenters the heart at the left atrium, which when full pumps into the left ventricle. When the left ventricle is full, blood is pushed into the aorta and on to the organs and extremities of the body.

8. A: The *cerebrum* is the part of the brain that interprets sensory information. It is the largest part of the brain. The cerebrum is divided into two hemispheres, connected by a thin band of tissue called the corpus callosum. The *cerebellum* is positioned at the back of the head, between the brain stem and the cerebrum. It controls both voluntary and involuntary movements. The *medulla oblongata* forms the base of the brain. This part of the brain is responsible for blood flow and breathing, among other things.

9. C: *Collagen* is the protein produced by cartilage. Bone, tendon, and cartilage are all mainly composed of collagen. *Actin* and *myosin* are the proteins responsible for muscle contractions. Actin makes up the thinner fibers in muscle tissue, while myosin makes up the thicker fibers. Myosin is the most numerous cell protein in human muscle. *Estrogen* is one of the steroid hormones produced mainly by the ovaries. Estrogen motivates the menstrual cycle and the development of female sex characteristics.

10. C: The parasympathetic nervous system is responsible for lowering the heart rate. It slows down the heart rate, dilates the blood vessels, and increases the secretions of the digestive system. The central nervous system is composed of the brain and the spinal cord. The sympathetic nervous system is a part of the autonomic nervous system; its role is to oppose the actions taken by the parasympathetic nervous system. So, the sympathetic nervous system accelerates the heart, contracts the blood vessels, and decreases the secretions of the digestive system.

11. B: Urea is formed during the breakdown of proteins. It is a nitrogen-rich substance filtered out of the bloodstream by the kidneys and expelled from the body in the urine. Individuals with an elevated level of urea in their bloodstream may be suffering from kidney failure. In humans and most animals, urea is the primary component of urine. However, urine also contains uric acid and ammonia. Both of these substances can be toxic to humans if they are not expelled from the body. This is one of the dangers of kidney disease and kidney failure.

12. A: A hinge joint can only move in two directions. The elbow is a hinge joint. It can only bring the lower arm closer to the upper arm or move it away from the upper arm. In a ball-and-socket joint, the rounded top of one bone fits into a concave part of another bone, enabling the first bone to rotate around in this socket. This connection is slightly less stable than other types of joints in the human body and is therefore supported by a denser network of ligaments. The shoulder and hip are both examples of ball-and-socket joints.

13. B: Smooth muscle tissue is said to be arranged in a disorderly fashion because it is not striated like the other two types of muscle: cardiac and skeletal. Striations are lines that can only be seen with a microscope. *Smooth* muscle is typically found in the supporting tissues of hollow organs and blood vessels. *Cardiac* muscle is found exclusively in the heart; it is responsible for the contractions that pump blood throughout the body. *Skeletal* muscle, by far the most preponderant in the body, controls the movements of the skeleton. The contractions of skeletal muscle are responsible for all voluntary motion. There is no such thing as *rough* muscle.

14. A: An adult inhales 500 mL of air in an average breath. Interestingly, humans can inhale about eight times as much air in a single breath as they do in an average breath. People tend to take a larger breath after making a larger inhalation. This is one reason that many breathing therapies, for instance those incorporated into yoga practice, focus on making a complete exhalation. The process of respiration is managed by the autonomic nervous system. The body requires a constant replenishing of oxygen, so even brief interruptions in respiration can be damaging or fatal.

15. D: *Plasma* cells secrete antibodies. These cells, also known as plasmacytes, are located in lymphoid tissue. Antibodies are only secreted in response to a particular stimulus, usually the detection of an antigen in the body. Antigens include bacteria, viruses, and parasites. Once released, antibodies bind to the antigen and neutralize it. When faced with a new antigen, the body may require some time to develop appropriate antibodies. Once the body has learned about an antigen, however, it does not forget how to produce the correct antibodies.

16. D: The force of *blood pressure* motivates filtration in the kidneys. *Filtration* is the process through which the kidneys remove waste products from the body. All of the water in the blood passes through the kidneys every 45 minutes. Waste products are diverted into ducts and excreted from the body, while the healthy components of the water in blood are reabsorbed into the bloodstream. *Peristalsis* is the set of involuntary muscle movements that move food through the digestive system.

17. A: *Insulin* decreases the concentration of blood glucose. It is produced by the pancreas. *Glucagon* is a hormone produced by the pancreas. Glucagon acts in opposition to insulin, motivating an increase in the levels of blood sugar. *Growth hormone* is secreted by the pituitary gland. It is responsible for the growth of the body, specifically by metabolizing proteins, carbohydrates, and lipids. The *glucocorticoids* are a group of steroid hormones that are produced by the adrenal cortex. The glucocorticoids contribute to the metabolism of carbohydrates, proteins, and fats.

18. A: The *hypothalamus* controls the hormones secreted by the pituitary gland. This part of the brain maintains the body temperature and helps to control metabolism. The *adrenal glands*, which lie above the kidneys, secrete steroidal hormones, epinephrine, and norepinephrine. The *testes* are the male reproductive glands, responsible for the production of sperm and testosterone. The *pancreas* secretes insulin and a fluid that aids in digestion.

19. C: Forty percent of female blood volume is composed of red blood cells. Red blood cells, otherwise known as erythrocytes, are large and do not have a nucleus. These cells are produced in the bone marrow and carry oxygen throughout the body. White blood cells, also known as leukocytes, make up about 1% of the blood volume. About 55% of the blood volume is made up of plasma, which itself is primarily composed of water. The plasma in blood supplies cells with nutrients and removes metabolic waste. Blood also contains platelets, otherwise known as thrombocytes, which are essential to effective blood clotting.

20. B: High-density lipoproteins (*HDL*) are considered to be the healthiest form of cholesterol. This type of cholesterol actually reduces the risk of heart disease. A lipoprotein is composed of both lipid and protein. These substances cannot move through the bloodstream by themselves; they must be carried along by some other substance. Although most people think of cholesterol as an unhealthy substance, it helps to maintain cell walls and produce hormones. Cholesterol is also important in the production of vitamin D and the bile acids that aid digestion. The other answer choices are low-density lipoproteins (*LDL*), very-low-density lipoproteins (*VLDL*), and very-high-density lipoproteins (*VHDL*).

21. C: The vocal cords are located in the larynx. These elastic bands vibrate and produce sound when air passes through them. The *larynx* lies between the pharynx and the trachea. The pharynx is the section of the throat that extends from the mouth and the nasal cavities to the larynx, at which point it becomes the esophagus. The *trachea* is the tube running from the larynx down to the lungs, where it terminates in the *bronchi*. The *epiglottis* is the flap that blocks food from the lungs by descending over the trachea during a swallow.

22. A: Gas exchange occurs in the *alveoli*, the minute air sacs on the interior of the lungs. The *bronchi* are large cartilage-based tubes of air; they extend from the end of the trachea into the lungs, where they branch apart. The *larynx*, which houses the vocal cords, is positioned between the trachea and the pharynx; it is involved in swallowing, breathing, and speaking. The *pharynx* extends

from the nose to the uppermost portions of the trachea and esophagus. In order to enter these two structures, air and other matter must pass through the pharynx.

23. B: *Axons* carry action potential in the direction of synapses. Axons are the long, fiberlike structures that carry information from neurons. Electrical impulses travel along the body of the axons, some of which are up to a foot long. A *neuron* is a type of cell that is responsible for sending information throughout the body. There are several types of neurons, including muscle neurons, which respond to instructions for movement; sensory neurons, which transmit information about the external world; and interneurons, which relay messages between neurons. *Myelin* is a fat that coats the nerves and ensures the accurate transmission of information in the nervous system.

24. A: The parathyroid gland is located in the neck, directly behind the thyroid gland. It is responsible for the metabolism of calcium. It is part of the endocrine system. When the supply of calcium in blood diminishes to unhealthy levels, the parathyroid gland motivates the secretion of a hormone that encourages the bones to release calcium into the bloodstream. The parathyroid gland also regulates the amount of phosphate in the blood by stimulating the excretion of phosphates in the urine.

25. B: In the lungs, oxygen is transported from the air to the blood through the process of *diffusion*. Specifically, the alveolar membranes withdraw the oxygen from the air in the lungs into the bloodstream. *Osmosis* is the movement of a solution from an area of low concentration to an area of higher concentration through a permeable membrane. *Dissipation* is any wasteful consumption or use. *Reverse osmosis* is a process for purifying a solution by forcing it through a membrane that blocks only certain pollutants.

Secret Key #1 - Guessing is not Guesswork

You probably know that guessing is a good idea - unlike other standardized tests, there is no penalty for getting a wrong answer. Even if you have no idea about a question, you still have a 20-25% chance of getting it right.

Most test takers do not understand the impact that proper guessing can have on their score. Unless you score extremely high, guessing will significantly contribute to your final score.

Monkeys Take the Test

What most test takers don't realize is that to insure that 20-25% chance, you have to guess randomly. If you put 20 monkeys in a room to take this test, assuming they answered once per question and behaved themselves, on average they would get 20-25% of the questions correct. Put 20 test takers in the room, and the average will be much lower among guessed questions. Why?
1. The test writers intentionally write deceptive answer choices that "look" right. A test taker has no idea about a question, so picks the "best looking" answer, which is often wrong. The monkey has no idea what looks good and what doesn't, so will consistently be lucky about 20-25% of the time.
2. Test takers will eliminate answer choices from the guessing pool based on a hunch or intuition. Simple but correct answers often get excluded, leaving a 0% chance of being correct. The monkey has no clue, and often gets lucky with the best choice.

This is why the process of elimination endorsed by most test courses is flawed and detrimental to your performance- test takers don't guess, they make an ignorant stab in the dark that is usually worse than random.

$5 Challenge

Let me introduce one of the most valuable ideas of this course- the $5 challenge:

You only mark your "best guess" if you are willing to bet $5 on it.
You only eliminate choices from guessing if you are willing to bet $5 on it.

Why $5? Five dollars is an amount of money that is small yet not insignificant, and can really add up fast (20 questions could cost you $100). Likewise, each answer choice on one question of the test will have a small impact on your overall score, but it can really add up to a lot of points in the end.

The process of elimination IS valuable. The following shows your chance of guessing it right:

If you eliminate this many choices:	0	1	2	3	4
Chance of getting it correct	20%	25%	33%	50%	100%

However, if you accidentally eliminate the right answer or go on a hunch for an incorrect answer, your chances drop dramatically: to 0%. By guessing among all the answer choices, you are GUARANTEED to have a shot at the right answer.

That's why the $5 test is so valuable- if you give up the advantage and safety of a pure guess, it had better be worth the risk.

What we still haven't covered is how to be sure that whatever guess you make is truly random. Here's the easiest way:

Always pick the first answer choice among those remaining.

Such a technique means that you have decided, **before you see a single test question**, exactly how you are going to guess- and since the order of choices tells you nothing about which one is correct, this guessing technique is perfectly random.

Let's try an example-

A student encounters the following problem on the Mathematics test:

What is $(x^2)(x^3)$ equal to?

    a. x^1
    b. x^5
    c. x^6
    d. x^9

The student has a small idea about this question- he is pretty sure that you are supposed to either add the two exponents (2+3 = 5), or multiply them (2*3 = 6) but he wouldn't bet $5 on either choice. He knows that it isn't any of the other choices and so he is willing to bet $5 on both choices a and d not being correct. So he is down to choices b and c. At this point, he guesses b, since b is the first choice remaining.

The student is correct by choosing b, since $(x^2)(x^3)$ is equal to x^5. He only eliminated those choices he was willing to bet money on, AND he did not let his stale memories (often things not known definitely will get mixed up in the exact opposite arrangement in one's head) about the rules for exponents influence his guess. He blindly chose the first remaining choice, and was rewarded with the fruits of a random guess.

This section is not meant to scare you away from making educated guesses or eliminating choices- you just need to define when a choice is worth eliminating. The $5 test, along with a pre-defined random guessing strategy, is the best way to make sure you reap all of the benefits of guessing.

Specific Guessing Techniques

Similar Answer Choices

When you have two answer choices that are direct opposites, one of them is usually the correct answer.
Example:
   a. forward
   b. backward

These two answer choices are very similar and fall into the same family of answer choices. A family of answer choices is when two or three answer choices are very similar. Often two will be opposites and one may show an equality.
Example:
   a. excited
   b. overjoyed
   c. thrilled
   d. upset

Note how the first three choices are all related. They all ask describe a state of happiness. However, choice d is not in the same family of questions. Being upset is the direct opposite of happiness.

Summary of Guessing Techniques

1. Eliminate as many choices as you can by using the $5 test. Use the common guessing strategies to help in the elimination process, but only eliminate choices that pass the $5 test.
2. Among the remaining choices, only pick your "best guess" if it passes the $5 test.
3. Otherwise, guess randomly by picking the first remaining choice that was not eliminated.

Secret Key #2 - Prepare, Don't Procrastinate

Let me state an obvious fact: if you take the test three times, you will get three different scores. This is due to the way you feel on test day, the level of preparedness you have, and, despite the test writers' claims to the contrary, some tests WILL be easier for you than others.

Since your future depends so much on your score, you should maximize your chances of success. In order to maximize the likelihood of success, you've got to prepare in advance. This means taking practice tests and spending time learning the information and test taking strategies you will need to succeed.

Since you have to pay a registration fee each time you take the test, don't take it as a "practice" test. Feel free to take sample tests on your own, but when you go to take the official test, be prepared, be focused, and do your best the first time!

Secret Key #3 - Test Yourself

Everyone knows that time is money. There is no need to spend too much of your time or too little of your time preparing for the test. You should only spend as much of your precious time preparing as is necessary for you to pass it.

Once you have taken a practice test under real conditions of time constraints, then you will know if you are ready for the test or not.

If you have scored extremely high the first time that you take the practice test, then there is not much point in spending countless hours studying. You are already there.

Benchmark your abilities by retaking practice tests and seeing how much you have improved. Once you score high enough to guarantee success, then you are ready.

If you have scored well below where you need, then knuckle down and begin studying in earnest. Check your improvement regularly through the use of practice tests under real conditions. Above all, don't worry, panic, or give up. The key is perseverance!

Then, when you go to take the test, remain confident and remember how well you did on the practice tests. If you can score high enough on a practice test, then you can do the same on the real thing.

General Strategies

The most important thing you can do is to ignore your fears and jump into the test immediately. Do not be overwhelmed by any strange-sounding terms. You have to jump into the test like jumping into a pool; all at once is the easiest way.

Make Predictions
As you read and understand the question, try to guess what the answer will be. Remember that several of the answer choices are wrong, and once you begin reading them, your mind will immediately become cluttered with answer choices designed to throw you off. Your mind is typically the most focused immediately after you have read the question and digested its contents. If you can, try to predict what the correct answer will be. You may be surprised at what you can predict.

Quickly scan the choices and see if your prediction is in the listed answer choices. If it is, then you can be quite confident that you have the right answer. It still won't hurt to check the other answer choices, but most of the time, you've got it!

Answer the Question
It may seem obvious to only pick answer choices that answer the question, but the test writers can create some excellent answer choices that are wrong. Don't pick an answer just because it sounds right, or you believe it to be true. It MUST answer the question. Once you've made your selection, always go back and check it against the question and make sure that you didn't misread the question, and the answer choice does answer the question posed.

Benchmark
After you read the first answer choice, decide if you think it sounds correct or not. If it doesn't, move on to the next answer choice. If it does, mentally mark that answer choice. This doesn't mean that you've definitely selected it as your answer choice, it just means that it's the best you've seen thus far. Go ahead and read the next choice. If the next choice is worse than the one you've already selected, keep going to the next answer choice. If the next choice is better than the choice you've already selected, mentally mark the new answer choice as your best guess.

The first answer choice that you select becomes your standard. Every other answer choice must be benchmarked against that standard. That choice is correct until proven otherwise by another answer choice beating it out. Once you've decided that no other answer choice seems as good, do one final check to ensure that your answer choice answers the question posed.

Valid Information
Don't discount any of the information provided in the question. Every piece of information may be necessary to determine the correct answer. None of the information in the question is there to throw you off (while the answer choices will certainly have information to throw you off). If two seemingly unrelated topics are discussed, don't ignore either. You can be confident there is a relationship, or it wouldn't be included in the question, and you are probably going to have to determine what is that relationship to find the answer.

Avoid "Fact Traps"

Don't get distracted by a choice that is factually true. Your search is for the answer that answers the question. Stay focused and don't fall for an answer that is true but incorrect. Always go back to the question and make sure you're choosing an answer that actually answers the question and is not just a true statement. An answer can be factually correct, but it MUST answer the question asked. Additionally, two answers can both be seemingly correct, so be sure to read all of the answer choices, and make sure that you get the one that BEST answers the question.

Milk the Question

Some of the questions may throw you completely off. They might deal with a subject you have not been exposed to, or one that you haven't reviewed in years. While your lack of knowledge about the subject will be a hindrance, the question itself can give you many clues that will help you find the correct answer. Read the question carefully and look for clues. Watch particularly for adjectives and nouns describing difficult terms or words that you don't recognize. Regardless of if you completely understand a word or not, replacing it with a synonym either provided or one you more familiar with may help you to understand what the questions are asking. Rather than wracking your mind about specific detailed information concerning a difficult term or word, try to use mental substitutes that are easier to understand.

The Trap of Familiarity

Don't just choose a word because you recognize it. On difficult questions, you may not recognize a number of words in the answer choices. The test writers don't put "make-believe" words on the test; so don't think that just because you only recognize all the words in one answer choice means that answer choice must be correct. If you only recognize words in one answer choice, then focus on that one. Is it correct? Try your best to determine if it is correct. If it is, that is great, but if it doesn't, eliminate it. Each word and answer choice you eliminate increases your chances of getting the question correct, even if you then have to guess among the unfamiliar choices.

Eliminate Answers

Eliminate choices as soon as you realize they are wrong. But be careful! Make sure you consider all of the possible answer choices. Just because one appears right, doesn't mean that the next one won't be even better! The test writers will usually put more than one good answer choice for every question, so read all of them. Don't worry if you are stuck between two that seem right. By getting down to just two remaining possible choices, your odds are now 50/50. Rather than wasting too much time, play the odds. You are guessing, but guessing wisely, because you've been able to knock out some of the answer choices that you know are wrong. If you are eliminating choices and realize that the last answer choice you are left with is also obviously wrong, don't panic. Start over and consider each choice again. There may easily be something that you missed the first time and will realize on the second pass.

Tough Questions

If you are stumped on a problem or it appears too hard or too difficult, don't waste time. Move on! Remember though, if you can quickly check for obviously incorrect answer choices, your chances of guessing correctly are greatly improved. Before you completely give up, at least try to knock out a couple of possible answers. Eliminate what you can and then guess at the remaining answer choices before moving on.

Brainstorm

If you get stuck on a difficult question, spend a few seconds quickly brainstorming. Run through the complete list of possible answer choices. Look at each choice and ask yourself, "Could this answer the question satisfactorily?" Go through each answer choice and consider it independently of the other. By systematically going through all possibilities, you may find something that you would otherwise overlook. Remember that when you get stuck, it's important to try to keep moving.

Read Carefully

Understand the problem. Read the question and answer choices carefully. Don't miss the question because you misread the terms. You have plenty of time to read each question thoroughly and make sure you understand what is being asked. Yet a happy medium must be attained, so don't waste too much time. You must read carefully, but efficiently.

Face Value

When in doubt, use common sense. Always accept the situation in the problem at face value. Don't read too much into it. These problems will not require you to make huge leaps of logic. The test writers aren't trying to throw you off with a cheap trick. If you have to go beyond creativity and make a leap of logic in order to have an answer choice answer the question, then you should look at the other answer choices. Don't overcomplicate the problem by creating theoretical relationships or explanations that will warp time or space. These are normal problems rooted in reality. It's just that the applicable relationship or explanation may not be readily apparent and you have to figure things out. Use your common sense to interpret anything that isn't clear.

Prefixes

If you're having trouble with a word in the question or answer choices, try dissecting it. Take advantage of every clue that the word might include. Prefixes and suffixes can be a huge help. Usually they allow you to determine a basic meaning. Pre- means before, post- means after, pro - is positive, de- is negative. From these prefixes and suffixes, you can get an idea of the general meaning of the word and try to put it into context. Beware though of any traps. Just because con is the opposite of pro, doesn't necessarily mean congress is the opposite of progress!

Hedge Phrases

Watch out for critical "hedge" phrases, such as likely, may, can, will often, sometimes, often, almost, mostly, usually, generally, rarely, sometimes. Question writers insert these hedge phrases to cover every possibility. Often an answer choice will be wrong simply because it leaves no room for exception. Avoid answer choices that have definitive words like "exactly," and "always".

Switchback Words

Stay alert for "switchbacks". These are the words and phrases frequently used to alert you to shifts in thought. The most common switchback word is "but". Others include although, however, nevertheless, on the other hand, even though, while, in spite of, despite, regardless of.

New Information
Correct answer choices will rarely have completely new information included. Answer choices typically are straightforward reflections of the material asked about and will directly relate to the question. If a new piece of information is included in an answer choice that doesn't even seem to relate to the topic being asked about, then that answer choice is likely incorrect. All of the information needed to answer the question is usually provided for you, and so you should not have to make guesses that are unsupported or choose answer choices that require unknown information that cannot be reasoned on its own.

Time Management
On technical questions, don't get lost on the technical terms. Don't spend too much time on any one question. If you don't know what a term means, then since you don't have a dictionary, odds are you aren't going to get much further. You should immediately recognize terms as whether or not you know them. If you don't, work with the other clues that you have, the other answer choices and terms provided, but don't waste too much time trying to figure out a difficult term.

Contextual Clues
Look for contextual clues. An answer can be right but not correct. The contextual clues will help you find the answer that is most right and is correct. Understand the context in which a phrase or statement is made. This will help you make important distinctions.

Don't Panic
Panicking will not answer any questions for you. Therefore, it isn't helpful. When you first see the question, if your mind goes blank, take a deep breath. Force yourself to mechanically go through the steps of solving the problem and using the strategies you've learned.

Answer Selection
The best way to pick an answer choice is to eliminate all of those that are wrong, until only one is left and confirm that is the correct answer. Sometimes though, an answer choice may immediately look right. Be careful! Take a second to make sure that the other choices are not equally obvious. Don't make a hasty mistake.

Check Your Work
Since you will probably not know every term listed and the answer to every question, it is important that you get credit for the ones that you do know. Don't miss any questions through careless mistakes. If at all possible, try to take a second to look back over your answer selection and make sure you've selected the correct answer choice and haven't made a costly careless mistake (such as marking an answer choice that you didn't mean to mark). This quick double check should more than pay for itself in caught mistakes for the time it costs.

Beware of Directly Quoted Answers
Sometimes an answer choice will repeat word for word a portion of the question or reference section. However, beware of such exact duplication – it may be a trap! More than likely, the correct choice will paraphrase or summarize a point, rather than being exactly the same wording.

Slang

Scientific sounding answers are better than slang ones. An answer choice that begins "To compare the outcomes…" is much more likely to be correct than one that begins "Because some people insisted…"

Extreme Statements

Avoid wild answers that throw out highly controversial ideas that are proclaimed as established fact. An answer choice that states the "process should be used in certain situations, if…" is much more likely to be correct than one that states the "process should be discontinued completely." The first is a calm rational statement and doesn't even make a definitive, uncompromising stance, using a hedge word "if" to provide wiggle room, whereas the second choice is a radical idea and far more extreme.

Answer Choice Families

When you have two or more answer choices that are direct opposites or parallels, one of them is usually the correct answer. For instance, if one answer choice states "x increases" and another answer choice states "x decreases" or "y increases," then those two or three answer choices are very similar in construction and fall into the same family of answer choices. A family of answer choices is when two or three answer choices are very similar in construction, and yet often have a directly opposite meaning. Usually the correct answer choice will be in that family of answer choices. The "odd man out" or answer choice that doesn't seem to fit the parallel construction of the other answer choices is more likely to be incorrect.

Additional Bonus Material

Due to our efforts to try to keep this book to a manageable length, we've created a link that will give you access to all of your additional bonus material.

Please visit http://www.mometrix.com/bonus948/hesia2 to access the information.

CPSIA information can be obtained
at www.ICGtesting.com
Printed in the USA
LVHW101354060219
606597LV00028B/336/P